SWITZERLAND

About the Author

John Marshall, M.A., graduated First Class Honours in Classics, was University prizeman in Classics, in Roman Empire History and later in Modern European History. After some years' teaching he was appointed Rector, North Berwick High School, and ten years later Headmaster of Robert Gordon's College, Aberdeen. For many years as a Trustee (and later Chairman) of Scottish Secondary Schools Travel Trust planned and led student travel trips in Europe and Mediterranean regions. He has travelled widely, showing preferences for areas where he can follow the local languages. He is also author of Moorland's 'Visitor's Guide to the Rhine and Mosel' and co-author of 'Off the Beaten Track in Switzerland.'

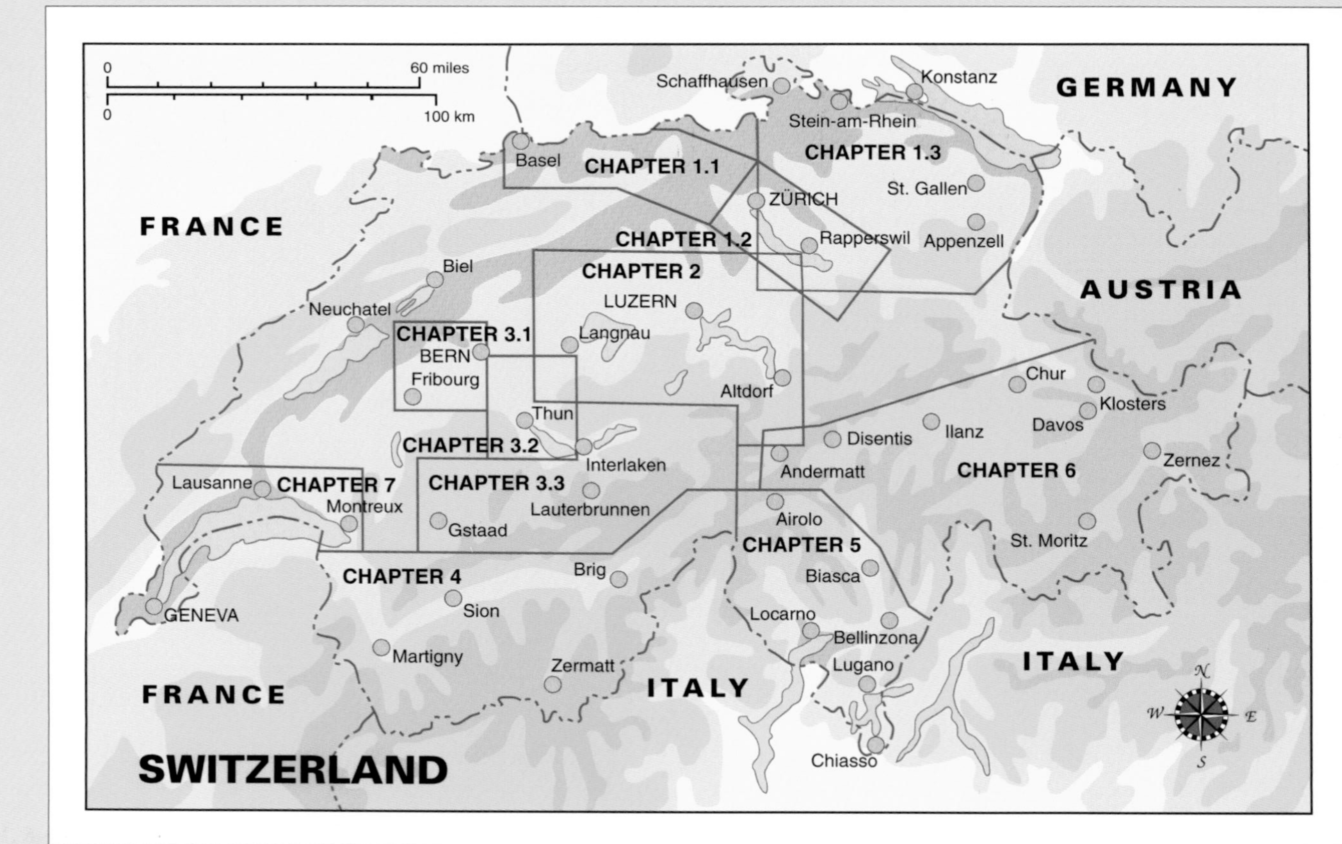

0
60 miles
0
100 km
GERMANY
AUSTRIA
FRANCE
FRANCE
ITALY
ITALY
SWITZERLAND
Schaffhausen
Konstanz
Stein-am-Rhein
CHAPTER 1.3
Basel
CHAPTER 1.1
St. Gallen
ZÜRICH
CHAPTER 1.2
Rapperswil
Appenzell
Biel
CHAPTER 2
LUZERN
Neuchatel
CHAPTER 3.1
Langnau
BERN
Fribourg
Altdorf
Chur
Klosters
Davos
Thun
CHAPTER 3.2
Interlaken
Disentis
Ilanz
Andermatt
Zernez
CHAPTER 6
Lausanne
CHAPTER 7
Montreux
CHAPTER 3.3
Lauterbrunnen
Gstaad
Airolo
CHAPTER 5
St. Moritz
CHAPTER 4
Brig
Biasca
Sion
GENEVA
Locarno
Bellinzona
Martigny
Zermatt
Lugano
Chiasso
N
W
E
S

VISITOR'S GUIDE
SWITZERLAND

John Marshall

MPC
HUNTER

Published by:
Moorland Publishing Co Ltd,
Moor Farm Road West, Ashbourne,
Derbyshire DE6 1HD
England

Published in the USA by:
Hunter Publishing Inc,
300 Raritan Center Parkway,
CN 94, Edison, NJ 08818

ISBN 086190 548 2

2nd edition (rev) 1995

British Library Cataloguing in Publication Data:
A catalogue record for this book is available from the British Library.

Colour origination by: Reed Reprographics, Ipswich

Printed in Hong Kong by: Wing King Tong Co Ltd

Cover photograph: Klausenpass

Rear Cover: William Tell statue at Altdorf

Page 3: Sign at Rigi

The illustrations are by Lindsey Porter and John Marshall

MPC Production Team:
Editor: Christine Haines
Designer: Dick Richardson
Cartography: ESR Ltd., Byfleet, Surrey
and Alastair Morrison

Contents

Key to Symbols Used in Text Margin and on Maps

- Church
- Castle
- Building of Interest
- Museum/Art Gallery
- Archaeological Site
- Winter Sports
- Other Place of Interest
- Beautiful View/ Natural Phenomenon
- Park
- Garden
- Mountain Peak

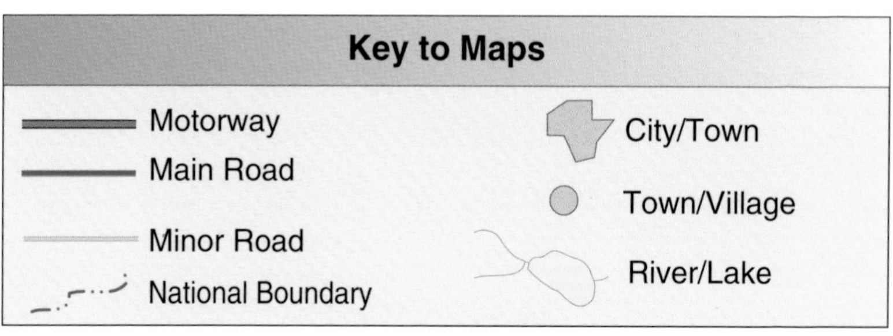

How To Use This Guide

This MPC Visitor's Guide has been designed to be as easy to use as possible. Each chapter covers a region and gives all the background information to help you enjoy your visit. MPC's distinctive margin symbols, the important places printed in bold and a comprehensive index enable the reader to find the most interesting places to visit with ease.

At the end of each chapter an Additional Information section gives specific details such as addresses and opening times, making this guide a complete sightseeing companion.

At the back of the guide the Fact File, arranged in alphabetical order, gives practical information and useful tips to help you plan your holiday before you go and while you are there.

The maps of each region show the main towns, villages, roads and places of interest, but are not designed as route maps and motorists should always use a good recommended road atlas.

Introduction

Switzerland is small in size even by European standards; its territory amounts to only about a quarter of that of England and Wales. Yet in that small area it shows extraordinary variety; variety of landscape and topography, of clime and flora and fauna, of the languages and the fascinating but diverse historical and cultural heritage of its people in the different parts of the country. Yet all this diversity is bound together with an exemplary cohesion.

Switzerland's history, more than that of most countries, was greatly shaped by its physical structure. In the past two centuries — since the European Romantics became seized with the natural beauty and fascination of this great Alpine region — the very name of Switzerland has conjured up appealing images of mountain grandeur. But in pre-Romantic eras the mountains do not seem to have been seen in the same attractive light but rather as inescapable environmental factors that dominated men's living patterns.

The Alps take up more than 60 per cent of Swiss territory. For centuries these great massifs and their high valleys locked communities away from one another. Yet the paradox exists that the Alps are not entirely a barrier to passage and to transport. Through their lateral valleys and over the passes they also form a link between peoples and their way of life and encourage commercial exchange. However, the limited and difficult nature of these passes greatly determined the extent of the mountain communities' contact with other societies. This is illustrated by the history of the Gotthard Pass.

One geographical fact about the nature of the Alps is likely to strike any observant traveller on the Gotthard route whether he passes by road or by rail: the Alpine massif's slopes to the north are relatively gentle compared to the steep, precipitous valley-steps and mountain faces that confront the south. Certain Roman historians maintain that in the days of the Roman Republic the Romans did not advance beyond the Alps with plans of empire; they did so because this difference between the north and the south faces of the massif made it much more difficult to hold a defensive line south of the great barrier than north of it. However that may be, from the time the Romans did cross the Alps, the main through routes linking Southern and Northern Europe have passed through what is nowadays Switzerland.

In the centre of the Alpine chain the Gotthard massif has been likened to the hub of a wheel with Andermatt, in the Urseren Valley, lying at dead centre. Alpine rivers form the spokes of the wheel. These have their sources at or near the passes. To the east flows the Alpine sector of the Rhine (its source lying in a lateral valley of the Oberalp Pass). To the west rises the Rhône at the Rhône Glacier near the Furka Pass. South of the Gotthard Pass lie the headwaters of the River Ticino, flowing to Lake Maggiore and the River Po. To the north down the narrow Schöllenen Gorge tumbles the River Reuss. Rather spoiling the symmetry of the wheel is a fifth spoke: to the north-east of the 'hub' the River Aare rises at the Grimsel Pass, linking it to the east Berner Oberland.

All these rivers are of European importance and their valleys have provided the channels for the communication routes of which the Gotthard is the strategic centre. To the south is the Gotthard Pass leading to Bellinzona and Italy, to the east the Oberalp Pass leading to Chur and Austria, to the west the Furka Pass leading to Lake Geneva and France, and to the north the Schöllenen Gorge leading to Central Switzerland and Northern Europe.

So when the Romans moved north of the Alps they did not do so in half-hearted style so as to leave these critical lines of communications in any border zone. They moved their frontiers forward to cover the angle between the main body of the River Rhine and that of the Danube. The area including what is now Switzerland was colonised, Romanised, and, as the province of *Rhaetia*, enjoyed centuries of peaceful development at the start of the Christian era.

Even after the effective collapse of Rome and the withdrawal of its legions this civilisation survived until in the sixth century *Rhaetia* was invaded by barbarians from two opposing directions. Burgundians from the west and Alemannic tribes from the north. Both groups pushed forward where they could until they met resistance; and the line along which they met remained astonishingly stable over the centuries as the boundary between the speakers of a Romance language (in modern times French in Western Switzerland) and those of a Germanic language (in modern times Swiss-German).

In the Middle Ages Switzerland (which English-speakers then frequently called High Germany) was incorporated in that rather loosely organised structure, the Holy Roman Empire of the German Nation. The feudal magnates in the settled, cultivated regions which the Swiss call collectively Mittelland varied as did local feudal rulers throughout Europe; but in the Oberland — the high valleys of the Alpine massif — feudal landlords were often absentees, and the communities were often left to organise their collective hard life on marginal grazing lands as best they could. They acquired, in short, liberties to live a very hard life in isolated and hostile natural environments without external help or interference. Even some of the Mittelland cities, such as Bern and Zürich, acquired freedom from local landlords by dispensations from a far-off emperor of 'free city' status.

Then, in the thirteenth century, the situation changed with two new factors. Firstly, by the application of wooden plank technology to the previously impassable Schöllenen Gorge below the Gotthard, the most direct pass road to Italy became a practical possibility; the herdsmen in the valleys of cantons Uri, Schwyz and Unterwalden could now drive their products to Italian markets and could make purchases from the fertile lowlands of the south. Secondly, a new breed of overlord was on the scene; the Habsburg family was sharp enough to see profit in having tighter control of so valuable a possession as the lands that commanded a major trade-artery. The men of the Alpine valleys responded by solemnly swearing mutual assistance against outside threats to inherited liberties in 1291. And the following century saw these men of the 'original forest communities', bound together as 'Confederates', take on as footsoldiers in battle, and defeat the armoured chivalry of the Habsburgs in 1315, 1339, 1386 and 1388.

Nothing succeeds like success, so the three first cantons became four when Luzern joined them in 1332 (hence the *vierwaldstätten*, ie, 'Four Forest Cantons' that gave their name to the Swiss lake they surround, the Vierwaldstättersee, which English speakers call Lake Luzern). By mid-century, with the accession also of Zürich, Zug, Glarus and Bern, there was a confederation that the Swiss call the 'Eight Cantons'. A century later, Charles the Bold, Duke of Burgundy, attempted to do in the west what the Habsburgs had failed to do in the centre. He too was bested.

It is difficult for moderns to think of the Swiss (from a country with a name associated with neutrality, the Red Cross and international agencies) ever being belligerent. But the disciplined infantrymen who had broken the Austrian and Burgundian knights-at-arms were next century in high demand as mercenaries in the then cockpit of Europe, Italy. They also took on Italian armies on their own account and in stages took over the lands to the south of the Gotthard, inhabited by Italian-speaking people of Lombardy stock, making them subject to the Confederates and ruled by Confederate bailiffs and governors. (It was not until the beginning of the nineteenth century that the Italian-speaking Ticino became an equal member canton of the Confederacy.) It took a very costly defeat at the hands of François I of France, at Marignano in 1515, to make the Swiss give up the organised practice of mercenary soldiering and to embrace the policy of neutrality.

Perhaps some accumulation of wisdom from these experiences helped the Confederacy to weather the tensions in the sixteenth century of Reformation and Counter-Reformation. For tensions, passions and strife there were. Zürich's leading light of the Reformation was Zwingli, Geneva's, stern Calvin. Luzern and Fribourg were citadels of the Catholic faith and the Counter-Reformation. Yet the loose ties of the Confederacy did not break, and the Confederacy kept clear of the Thirty Years War that ravaged the German lands. (At the end of the day most of French-speaking Switzerland is Protestant, excepting Fribourg, the Valais and the Jura; the Four Original Cantons of Central Switzerland and Zug, Solothurn, St Gallen, Ticino also remain Catholic, while the north and east are Protestant.)

At the end of the eighteenth century the influence of the French Revolution had destabilising effects in Switzerland. In 1798 French armies invaded to help 'free' the Swiss; a Helvetian Republic was set up reflecting French centralised conceptions of government. This did not work with the Swiss and in 1803 Napoleon restored the Confederal constitution of equal cantons, increasing the number to nineteen but retaining Geneva and Valais as French. At the Congress of Vienna after Napoleon's defeat twenty-two cantons were recognised as sovereign within the Confederation and Switzerland's neutrality was guaranteed.

Many visitors find admirable in Switzerland the tolerance extended to fellow citizens of different religion, of different racial stock and language.

The Languages

The brief history above has shown how Switzerland has come to demonstrate an unquestionable sense of unity but recognises a diversity of national languages and cultures. Strictly speaking, the Swiss constitution recognises three languages as *official*: German (in its Swiss-German forms the mother-tongue of 65 per cent of the Swiss, in Central, North-Eastern

Traditional transport at Interlaken

and Eastern Switzerland); French (18 per cent — predominantly in Western Switzerland); Italian (10 per cent — in Southern Switzerland). Since early in the twentieth century a fourth language (or rather group of languages) has been recognised as a *national* language: Romansch (including its near relative, Ladin), the language derived from the vernacular Latin spoken in the isolated valleys of the Roman province of *Rhaetia* (1 per cent — in the Graubünden of South-Eastern Switzerland).

The situation of German is rather complicated. All ranks and classes in German-speaking Switzerland in their everyday life speak an Alemannic dialect described as *Schwyzertütsch* (the spelling varies and so too does the language even between residents of the great cities of Basel, Bern and Zürich). But the language of officialdom, of schools and universities, of pulpit and formal lecture, of radio, television and the newspapers is Standard German which can be understood readily in other German-speaking countries. (It should perhaps be added that even in the case of highly educated Swiss people speaking Standard German, their 'Swiss accent' still identifies them.) Finally, most Swiss in positions of any responsibility speak at least one other of the national languages. Officials at the information desks of railway stations, and in banks, airports, fashion-

Typical Swiss mountain scenery – the Jungfrau region in June

able shops and large hotels are likely to speak all three official languages and also the unofficial world language, English.

A humorous cynic once made the point that the great attraction of Switzerland for English-speakers was that it gave them all the novelty and exhilaration of sampling life 'abroad' in a French, an Italian or a German atmosphere without depriving them of the comforting Victorian security of the English-speaking world!

The Swiss Constitution

Different languages imply some degree of difference in traditions and heritage as well. How does the Swiss nation maintain its apparent cohesion? It would seem that the Swiss acquired the message that tolerance of differences between communities is most likely to take root if the communities in question can take pride in their own sovereignty — which is what the Confederal constitution is mostly about.

Each of the twenty-six cantons of the Confederation remains sovereign, having its own legislative body and a constitution. Indeed, a few mountain cantons and half-cantons (such as in Appenzell where the half-canton was found to be a solution for the religious differences which in other parts of Europe kindled thirty years of war) still practise direct democracy in the form of the spring assembly of the *Landsgemeinde* when all citizens gather in the open square of the principal village to discuss and vote on the business of their land.

At federal level two assemblies work hand in hand, one, the Council of States (two members from each canton) and the other the National Council where the number of representatives elected from any given canton is proportional to its population. The two together form the legislative body for the country. The executive power lies with a seven-member Federal Council, elected by the combined Assembly; each of the seven is responsible for what could be called a ministry. But at the end of the day, any legislative decision made by the Federal Assembly may be subject to the whole people's right to be consulted by a referendum if within three months a specific number of citizens sign a demand for it. Active citizens can also band together to demand the initiation of constitutional amendments depending on the support they can win for their plea.The whole system is the antithesis of centralisation and reflects the process of growth that led so many once-isolated mountain and valley communities into the beginnings of a Confederation.

The Swiss Economy

Even a brief visit to Switzerland leaves the visitor with the impression of a populace enjoying a generally high standard of life. Yet the country clearly has few natural resources. As the director of a Swiss institute concerned with the environment has summed it up: 'About one-quarter of Swiss territory is unproductive. Most of it lies in the high mountain areas consisting of rock, boulders and glaciers. All the rest with the exception of built-up areas and communications has for centuries been developed for agriculture and afforestation'.

In forest products, in fact, Switzerland is self-sufficient. Not so in food production in which it ranks next to the United Kingdom in the level of importation of foodstuffs per capita. What then makes its economy tick? The nature of the land encouraged specialisation in dairy farming: milk production was maximised and its uses diversified with cheese-making and the manufacture of malted milks and milk chocolate for a world-wide market. The textile industry, starting as a cottage industry, developed into a highly organised manufacturing branch; colour research for the textile industry led the way into chemical and pharmaceutical industry on a world-market scale as is now well known through familiar brand names. Textile mills too led the way into machine production and precision engineering of machine tools. Industry, in short, has one common factor in this country. Having no raw resources of their own the Swiss specialise in the high levels of skill and precision work they put into manufactured products which have a very high value relative to their bulk: machine tools, surgical instruments, optical instruments, electrical and electronic engineering products — and of course watches and chronometers. In all these fields they were pioneers — and also in hydro-electric power, and indeed also nuclear power. This industry they manage to conduct profitably while yet showing sensitivity to the environment in the manufacturing towns.

And of course they were world pioneers in tourism and have for long been renowned for skills in the provision of banking services.

Traditional Ceremonies

Of festivals (whether folk, musical, floral or national), processions and ceremonial events, there is never any lack in Switzerland. A people with such justifiable pride in the diversity and colourful nature of its heritage has ample scope for sharing in celebrations. In this context, too, the SNTO branches can be relied upon as a source of annual lists of the events that are planned for each week of the year and for each region. If any one can be singled out as a specially moving as well as a colourful occasion it is National Day, 1 August, in canton Schwyz, when people from all parts of the Confederation arrive in Brunnen almost in the spirit of pilgrims, to be conveyed by boats shuttling across the waters of Lake Luzern to assemble, beneath the beetling Seelisberg cliffs, on the Rütli meadow.

1

THE NORTHERN CITIES

Switzerland's largest city, Zürich, and second-largest, Basel, both lie in the north of the country and a great majority of English-speaking visitors to Switzerland seem to prefer the traditional route used by travellers from Northern Europe, and enter Switzerland via Zürich (by plane) or via Basel (by road or rail).

1.1 Basel

Basel in fact might fairly be described as being situated on the country's northern entrance 'porch'. It lies outside the Jura highland range which forms the north-western rim of Switzerland, on a corridor tightly constrained by the French and German borders where the River Rhine makes a right-angled bend as it flows north to leave Switzerland. The ancient Romans, with their customary appreciative eye for the strategic values of a site, seized upon this one. And when the first Rhine bridge was built in the thirteenth century, the city which straddled it was set to become an important centre for trade and the transit of goods, skills and ideas at international level. The city's cramped geographic confines are today illustrated by the fact that Basel's airport and much of its great pharmaceutical industrial production is situated on French soil.

Having acquired a university in 1460 and having been strongly influenced by Renaissance movements, Basel became famed for its receptivity to liberal humanism. It was won over to the Reformation in 1529. When in the following era the Counter-Reformation became most active in France and Italy, the city, so noted for its liberal philosophy, became a sanctuary for Protestant refugees including many practitioners in skills and crafts, arts and sciences that contributed to the diversification of the city's economy and also its culture.

Today Basel is very prosperous, having about the highest level of income per head of population in Europe; the centre of the great Swiss pharmaceutical industry, of insurance and banking operations. It is a

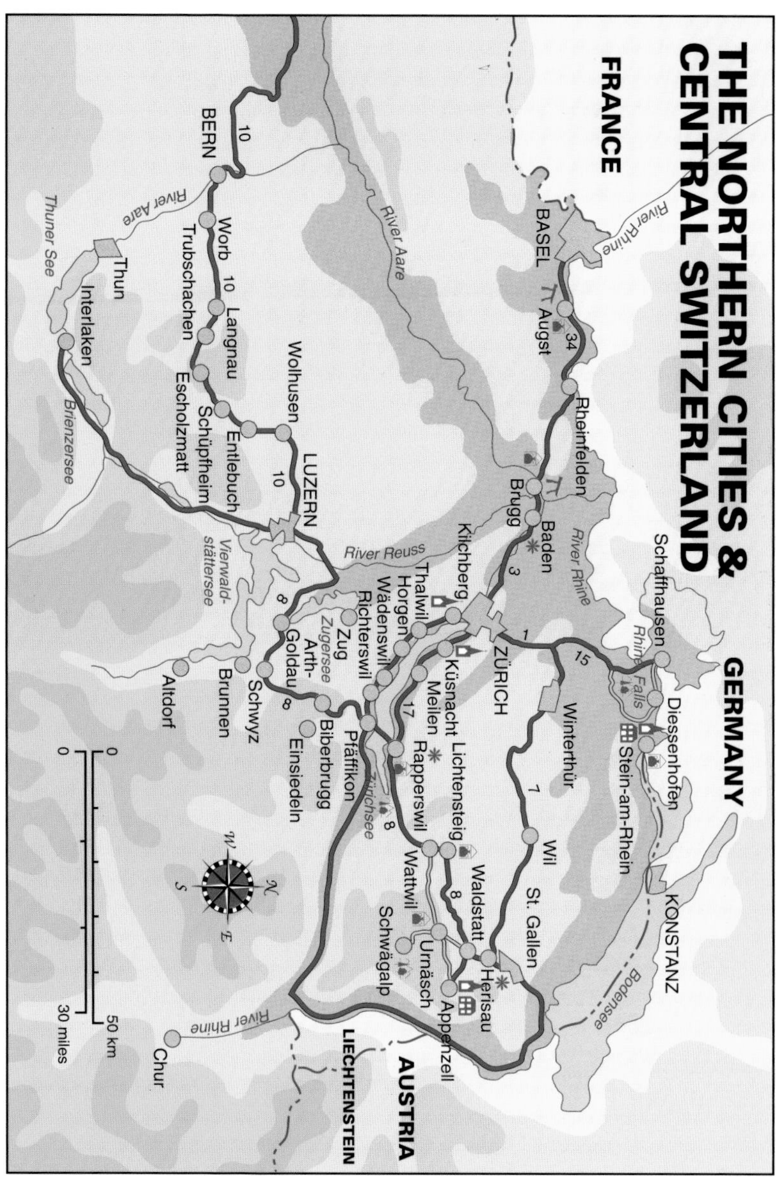

major port on the Rhine, Europe's great artery of transport, handling much of Swiss foreign trade. It has been said that of the great Swiss cities Basel is the one that 'turns its back to the Alps and faces northwards towards Alsace in France, the Upper Rhine plain and the Black Forest in Germany'. Its position as a centre of railway communications illustrates this point. It has three main terminal stations, one each for Swiss, French and German railways.

The *Hauptbahnhof*, central railway station, of Swiss Federal Railways (Schweizerische Bundes-Bahn, usually called by its initials SBB) is a convenient starting point for a short tour of the heart of the city, the *Altstadt* (Old Town), which is grouped around an eminence, overhanging the river's left bank, on which the great Gothic Minster stands today, and where the Roman fort stood two millennia ago.

From the *Centralbahnplatz* (the Station Square) either walk the 1½ km (about a mile) or take a line 1 tram to the **Marktplatz** (**Market Square**) which is the Old Town's main square and, with its timbered houses, is held to be one of the finest-proportioned examples of its kind in Europe. In it stands the impressive red-sandstone **Rathaus** (**Town Hall**), built in late Gothic style; the middle block with its three arcades dates back to 1512 but it incorporates later alterations.

From the north-east corner of the square runs Eisengasse. (A *gasse* is a built-up street or lane, while *-strasse* implies more width and spaciousness.) Follow this in the direction of the river bridge. On the unobstructed river bank to the left of the bridge is the **Schifflände**, the historic landing place for river vessels.

(**Note**: the Tourist Information Office is only a few steps beyond the Schifflände, at Schifflände No 5. Private motorists in particular should call there early in their visit to request a copy of the useful leaflet with information, especially on parking, for motorists.)

Before the bridge there is a lane to the right, the Rheinsprung, which leads up the steep Minster Hill. It is lined with imposing late medieval houses (originally half-timbered buildings), many of them former official residences of patricians, clergy and even nobility. No 11, however, was the first faculty building of the University (founded in 1460). A narrow lane goes off the Rheinsprung to the right leading to the city's oldest parish church, St Martin's, in its narrow square with an interesting fountain. Take however the Augustinergasse (where the **Museum of Natural History** and **Museum of Ethnology** are both to be found) in order to reach the beautifully conceived large square, the Münsterplatz dominated by the front towers of the **Minster**. The splendid residences surrounding the square are a reminder that here was the centre of power in the era when the Bishop ruled in Basel. Excavations have shown that the present Minster had several predecessors. An earthquake in 1356 destroyed many parts of the late Romanesque twelfth-century building that had thirteenth-century high Gothic additions. Reconstruction was completed around 1500. The façade is richly decorated; sculptured treasures abound in the friezes above and on the sides of the main doorway. Note especially the glorious twelfth-century St Gallus doorway (north-west) in the form of a triumphal arch and the associated Wheel of Fortune; it is the oldest figured doorway in the German-speaking lands. Among numerous treasures in the interior is a memorial to the great Renaissance scholar Erasmus who died in Basel in 1536.

From the Gallus portal, passing between the Minster (right) and the

Pisoni fountain (left) one reaches the great Rhine terrace, poised above the river, which is known as the **Pfalz** (a name that has connotations with palace'). From it there is a noble prospect over the river to Greater Basel's traditional rival and sister town, Kleinbasel, Lesser Basel, at a lower level on the right bank opposite. The view takes in the medieval town between the surviving buildings of the thirteenth-century Klingental Convent and those of the former fifteenth-century Charterhouse, later a city orphanage (*Waisenhaus*).

Walk from the Pfalz via the square into the Rittergasse which as its name hints (*Ritter* means Knights) has its palatial mansions such as the fifteenth-century Bishop's Court. From Rittergasse's end turn right into St Alban Graben where the **Kunstmuseum (Fine Arts Museum)** is on the left-hand side. It has one of the most comprehensive collections in Europe including many works of Hans Holbein the Younger, Cranach, Konrad Witz, and Grünewald. From here it is no distance to the hub of Basel life, the **Barfüsserplatz** (**Square of the Barefoot Friars**) where a fourteenth-century Franciscan church houses a historical museum with rich relics and elements from the life of the medieval city. This square is near the southern end of the Freie Strasse which is the Old Town's most exclusive shopping street, and which leads back northwards direct into the Market Square.

Even in the briefest of visits two other things are worth trying to fit into the timetable. Firstly, apart from the bridges that cross the Rhine and link Grossbasel with Kleinbasel, there are also four unpowered ferries. Each is attached to a pulley running on an overhead cable stretching across the river; it is propelled by the pressure of the river current on the rudder-sweep. It is an enchanting — and in this locality somehow quite appropriate — experience to be ghosted across the river in such unusual freedom from modern motor noise. One of them operates from just below the Minster and Pfalz terrace on the left bank to the opposite Kleinbasel river front near the fifteenth-century Carthusian monastery buildings which were taken over in 1669 by the city orphanage; the buildings and small cloister have substantially retained their fifteenth-century form.

From the orphanage it is a favourite tour route then to proceed north, ie, downstream, on the Kleinbasel side past the riverside houses, to enjoy the famous view of the Minster Hill opposite with its impressive grouping of buildings above the tree-framed Pfalz terrace, the whole crowned by the twin towers and the coloured tile-roofs of the Minster. It is only a short distance to the Mittlere Brücke (Central Bridge) by which one can recross the river and rejoin the Eisengasse back to the Market Square.

Secondly, from the Market Square it is well worth while to walk by way of the line of streets named the Hutgasse, Spalenberg and Spalenvorstadt to reach the limit of the historic medieval Old Town. This limit is marked by the presence of the fourteenth-century **Spalentor**, the city gate which in the former fortifications faced Alsace. It is one of the country's most handsome and imposing.

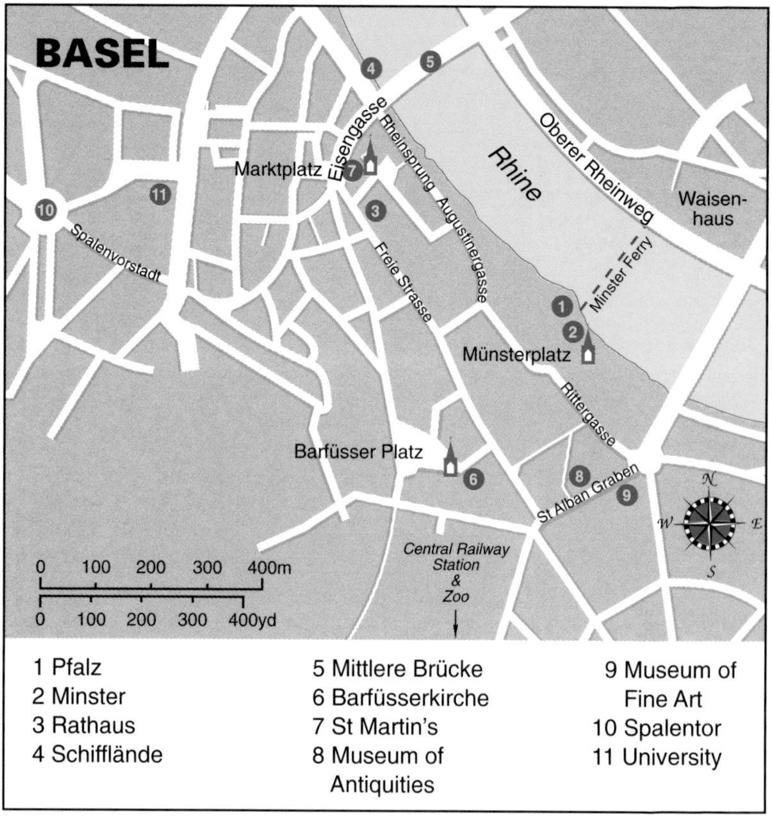

BASEL

1 Pfalz	5 Mittlere Brücke	9 Museum of Fine Art
2 Minster	6 Barfüsserkirche	10 Spalentor
3 Rathaus	7 St Martin's	11 University
4 Schifflände	8 Museum of Antiquities	

Opposite: The impressive red-sandstone Rathaus on Markplatz, Basel

Basel Minster

BANK
(Schweiz) CREDIT INDUSTRIEL D'ALSACE ET D
HERREN GLOBUS
TELEFON

Basel has innumerable other places worthy of a visit. Behind the main railway station is its renowned **zoo**. The city has more than two dozen museums with collections covering many specialised interests such as river navigation, paper, musical instruments, film, sport, the Jewish religion and culture and many more.

Excursions in the Neighbourhood

Situated as it is on a communications 'hub' Basel provides a great variety of excursions, not only into Swiss territory but into neighbouring Alsace, the French Jura and German Black Forest areas. (Information on this is readily available from the Tourist Office.) In the very immediate vicinity there are one or two unique places of interest.

1 *Dreiländereck*

The 'Three-Countries Corner' is a promontory jutting into the Rhine river port here Switzerland, France and Germany meet. A trip to it also opens one's eyes to the scope of the Rhine Harbour which is the Swiss home port for some 500 river vessels. Take the 25-minute tram ride from the Market Square to the Kleinhüningen terminus (line 14). (The tram route passes famous chemical industrial plants.) Go along the left bank of the Wiese Rhine tributary on the Hochbergerstrasse to the shipping exhibition in the harbour areas 'Our Way to the Sea' (open daily March to October). From it a 15-minute stroll along the Westquaistrasse (parallel to the Rhine) brings you in sight of a pylon which marks where the three frontiers meet.

2 *Boat trip to Augst and Rheinfelden*

A passenger steamer plies daily in summer on the Rhine from the pier at the Schifflände immediately below the Mittlere Rheinbrücke (Central Bridge referred to above). There are short trips to the Rhine Harbour downstream. But there is an upstream journey taking 2 hours which offers two interesting destinations, with 1½ or 2 hours ashore respectively.

Augst is the option after 1½ hours sailing upstream, allowing a 2-hour stay ashore. The important and well-excavated site of the Roman trading town colony of *Augusta Raurica* (founded 44BC) has a large theatre, remains of temples, a forum with a basilica as well as commercial and domestic buildings. The near end of the site has a reconstructed Roman house to which is attached a museum displaying important finds. Remains of an amphitheatre have also been found in the south-west corner of the site.

Half-an-hour further upstream is **Rheinfelden**, a picturesque, fortified small town that was originally built by using the stone debris of *Augusta Raurica*. Further details of both this and Augst are given below.

From Basel to Zürich by road

The Roman site of Augst, only 11km (7 miles) from Basel, is also easily reached by motorists, heading east either on the express motorway or on road No 3 on the south bank of the Rhine. The site is about half a kilometre from Augst, across the tributary Ergotz, on a plateau. The Roman house, museum and theatre are at the near end of the site. Towards the north of the site, on the river bank (at the village of Kaiseraugst) are the remains of a later (fourth-century) Roman fortress guarding the bridgehead.

The main road continues along the line of the river to **Rheinfelden** (7km, 4 miles), a health resort (spa) which is also the uppermost port of Rhine navigation. It was once an imperial free city, if a small one. Much of the medieval character of the small town — with its fine Town Hall, its gate towers and old city walls — one of the most picturesque and dramatic in Europe, has survived unspoiled. The Old Catholic church of St Martin and the fifteenth-century chapel of the Order of St John are worth a visit. There is also a picturesque bridge over the river.

In 11km (7 miles) beyond Rheinfelden, at Stein, fork right, leaving the riverside road, and pass beneath the motorway near Frick. The road ascends a minor pass and descends to reach **Brugg**, 15km (9 miles) beyond Stein. It lies on the River Aare near where the River Reuss joins it after flowing north from the Luzern area. Brugg is an ancient town, founded in the twelfth century by the Hapsburgs at the point where the Aare could be bridged (hence its name). In recent times industrialised, it yet conserves a very impressive Old Town area on the main street approaching the bridge. West of the town are remains of a late Roman river fort. At Brugg the Vindonissa Museum has exhibits of finds from the key Roman military camp and colony of *Vindonissa* (which is sited at present-day Windisch, about 1½km east of Brugg).

The main road crosses the river at Windisch and in a northern curve provides a view over the junction of the Aare and Reuss with the third river, Limmat, before continuing east to **Baden** (in 10km, 6 miles). Baden, now an industrial town, a noted centre of electrical engineering, is, as its name indicates, also a spa. It was known as such (*Aquae Helveticae*) to the Romans and was in late medieval times still one of the best known. It still has a medieval corner and also a well-preserved ancient covered wooden bridge over the Limmat. Before the transport revolution in the early nineteenth century Baden was a greatly favoured resort for the well-to-do citizens of Zürich which is only 22km (14 miles) away. In fact Switzerland's first railway was the Zürich-Baden line opened 1847. Nowadays Zürich is most conveniently reached by the N1 motorway which can be joined just south of Baden as it comes in from the Bern direction.

Public Transport Option

The route described above for private motorists can also be closely followed by public transport on the SBB line Basel-Zürich (Official Timetable 700). Expresses stop only at Brugg and Baden, regional trains at numerous stops including Kaiseraugst and Rheinfelden.

P
CH

Dreiländereck, where three frontiers meet, showing the flags of France, Germany and Switzerland

Opposite: Basel's medieval Spalentor city-gate

1.2 Zürich

Zürich, like many historic Swiss cities, is situated at the end of a lake where the lake's outflow river could be bridged. The River Limmat which flows out of Lake Zürich (Zürichsee) is joined at an acute angle by a tributary River Sihl. The city developed on the banks of the Y-shaped water-course thus formed and its riverside promenades called *Quais* are one of its pleasing features. Zürich's historic *Altstadt*, Old Town, lies on both banks of the Limmat between the lake and the junction of the rivers.

(**Note**: in Zürich the Tourist Information Office is at the Main Railway Station. Private motorists in particular should call there and pick up the useful leaflet with information for motorists, especially on parking.)

The city is best known to strangers nowadays as a great financial centre with world-wide influence as well as being the largest city in Switzerland. It has many modern buildings yet it is also a particularly charming, graceful and fascinating city. This is brought home on a walk through the Old Town on both sides of the Limmat.

Left Bank Old Town

The walk begins at the *Hauptbahnhof* (Main Station). Facing the main exit from the station are the escalators that lead down to an underground modern shopping mall; pass through to another escalator that leads to the **Bahnhofstrasse** heading away from the station. This street, for most of its length traffic-free except for the trams and lined with linden trees, is the home of the great banks and also of the most exclusive and upmarket shops. On a first walk, however, resisting the temptation to window shop, continue along the left-hand pavement. Although the street carries on all the way to the lakeside, turn off into the Rennweg which goes off left at an angle and turn left again, at the first intersection, into the Fortunagasse. This street shortly intersects the Lindenhofstrasse, into which turn right to climb the slope to the Lindenhof.

The **Lindenhof** is Zürich's scenic as well as its historic centre; tree-shaded, as its name suggests, it is a park-like belvedere on a little plateau where a late Roman fort once stood. It offers fascinating panoramic views across the Limmat, which it overhangs, to the other medieval quarter of Zürich on the right bank opposite. There are relics of Roman stonework and of a medieval imperial residence, park benches, a fountain, a giant chessboard and chess pieces under the trees. Below at street level there are glimpses of a maze of fascinating, uneven, winding medieval alleyways to be explored.

From the south end of the Lindenhof steps descend into the Pfalzgasse and by way of Strehlgasse and Widdergasse reach the curving Augustinergasse with its old-world oriel windows. The thirteenth-century Old Catholic **Augustinian church** in the Münzplatz (Mint Square), off Augustinergasse, was secularised at the Reformation and the city mint located in it in 1596. In the nineteenth century the nave was restored in

Gothic style for Catholic worship. Part of the Augustinian monastery wing served as Zürich's first university between 1837 and 1864.

Return to the curved upper section of Augustinergasse to reach the picturesque and peaceful square called **St Petershofstatt**, surrounded on three sides by fine houses; one side of the square is taken up by St Peter's, the city's oldest parish church (Protestant). Its sturdy square-built thirteenth-century Romanesque tower (heightened in the sixteenth century and the clock added) contrasts with the baroque nave inside. The clock face is the largest in all Europe. One of the fine houses in the square, No 6, was once the home of St Peter's most famous incumbent, the theologian, author and preacher Lavater, friend and host to the great German writer Goethe.

From St Petershofstatt the Schlüsselgasse leads down to the Münsterhof (Minster Square). The tall, delicate spire of the **Fraumünster** is as much a landmark of the left bank of the Old Town as the twin towers of the Grossmünster are of the right bank opposite. The Fraumünster originated as the church of a convent for noblewomen founded in the ninth century by a grandson of Charlemagne, King Ludwig the German. And the abbesses of the foundation were the city's effective rulers until 1522. The main parts of the building are early Gothic but there have been reconstructions and additions throughout its history, including the great painted glass windows (1970) by Marc Chagall.

The Münsterhof has two impressive guild halls, one of which, the rococo **Zunfthaus zur Meisen** on the riverbank houses the Ceramic Collection of the Swiss National Museum.

The Wühre passage along the river front leads downstream through a hotel's arcade to the charming **Weinplatz**, with its tall Gothic buildings bearing sixteenth-century house signs. This is the city's oldest market square and a former site of its corn exchange. Once an unloading place for goods conveyed on lake and river, it is today a calling place for the water-buses that carry out river excursions.

Equally picturesque and evocative of the medieval city is the water's edge passage called the Schipfe on the wharf-line where boat landings and transhipments between lake and river vessels were once made. The complexly-stacked Schipfe row of sixteenth-century buildings nestling into the side of the steep slope of the Lindenhof is perhaps seen more clearly from the opposite side of the Limmat which is the scene of the second part of this Old Town walk.

Right Bank Old Town

The starting point is the Münsterbrücke (Minster Bridge) which directly links the two cathedral churches, the Fraumünster on the left bank and the Grossmünster on the right. However, before visiting the Grossmünster complex, two buildings upstream, ie, to the right of the bridge, merit some attention. The nearer, the **Helmhaus**, once a law court but now used for non-permanent exhibitions, is an interesting example of late baroque

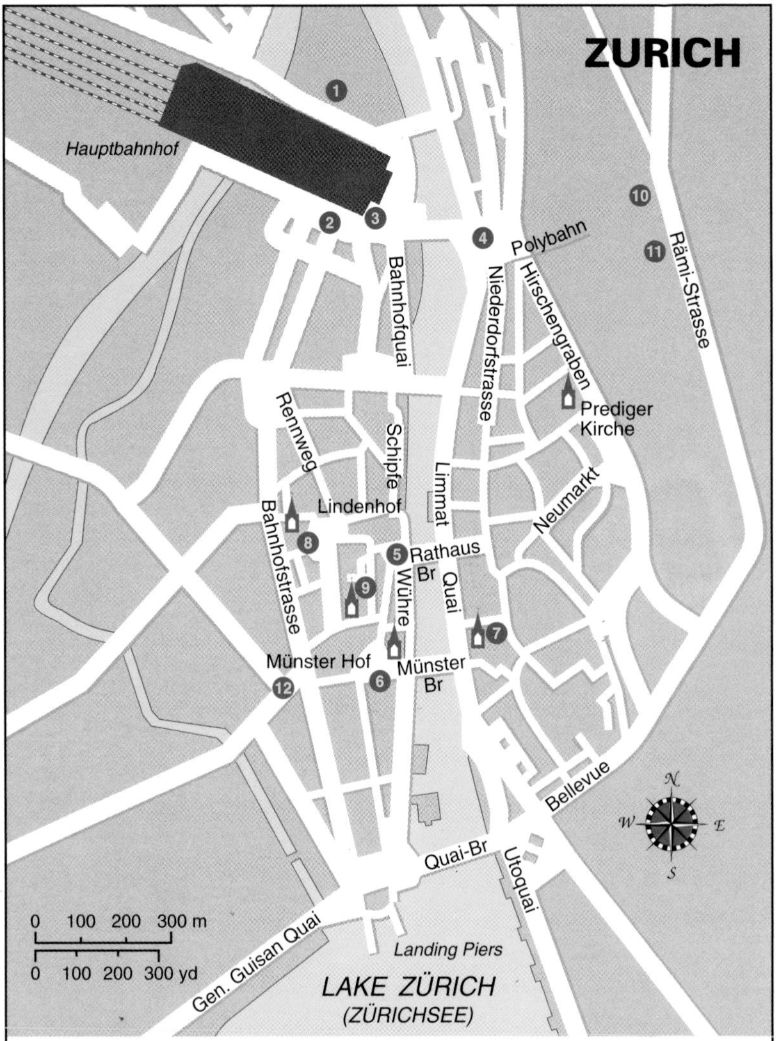

ZURICH

1 Landesmuseum	5 Weinplatz	9 Peterskirche
2 Bahnhofplatz	6 Fraumünster	10 Technical College
3 Tourist Information	7 Grossmünster	11 University
4 Centralplatz	8 Augustiner Kirche	12 Paradeplatz

The village of Herrliberg on Lake Zürich

classic style but has long had a close relationship with its neighbouring late Gothic 'preaching' church, with the small ridge-turret, known as the **Wasserkirche** (moated church) as the two buildings formerly stood on an island.

Seen from the bridgehead looking downstream, ie, away from the Helmhaus, the several guild halls on the right bank Limmatquai make an impressive group — the Carpenters' Guild Hall, the neighbouring banqueting hall of the former nobility, standing above its riverside arcades, and the Hall of the Guild of Spice Merchants. Beyond the riverside guild halls, however, stands a late seventeenth-century building of exemplary dignity, the Renaissance and early baroque **Rathaus (Town Hall)** built over the tunnel vault of its predecessor. Zürich cantonal councils still meet here.

The whole area of the Old Town right bank lying deep behind the Limmatquai, with cobblestoned streets and alleyways, and squares with fountains, carved coats of arms, medieval houses, quaint restaurants, antique shops and galleries, has an unforgettable atmosphere. The river bridges offer the chance of varying the viewpoints, eg, after visiting the Town Hall, cross the river by the Rathausbrücke (Town Hall Bridge) back to the Weinplatz to see it in fresh perspective.

From the long list of fascinating corners in this area, two further items single themselves out: the former Dominican monastery with its masterpiece church of thirteenth- and fourteenth-century craftsmanship, the **Predigerkirche**; and the walk along the charming Predigergasse which leads from the church to the **Neumarkt**, one of the Old Town's most colourful streets.

The highlight of the circuit is then reached by continuing south along the Münstergasse to the **Grossmünster**, Zürich's landmark and emblem. The Minster complex dominating the upper Limmat links several right bank street and terrace levels and is accessible from several angles.

Until the Reformation this was a canonry. The oldest parts of the building go back to the eleventh and twelfth centuries, other principal structures to the thirteenth. The towers, originally low, were raised at the end of the fifteenth-century and the existing domes added after a fire in the late eighteenth century. Exterior and interior features are of great architectural interest. Adjacent is the Minster Schoolhouse, nowadays providing premises for the University theological faculty.

Water-bus excursions on the river and lake provide an excellent opportunity for gaining a general impression of the right and left bank areas of the Old Town. The boat trips start from the quay at the **Landesmuseum**, Swiss National Museum, behind the Main Railway Station, with departures at half-hourly intervals during the season. On reaching the lake the boat continues as far as the Zürichhorn, making a landing at the recreational area there.

Zürich has many museums, but in scope and in variety of interest, first and foremost is the Landesmuseum with a wealth of exhibits on aspects of Swiss life, culture, environment, art and history.

An entirely different perspective of Zürich can be had from the funicular rail that runs from the Central Square, a very short distance from the far side of the Bahnhofbrücke (Main Station Bridge) on the Limmatquai. The Polybahn coach runs every three minutes to a terrace overlooking the city, giving a view of the Alps. The funicular also spares its passengers a steep climb on foot to reach the University and Technical High School which lie at terrace level above the central part of the city.

Apart from the river trips, lake steamer trips of varied duration depart from the landing stage at the lake end of the Bahnhofstrasse.

The Zürichsee with 88sq km (34sq miles) surface area is the third largest lake within the boundaries of Switzerland. Today it largely serves recreational needs but historically it was the vital water route for commerce and for travel between Zürich and Central Switzerland, Glarus and St Gallen. A round trip on the lake, lasting 4 to 5 hours, is a rewarding and interesting experience. Even tourists who have their own private motor transport can profit from the trip.

Excursions from Zürich

1 *Round Trip to Rapperswil by Road*

Leave Zürich from the Quaibrücke (where the River Limmat leaves the lake) heading west by General Guisan Quai along the lakeside following road signs in the 'Chur' direction. In 5km (3 miles) **Kilchberg** is the first village on the west shore with its fifteenth-century church of St Peter providing its landmark on the hill. Thomas Mann, the great German twentieth-century novelist, for long an exile in Switzerland, is buried here. On the lake shore was situated the famous eighteenth-century Zürich porcelain works. Four kilometres (2½ miles) further on is **Thalwil**, the important rail junction for Chur and Luzern-Gotthard lines. A textile town still, in the nineteenth century it was a great centre of the silk industry. **Horgen** (in 5km, 3 miles), once a wine-growing village, is now an industrial centre. From Horgen a modern car-ferry runs across the lake to Meilen on the east shore.

After Horgen is a more open stretch of the lakeside (although the railway line runs between shore and road). In 4km (2½ miles) is the peninsula of **Au**, an attractive nature reserve with orchards and vineyards managed by the Swiss Fruit and Wine College in the neighbouring industrial town of **Wädenswil** (3km, 2 miles). The Federal Research Institute for Fruit-growing, Viniculture and Gardening is housed in the castle above the town. **Richterswil**, just 4km (2½ miles) further on, has a particularly unspoiled village centre; there are fine views from the terrace above the village on which stand two churches. The offshore islands of Ufenau and Lützelau, nature reserves and bird sanctuaries, can be seen on the left during the next stretch of road to **Pfäffikon**, 7km (4½ miles) further on, which lies in canton Schwyz and is a rail junction. The castle here, which belonged to the famous Einsiedeln Abbey, has an interesting thirteenth-

Hotel
Freihof
MUSIKHAUS

The left bank of the Limmat in Zürich Old Town

Opposite: Rapperswil, the castle and square

The lake front, Rapperswil

century tower. From here a causeway runs across the lake to Rapperswil (4km, 2½ miles) on the further shore, damming off the main body of the lake from the Obersee (Upper Lake).

Rapperswil has an enchanting old-world atmosphere, sited so picturesquely on a peninsula. Founded about AD1200, the small town was, for a period in the fifteenth century, an imperial free city and has been part of canton St Gallen since 1803. The thirteenth-century castle towers impressively above the town; a broad flight of steps links it with the medieval heart of the town, including high-arcaded Hintergasse and central Hauptplatz (Main Square) and the *Rathaus* with a fifteenth-century Council Chamber. The castle houses the interesting Burgenmuseum (Castles Museum) illustrating life in the age of chivalry. A bastion shaded by trees gives fine views over the town below and the colourful harbour and lakefront.

Returning now on the north-east shore of the lake, road No 17 reaches **Stäfa** after 5km (3 miles), the largest wine-growing village in the canton. Seven kilometres (4½miles) further is **Meilen**, a prominent town in the chain of attractive residential lakeside communities with beaches in front and vineyards on the hillsides behind (commonly known to Zürichers as the 'Gold Coast'). Herrliberg-Feldmeilen (3km, 2 miles) and Erlenbach (6km, 4 miles) are similar communities.

Küsnacht lies 2km (1¼ miles) on. Its fifteenth-century church has frescos of similar date in the chancel. A former estate house of the Knights of St John (the Hospitallers' Commandery here having been founded in 1358) now serves as a Teacher Training College. In 6km (3¾ miles) the road reaches Bellevue Square in Zürich.

Needless to say, the attractive residential communities on the lakeside just described are served by a regular railway commuter service running to Rapperswil, which can therefore be reached by rail in about 50 minutes (Timetable 730).

2 *Excursion to Einsiedeln*

Either as a side-trip in the course of the Rapperswil excursion, or as a separate day excursion, a trip from Zürich to Einsiedeln, the famous Swiss pilgrimage destination, so close by in the pre-Alpine region between Lake Zürich and Lake Luzern, is a must.

If travelling direct to Einsiedeln from Zürich, it is better to take the N3 motorway east-bound (direction Chur) beyond Wädenswil to the exit indicated for Einsiedeln and Schwyz. Turning south, in some 6km (3¾ miles) the Biberbrugg crossroads are reached. There turn off left for Einsiedeln.

The small town of Einsiedeln, set in its high valley in pre-Alpine country, as a summer and winter resort is in itself unremarkable. What brings most visitors — and devout pilgrims — here is its great abbey. For more than a thousand years there has been a monastic community here, for most of that time a monastery under the Benedictine rule. In its present form it was rebuilt in the mid-eighteenth century, one of Europe's greatest baroque buildings, with the monastery church embodied as centrepiece of the great façade. Its *Gnadenkapelle*, Chapel of Grace, enshrines the Black Madonna venerated by pilgrims. The abbey possesses a wealth of art and architectural treasures. In the abbey Great Hall (accessible to visitors from the south side of the monastery) special exhibitions are assembled from these art collections.

Public Transport Option

The frequent rail service from Zürich to Pfäffikon (Timetable 720), a half-hour trip, has a regular connection at Wädenswil through to Einsiedeln via Biberbrugg (Timetable 672). (Einsiedeln can also be visited fairly conveniently from Luzern and Arth-Goldau in Central Switzerland.)

1.3 North-East Switzerland

North-east Switzerland — the region that faces South Germany across the River Rhine on that east-west part of its course from Lake Constance — is probably the area least well known to English-speaking visitors. Yet much of its great interest can be absorbed in comparatively brief tours from Zürich. (**Note**: the routes in this section are described as road journeys, but can be carried out equally well by public transport — of which there are details.)

Zürich to Stein-am-Rhein, Schaffhausen, Rhine Falls

From the city centre take roads indicated by signposts 'Winterthür' so as to join the N1 motorway; but in 25km ($15^1/_2$ miles) leave the N1, turning off at the exit indicating 'Schaffhausen'. Bypassing Winterthür, continue to follow 'Schaffhausen' signs on to the N4 expressway until, in 9km ($5^1/_2$ miles), the exit sign for 'Stein-am-Rhein'. Continue to follow this side road so signposted, through the picturesque wine-growing villages of Lower and Upper Stammheim, until in 19km (12 miles) **Stein-am-Rhein** is reached. It is situated in an enclave on the north bank of the Rhine near its out-flow from Lake Constance (known as the Bodensee). Stein too is set among vineyards. It is a favourite tourist destination, having retained so many features and so much atmosphere of a small medieval town, with fountains, half-timbered buildings, colourful façades, houses with exquisitely carved and decorated oriel windows projecting into the street. Its Market Place has a *Rathaus* with fifteenth-century stained-glass windows. Its Benedictine monastery of St George (dissolved 1525) is famed for its interior paintings and decorations, and is held to be the best-conserved medieval monastic complex in the German-speaking lands. It is now a national monument and houses a museum. The former abbey church, St

The Munot Tower and fortifications, Schaffhausen

Opposite: The lower Town Gate, Stein-am-Rhein

A fountain in Schaffhausen Old Town

Schweizer Heimatwerk

George's, is a Romanesque twelfth-century basilica.

From Stein recross to the south bank of the Rhine and take road No 13 west towards Schaffhausen, 19km (12 miles) distant. However, in 9km (5½ miles) another quaint little medieval bridge town, **Diessenhofen**, may prove a tempting halt, with its many Gothic buildings. Its wooden Rhine bridge has been often rebuilt, after destruction by the Russians for instance in 1799, and again in 1945 after wartime bombing.

Schaffhausen, with a population of about 40,000, is an important industrial town. Town and canton also form an enclave on the north bank of the Rhine. It owed its existence to the need here for quays and a workforce for the transhipment and portage of waterborne freight on a section of the Rhine with hazardous rapids and falls. It joined the Swiss Confederation in 1501 as a defensive move against Hapsburg threats to its independence. In more modern times (1866 onwards) it exploited the hydro-electric power potential of the Rhine and pioneered its application to the production of aluminium.

However, it has cherished and conserved the character and charm of the historic medieval quarter of the town, including the two remaining elements of the former city fortifications, the Upper Tower and the Swabian Gate (its portals for trade routes into Germany) as well as its cloistered Romanesque Minster. In a stroll through the winding streets of the traffic-free old quarter of the town the visitor can admire some of the numerous richly decorated oriel windows that were clearly a status symbol among its burghers, and the sculptured façades of ornate burgher houses. (One of them, the fresco-decorated Haus zum Ritter ie, the House at the Sign of the Mounted Knight, ranks as the finest example of German late Renaissance work.) There still exist, too, no less than twelve guild halls — some serving nowadays as restaurants. Other highlights are Allerheiligen (All Saints), a former Benedictine abbey, with its Minster church; and above all, literally, as it presides over the city, the sixteenth-century Munot Fortress, of which the picturesque outline is emblematic of Schaffhausen. Long flights of steps lead up to its rooftop outlook which provides a fine view of the city. The monastic buildings accommodate a museum which is open daily, except Mondays.

The magnificent **Rhine Falls** near Schaffhausen, the highest in Europe, are an added attraction to the city. They are especially impressive in early high summer when the river is at its height, swollen with the melting snows from the mountains of canton Graubünden.

By road the falls are reached from Schaffhausen by following first the signposts for Zürich. After 3km (2 miles) look out for the signpost 'Laufen: Rheinfall'. In 1½km (1 mile) the Laufen Castle's parking place is reached, from which a pathway leads to the two viewpoint terraces giving an outlook on the 21m (69ft) high and 150m (492ft) wide falls.

Return by main road N4 (signposted for Zürich) by way again of the Winterthür bypass, and then by N1 south to Zürich. Alternatively, if there is no need to return to Zürich, at this point it could be convenient to start off on the next excursion (by turning into the N1 not towards Zürich but in the opposite direction, eastward to Wil and St Gallen).

Public Transport Option

Swiss Transport: Official Timetables

The word 'Timetable' followed by a number frequently occurs in connection with transport. The reference is to the publication (obtainable from Swiss National Tourist Offices in Switzerland and abroad), 'Official Timetable' of all public transport (see Introduction).

By rail the above excursion is more conveniently carried out in reverse order, taking the Zürich-Schaffhausen train (Timetable 760) and first making the tour of Schaffhausen; then do the Rhine Falls excursion by using the train service Schaffhausen-Winterthür (Timetable 762) which runs every hour, taking only a 5-minute journey to the second stop, which is Laufen Castle and Rhine Falls. (This Laufen stop operates from May to October.) The excursion to Stein-am-Rhein can be made on the Schaffhausen-Rorschach train (Timetable 820) which takes around 20 minutes to Stein-am-Rhein. An attractive alternative is to take advantage of the river-boat excursion on the Rhine, lasting 1¾ hours upstream to Stein and 1 hour return downstream, also calling in at Diessenhofen (Timetable 2820).

A Round Trip: Zürich to St Gallen and Appenzell

If starting the trip from Zürich city centre take roads indicated by signposts 'Winterthür' bringing you onto the N1 motorway but thereafter disregard exit signs for Winterthür, remaining on the N1 to bypass Winterthür and continue eastward to reach Wil in 24km (15 miles). There is a glimpse of the Appenzeller mountains in the south-east as the Wil exit is approached.

Wil is another small industrial town that retains a most charming Old Quarter on a typical hill site. It was founded in the twelfth-century by the Counts of Toggenburg and since the early nineteenth century has been the main town of the Toggenburg district, a very attractive area of varied hill and valley landscape extremely popular with ramblers and hikers. Having been the favoured summer country seat of the St Gallen abbots, Wil has some particularly fine fourteenth- to eighteenth-century buildings on Marktgasse and Hauptplatz with the abbots' palatial castle (the *Hof*) centrally sited.

From Wil in 29km (18 miles) the motorway reaches **St Gallen**. St Gallen's recorded history goes back to AD612 when the Irish missionary

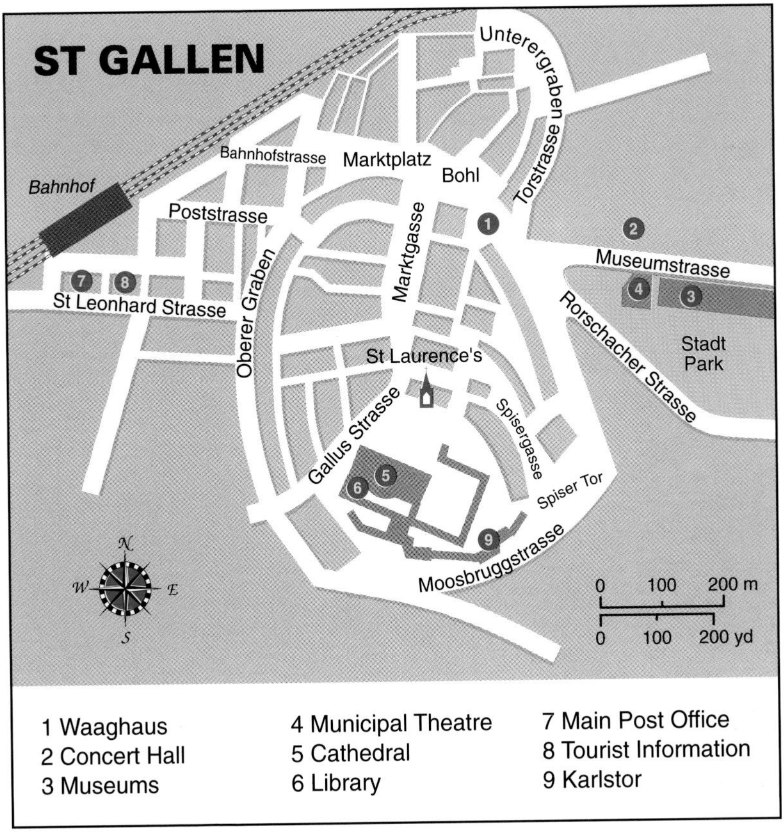

ST GALLEN

Untergraben
Bahnhofstrasse
Marktplatz
Bohl
Torstrasse
Bahnhof
Poststrasse
Marktgasse
Museumstrasse
St Leonhard Strasse
Oberer Graben
Rorschacher Strasse
Stadt Park
St Laurence's
Gallus Strasse
Spisergasse
Spiser Tor
Moosbruggstrasse
N
W
E
S
0 100 200 m
0 100 200 yd

1 Waaghaus
2 Concert Hall
3 Museums
4 Municipal Theatre
5 Cathedral
6 Library
7 Main Post Office
8 Tourist Information
9 Karlstor

Opposite: Cathedral façade from Klosterhof, St Gallen

The Brewery, Appenzell

Gallus established his hermit cell in the Steinach high valley in pre-Alpine green hill country. By the eighth century it had become the nucleus of an abbey around which arose a settlement of peasants and craftsmen that expanded into the town which in AD1212 gained the charter of a free imperial city, the abbey itself developing into the most important religious community in the area of Lake Constance. In 1454 the town joined the Swiss Confederation. And in 1524 it opted for the Reformation, while the abbey maintained its rights and influence in the surrounding area which remained Catholic. The town prospered in textile crafts firstly with linen-making; and later with cotton weaving and cotton embroidery which it developed into a great export industry, influencing the development of textile craft-work in the neighbouring countryside.

Tour of St Gallen

The town walls were removed early last century, but even so the circular (or slightly oval) shape of the medieval city grouped round the abbey precinct is obvious. It is easily reached from the station by walking south from the Bahnhofplatz into St Leonhardstrasse, turning left to go east, crossing at right angles the Kornhausstrasse (noting the Tourist Information Office at the corner) to enter the Oberer Graben avenue which marks the beginning of the Old Town. (**Note**: *'Graben'* often occurs as a name for a wide street in historic towns. The word means a 'trench' and indicates a filled-in moat on the line of demolished fortified walls.) Follow the Oberer Graben north until the wide Marktplatz (Market Square) opens up to the right. From the Square turn again right to head south down Marktgasse (passing on the left the restored St Lawrence church) to reach the spacious Klosterhof (Abbey Courtyard) surrounded by buildings of the former Benedictine abbey (dissolved in 1805) including the **Cathedral church**. Entrance to the Stiftsbibliothek (Abbey Library) is obtained from an inner courtyard to the south. The three-aisled baroque Cathedral was built between 1755 and 1767, decorated by leading South German masters. In 1983 the Cathedral and entire abbey precinct were listed by UNESCO as protected buildings of world cultural importance.

The west wing of the monastery quadrangle is occupied by the **Abbey Library**. Its hall ranks as Switzerland's most beautiful secular rococo interior. The Library's contents survived secularisation unscathed and undiminished and it is now a foremost research library open to the public. Its 130,000 volumes include 2,000 manuscripts and 1,650 early printed books.

To the west of the Cathedral is the Gallusstrasse with attractive burghers' houses of the seventeenth and eighteenth century. There are others in the Moosbruggstrasse to the south of the abbey quarter. Also on the Moosbruggstrasse is the Karls Tor, a surviving element from the old town walls.

Returning back north on the Marktstrasse and turning right into the eastward extension of the Marktplatz one arrives at a broad street named the Bohl. At its east end is a medieval building with crow-stepped gables, the sixteenth-century Waaghaus (weigh-house) with Council Chamber on upper floor. Across the Torstrasse from the Bohl (and so outside the limits of the Old Town) running north-east is the modern Museumstrasse in which are sited the Concert Hall, Municipal Theatre and museum buildings. To its south lies the Municipal Park.

From St Gallen a round trip can be made by returning to Zürich via Wattwil and Rapperswil.

St Gallen to Wattwil and Rapperswil

Leave St Gallen by the west suburbs but instead of joining the N1 motorway take road No 8 signposted Wattwil. In 10km (6 miles) **Herisau** is reached, another ancient town, which began as a property of the St Gallen abbey. It is the main town of the Protestant half-canton of Appenzell and has a number of interesting precincts. Four kilometres (2½ miles) further on is Waldstatt from which two roads branch off south-east into the canton of Appenzell. Continue on road No 8 from Waldstatt as it climbs through attractive wooded hill country, passing within sight of the ruined castle of Neu-Toggenburg before descending in steep zigzags, with the Köbelis (1,046m, 3,432ft) towering on the left, to intersect at Lichtensteig with road No 16 (which comes down through the Toggenburg district from Wil). **Lichtensteig**, a quaint little town situated on a rocky spur above the River Thur, is the principal place of the Toggenburg region. It has some charming old half-timbered houses raised on arcades in the main street; near the Town House is the Toggenburger Heimatmuseum (folk museum). From Lichtensteig on road No 16 heading south, **Wattwil** is reached in 2km (1¼ miles). This long town is the economic centre of the Toggenburg, and has a textile college. Above the town is the fortress-like walled Capuchin convent of St Mary among the Angels.

Leave Wattwil by road No 8, heading south-west and climbing out of the Toggenburg valley to reach the Ricken Pass (780m, 2,559ft) in 6km (3¾ miles). From the pass a gentle descent, offering panoramic views to the south-east, leads past St Gallenkappel on to Jona on the outskirts of Rapperswil in 18km (11 miles). Near Jona on the lakeside is **Wurmsbach**, and the Cistercian convent of Mariazell; the nearby one-time parish church, St Dionys, fifteenth century, has late Gothic wall paintings. From Jona, **Rapperswil** is 2km (1¼ miles) away and a return to Zürich can be made on either side of the Zürichsee (as detailed in the Rapperswil excursion from Zürich in the previous section).

Appenzell

The canton of Appenzell is especially noted for its adherence to traditional ways and customs. Since 1597 the canton has been divided into two half-cantons, Catholic Innerrhoden and Reformed Ausserrhoden. (The word *Rhoden* here indicates a medieval tax district.) Ausserrhoden's economy has rested mainly on the famed Appenzeller industries of weaving and

DENNER-

In autumn the cows are brought down from the Alps at Weissbad, Appenzell

Gais lies on the road between St Gallen and Appenzell

embroidery; while Innerrhoden's has been essentially high Alpine agriculture. (Incidentally, the whole canton of Appenzell lies within the St Gallen canton.) Both half-cantons are noted for their democratic form of local government by the *Landsgemeinde*. On the last Sunday in April each year the meeting of the *Landsgemeinde* takes place — the formal assembly of all vote-holding citizens of the canton (men above the age of 20, carrying swords as a symbol of their right to vote). This assembly forms the half-canton's law-giving governing body.

To give motorists with private transport an opportunity to sample something of the unique atmosphere of Appenzell an excursion on good roads can be made from the road junction at Waldstatt referred to above, 14km (8½ miles) from St Gallen, where there is a choice of two roads into Appenzell. A short triangular trip can be made by using both. Leave Waldstatt by road No 152 for **Urnäsch** (14km, 8½ miles), the largest commune in Ausserrhoden, with its traditional, colourful, immaculately maintained wooden houses. It is noted for traditional observances and activities such as yodelling, playing the alpenhorn, wood-carving, and folk-dancing. There is a museum to these traditions. Visitors interested in hill walking have ample opportunities in this district.

There is a secondary road which goes straight from Urnäsch in a southerly direction, climbing up a valley in the mountains to the Schwägalp high pastures. At **Schwägalp** is a large mountain inn, facing the precipitous north face of Säntis, the outstanding mountain of this region. Nearby the inn is the bottom station of one of Switzerland's most daring suspended cablecar lines (Timetable 1730) that runs to near the summit (2,483m, 8,147ft) of the Säntis, which provides spectacular panoramas. The Urnäsch-Schwägalp trip can also be taken by Postbus (Timetable 854.20).

The principal road, No 152, turns east (to the left) from Urnäsch, however, and via Gonten covers 11km (7 miles) to arrive at **Appenzell**, the principal village of Innerrhoden, set in its pastoral valley. Its main street (Hauptgasse) also has a row of picturesque houses built of wood, brightly painted and with curved gables facing the street. It has a sixteenth-century *Rathaus* with historical frescos; also a friary and a convent of the Capuchin order. Of special interest is the Landsgemeindeplatz, the great square in which the annual meeting of vote-holding citizens takes place.

Leave Appenzell by road No 151 for Waldstatt (12km, 7½ miles). The route is via **Hundwil** in Ausserrhoden, which alternates with Trogen in hosting the annual meeting of their half-canton's *Landsgemeinde*. Hundwil's centre of gravity rather shifted from the historic sixteenth-century Dorfplatz (Village Square) with the building of seventeenth- and eighteenth-century houses around the greater square of the Landsgemeindeplatz further west. From Waldstatt one can return to St Gallen, or rejoin the N1 motorway westbound for a rapid return to Zürich, or complete the round trip back to Zürich via Wattwil and Rapperswil as described above.

Public Transport Option

There is an excellent rail service to St Gallen from Zürich (Timetable 850) via Winterthur and Wil. Almost all these trains also stop at Zürich airport (*'Flughafen'* on the timetable). The return journey can also be carried out to make a round trip by using the St Gallen-Wattwil-Rapperswil service (Timetable 870). This is, in any case, a fascinating railway journey. Soon after leaving St Gallen the line crosses the highest railway bridge in Switzerland over the deep gorge of the River Sitter, supported on two piers 98m (320ft) high; the metal main span of the bridge is 120m (394ft) long. (This part of Switzerland may not have any great mountain peaks, but it has a part-cultivated, part-afforested landscape strikingly furrowed by very deep valleys.)

The town of Herisau (10km, 6 miles from St Gallen) is also crossed by the railway on a great stonework viaduct reminiscent of ancient aqueducts. And there are some notable tunnels that take the line through from one valley to another, the longest being the 8½km (5 miles) long tunnel that bores down through the Ricken in a southerly direction from near Wattwil, taking the rail from the Toggenburg valley through to the upper lakeside of Zürichsee. Between Wattwil and the tunnel entrance there is a fine view to the left of the jagged sierra of the Churfirsten range (highest peak 2,309m, 7,575ft) that shelters the Walensee from the north; and on leaving the tunnel nearly 9km (6 miles) on, there is a splendid view ahead of the great Glarus Alps further south (highest peak 3,614m, 11,857ft).

For the Appenzell excursion a round trip by rail is also possible from St Gallen. Alongside the St Gallen *Hauptbahnhof* is a smaller station, terminus of the St Gallen-Appenzell railway (Timetable 855). Its motor-coaches are equipped for the steep start of the journey to reach high ground where there are wide views over the canton — with Säntis ever-prominent in the south. The line runs by way of Gais, after which it takes a steep descent down to reach Appenzell village. The return from Appenzell can be made by the other line, the Appenzeller Bahn (Timetable 854) by way of Urnäsch to Herisau, where one changes to the Swiss Federal Railways (SBB) line (Timetable 870) either to reach St Gallen or to travel on, in the opposite direction, via Wattwil and Rapperswil.

Note: travelling by the Appenzeller Bahn via Urnäsch enables the trip from that village by Postbus (Timetable 854.20) to Schwägalp and thence to Säntis summit by cablecar (Timetable 1730). The *Official Timetable* volume 2 (Buses) 854.20 shows not only the actual Schwägalp Postbus timings but also the connecting times of suitable trains to Urnäsch from St Gallen and even Zürich, as well as connecting times of the cablecar.

Additional Information

Places to Visit

Appenzell
Heimatsmuseum
Rathaus, Hauptgasse
CH-9050 Appenzell
☎ 071/59 17 33
Folk museum reflecting local history and customs.
Open: July to mid-September, daily 1.30-5pm; May, June, mid-September to end October, Sundays 1.30-5pm.

Retonios Mechanisches
Musikmuseum
Bankgasse 6,
CH-9050 Appenzell
☎ 071/87 41 22
Automatic dolls and toys, mechanical musical instruments. Guided tours: July to October daily 10.30am/2.30pm/3.30pm; November to June Tuesday to Sunday only 2.30pm.

Augst
Römermuseum Augst
Giebenacherstrasse 17
CH-4302 Augst
☎ 061/811 11 87
Roman House and museum open Monday 1.30 to 6pm; Tuesday to Sunday 10am-12noon, 1.30-6pm. Museum and reconstructed house are only part of the very extensive site of Roman *Augusta Raurica* which includes a very large reconstructed theatre and other buiildings.

Baden
Historisches Museum der Stadt
Landvogteischloss
CH-5400 Baden
☎ 056/22 75 44
Historical, exhibits include porcelain, ceramics, housed in keep of old castle.
Open: Tuesday to Sunday, 10am-12noon, 2-5pm.

Basel
Kunstmuseum
(Museum of Fine Arts)
St Alban Graben 16
☎ 061/271 08 28
A unique collection of old masters and twentieth-century artists.
Open: June-Sept, Tuesday to Sunday 10am-5pm; October to May, Tuesday to Sunday 10-12am, 2-5pm.

Antikenmuseum
(Museum of Ancient Art)
St Alban Graben 5
Ancient Greek and Italian works of art.
Open: Tuesday to Sunday 10am-12noon, 2-5pm.

Historisches Museum
(Museum of History) in two parts:
1 Kirschgarten Museum, Elisabethenstrasse 27, illustrates eighteenth-century life and domestic culture. And quite close.
2 Barfüsserkirche (former Franciscan church), Barfüsserplatz, with local treasures including those of the Minster.
Open Tuesday to Sunday 10am-12noon, 2-5pm.

Basler Papiermühle Museum
(Museum of Paper and the Book)
St Alban Tal 35
CH-4052 Basel
☎ 061/272 96 52
In a former medieval paper mill (working).
Open: Monday to Saturday 2-5pm; Sunday 10am-12noon, 2-5pm.

Sammlung alter Musikinstrumente
Leonhardsstrasse 8
CH4051 Basel
Collection of old musical instruments.
Open: Wednesday & Friday, Sunday 10am-12noon, 2-5pm.

Jüdisches Museum der Schweiz
(Swiss Jewish Museum)
Kornhausgasse 8
CH-4051 Basel
☎ 061/261 95 14
Exhibits which illustrate Jewish religious customs.

Open: Sunday 10am-12noon, 2-5pm; Monday and Wednesday, 2-5pm.

Schweizerisches Pharmazie-Historisches Museum
Totengässlein 3
CH-4051 Basel
☎ 061/ 261 79 40
Reconstructed eighteenth-/nineteenth-century pharmacies.
Open: Monday to Friday 9am-12noon, 2-5pm, or by arrangement.

Rheinschiffahrtsausstellung 'Unser Weg zum Meer'
(The exhibition on Rhine Navigation — 'Our Route to the Sea') at Kleinhüningen harbour
Wiesendamm 4, CH-4019 Basel
☎ 061/66 33 49
Open: daily March to October 10am-12noon, 2-5pm; in winter only on Sundays.

Basel's Zoologischer Garten
(Zoo) is outstanding; conveniently situated in the city.
Open: summer 8am-6.30pm, winter 8am-5pm.

Brugg
Vindonissa-Museum
CH-5200 Brugg
☎ 056/41 21 84
Archaeological finds from Roman legionary camp *Vindonissa.*
Open: Tuesday to Sunday, 10am-12noon, 2-5pm.

Lichtensteig
Fredys Mechanisches Musikmuseum
Zur Frohburg
CH-9620 Lichtensteig (SG)
☎ 074/7 37 66
Historical music boxes (1780 to 1928); guided tours Wednesday, Saturday, Sunday 2.30pm and 4.30pm. Closed 1st and 3rd Sunday in month.

Rapperswil
Medieval castle
Open daily except Tuesday.

St Gallen
Stiftsbibliothek
Abbey Library, possesses outstanding works, especially illuminated books, from eighth- to eleventh-century abbey school. For times of access inquire locally (☎ 071/22 57 19).

Kirchhofer Museum
Museumstrasse 27
CH-9000 St Gallen
☎ 071/24 75 21
Silver vessels from High Renaissance and baroque periods.
Open: June to September, Thursday to Sunday, 10am-12noon, 2-5pm. October to May, Thursday to Saturday, 2-4pm and Sunday 10am-12noon, 2-4pm.

Textilmuseum
Vadianstrasse 2
☎ 071/22 17 44
Embroidery and lace collection from sixteenth to nineteenth centuries.
Open: Monday to Friday, 10am-12noon, 2-5pm.(also on Saturday, April to end Sept).

Historisches Museum
Museumstrasse 50
☎ 071/24 78 32
Regional heritage, historical and cultural; includes tapestries, embroidery and porcelain.
Open: June-September, daily (except Monday), 10am-12noon, 2-5pm; October to May, Tuesday to Saturday 2-4pm, Sunday 10am-12noon and 2-4pm; closed Monday.

Schaffhausen
Museum zu Allerheiligen
(All Saints' Museum)
Klosterplatz 1
☎ 053/25 43 77
Fifteenth-century MSS and early printed books from former abbey. Swiss art from fifteenth to twentieth century. Local industries with working models.
Open: Tuesday to Sunday 10am-12noon, 2-5pm. Closed Monday.
Munot fortress with tower and parapet walks
Open: May to September, daily 8am-8pm; October to April, daily 9am-5pm.

Stein-am-Rhein

Puppenmuseum
Schwarzhorngasse 136
☎ 054/41 39 66
Collection of dolls, some automat, doll houses.
Open: mid-March to end October, Tuesday to Sunday, 10am-5pm.

Historische Sammlung
(Historic Museum)
Am Rathaus
☎ 054/8 61 27
Weapons, porcelain, stained glass illustrate the past.
Open: March to November, Tuesday to Sunday 10am-12noon, 1.30-5pm.

Urnäsch

Museum für Appenzeller Brauchtum
(Museum of Appenzeller Tradition and Way of Life)
Dorfplatz
☎ 071/58 23 22
Exhibits illustrate way of life of a community deeply attached to traditional observances.
Open: July to October, daily 2-5pm; April to June, Wednesday, Saturday and Sunday 2-5pm.

Zürich

Schweizerisches Landesmuseum
(Swiss National Museum)
Museumstrasse 2
☎ 01/221 10 10
Aims to illustrate the history of Switzerland, its culture and its arts. Pre-Romanesque and Romanesque church art, Gothic sculpture, ceramics, gold and silver ware.
Open: mid-June to mid-September Tuesday to Friday, and Sunday, 10am-12noon, 2-5pm, Saturday 10am-4pm; mid-September-mid-June, Tuesday to Friday, Sunday, 10am-12noon, 2-5pm, Saturday 10am-12noon, 2-4pm.

Keramiksammlung
(Ceramic Collection)
Zunfthaus zur Meisen
Münsterhof 20
☎ 01/221 28 07
Eighteenth-century porcelain displayed in rococo rooms, Tuesday to Friday, Sunday 10am-12noon, 2-5pm, Saturday 10am-12noon, 2-4pm.

Medizinhistorisches Museum der Universität Zürich
Rämistrasse 71
☎ 01/257 22 04
Medical apparatus from the Middle Ages onwards.
Open: Wednesday and Thursday 2-5pm, Sat 10am-12noon.

Kunsthaus
(Museum of Art)
Heimplatz 1
☎ 01/251 67 55
Western painting and sculpture from ancient times to present day. International repute for special exhibitions in exhibitions wing.
Open: Tuesday to Friday 10am-9pm, Saturday to Sunday 10am-5pm, Monday 2-5pm.

Museum Rietberg
Gablerstrasse 15
☎ 01/202 45 28
One of world's greatest museums for non-European art, displayed in a handsome villa.
Open: Tuesday to Sunday 10am-5pm (Wednesday also until 9pm); Monday closed. Tram Nos 7 and 10 to museum.

Sammlung EG Bührle
Zollikerstrasse 172
☎ 01/55 00 86
One of the finest private collections of European art, especially nineteenth-century French painting. On tram routes Nos 2 and 4. Open: only on Tuesday and Friday, 2-5pm.

Jacobs Suchard Museum
Seefeldquai 17
☎ 01/385 12 83
Collection on cultural history of coffee.
Open: Friday 3-6pm, Saturday 10am-4pm. Closed on public holidays, Saturdays before Easter and Whitsun, and week between Christmas and New Year's Day.

Züricher Spielzeugmuseum (Sammlung Franz Carl Weber)
Fortunagasse 15
☎ 01/211 93 05
Toys from past centuries, dolls, dolls' houses, mechanical toys, railways, steam engines, toy soldiers etc. Fascinating for children.
Open: Monday to Friday 2-5pm.

Tourist Information Offices

Regional Tourist Offices

North-west
Verkehrsverein Basel und Umgebung
Blumenrain 2
CH-4001 Basel
☎ 061/261 50 50

Zürich Region
Verkehrsverein Zürich u. Umgebung
Bahnhofbrücke 1
CH-8023 Zürich
☎ 01/211 12 56

Eastern Switzerland
Verkehrsverband Ostschweiz
Bahnhofplatz la
CH-9001 St Gallen
☎ 071/22 62 62

Local Offices
In German-speaking regions the usual word for a Tourist Office is *Verkehrsbüro* or *Verkehrsverein* followed by the resort name, eg Verkehrsverein Basel). Hours of opening are usually from 8am to 5.30pm, although in some smaller places they close for lunch.

Appenzell Innerrhoden
Verkehrsbüro
Hauptgasse 19
CH-9050 Appenzell (AI)
☎ 071/87 41 11

Baden
Kur- und Verkehrsbüro
Bahnhofstrasse 50
CH-5400 Baden
☎ 056/22 53 18

Basel
Verkehrsbüro Basel
Schifflände 5
CH-4000 Basel
☎ 061/261 50 50

Rapperswil
Verkehrsbüro
Am Seequai
CH-8640 Rapperswil
☎ 055/27 70 00

St Gallen
Verkehrsverein
Bahnhofplatz
CH-9001 St Gallen
☎ 071/22 62 62

Schaffhausen
Verkehrsverein
Fronwagturm
CH-8200 Schaffhausen
☎ 053/25 51 41

Stein-am-Rhein
Verkehrsbüro
Oberstadt 10
CH-8260 Stein am Rhein
☎ 054/41 28 35

Zürich
Offizielles Verkehrsbüro
Bahnhofplatz 15
Hauptbahnhof
CH-8000 Zürich
☎ 01/211 40 00

Sport and recreation

Local tourist offices invariably can supply information, usually in leaflet form, on tennis, swimming, golf, outdoor and indoor sport centres, and the popular 'Fitness Parcours' tracks for jogging as well as cycle tracks.

Public Transport

The steamer services on Lake Zürich are carried out by the Zürichsee Schiffahrtsgesellschaft
Mythenquai 333
CH-8038 Zürich
(☎ 01/482 10 33)
Timetable 2730-4

2

Luzern and Central Switzerland

From St Gallen there is a short and interesting (indeed, historic) route to the very heart of Switzerland, the region that the Swiss themselves know as the Zentralschweiz (Central Switzerland), with Luzern as its principal town.

Motorists in a hurry might prefer to take the somewhat longer but faster route using the N1 motorway from St Gallen to Zürich; there use the 'through traffic' routes signposted Gotthard/Luzern on to main road No 4 along the valley of the River Sihl to Zug (29km, 16 miles); taking the N4 motorway from Zug to Luzern (24km, 15 miles).

But the most scenic and instructive route follows in its first stretch the route described in Chapter 1 (North-East Switzerland), from St Gallen via Herisau and Wattwil across the Toggenburg to **Rapperswil** (see Chapter 1 – Zürich).

From Rapperswil go across the lake causeway to **Pfäffikon** (4km, 2½ miles). There join the N3 motorway westbound (towards Zürich) but travel only 6km (3¾ miles) to the Wollerau exit, joining the main road No 8 following the signposts Biberbrugg/Einsiedeln. For travellers who have not yet found an opportunity to visit the great baroque monastery of **Einsiedeln** the short detour from the Biberbrugg crossroads, involving only 6km (3¾ miles) each way, to the world-famous pilgrimage destination is difficult to resist.

Picking up road No 8 again at Biberbrugg, the route continues (to the left) in the Gotthard/Luzern direction, climbing over a moorland plateau and then descending again to reach Sattel (meaning 'saddle') where roads meet. From here there are views of prominent landmarks of Central Switzerland, with huge Rigi's summit (1,798m, 5,899ft) to the south-west, the Rossberg (1,581m, 5,187ft) to the west, while the two Mythen peaks (1,811m [5,942ft] and 1,899m [6,230ft]) to the south-east stand as sentinels to the historic old town of **Schwyz**, capital town of the canton of the same name which gave its name to the whole country. Road No 8 carries on to reach Schwyz in 9km (5½miles).

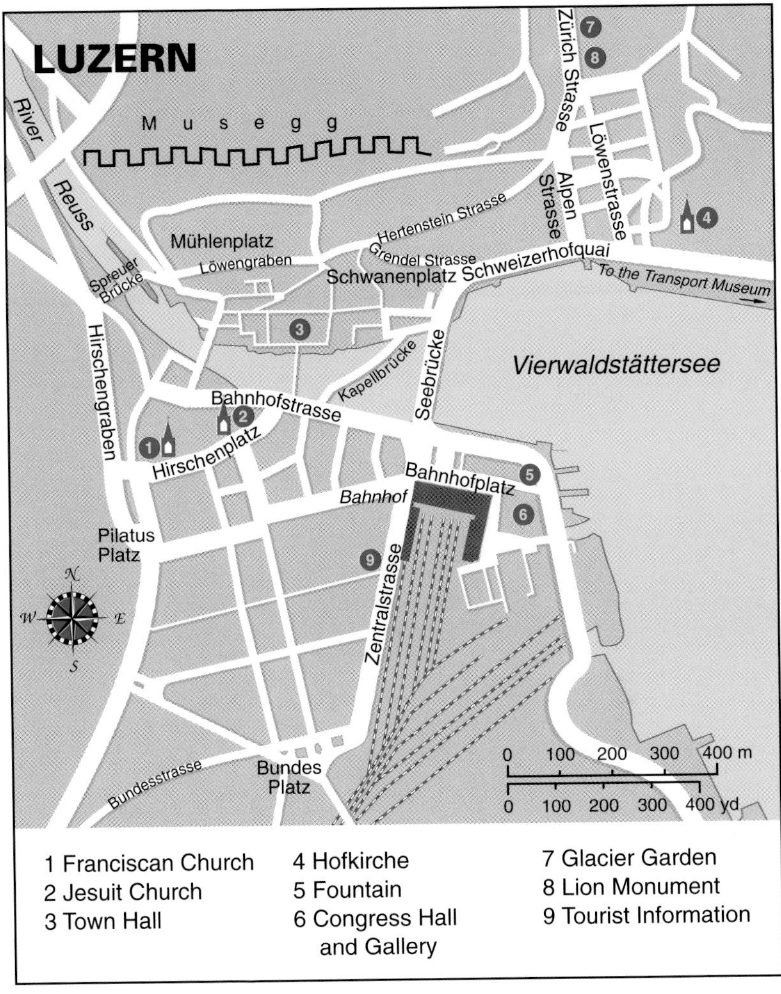

Its delightful situation in a wide fertile valley framed by the twin craggy peaks of the Mythen standing behind is particularly picturesque when the cherry orchards that surround it are smothered in blossom. The old town well merits a day's visit, with its many handsome seventeenth-century patrician mansions and Town Hall façade painted with frescos of significant moments in Swiss history. Prominent among the patrician mansions is the Ital-Reding Haus of 1609, in its handsome estate so close to the town centre. Sited also in the Ital-Reding estate is the Haus Bethlehem, Switzerland's oldest wooden 'chalet' style dwelling house. It is appropriate, too, that an attractive modern building here, the Bundesbriefarchiv, houses the country's Federal Archives — containing the solemn Pact of 1291, the signing of which by representatives of Schwyz, Uri and Unterwalden was the decisive step in the evolution of Switzerland.

Public Transport Option

A direct rail link from St Gallen to Luzern is provided by one of Switzerland's most attractive cross-country rail routes which largely follows the motor route just described. The main features of the first section of it, from St Gallen to Rapperswil (Timetable 870) via Herisau and Wattwil, are outlined towards the end of Chapter One (North-East Switzerland).

From Rapperswil the line (Timetable 670) crosses the Zürichsee on the causeway to Pfäffikon, the junction point on the mainline Zürich-Chur. Passing through the junction it swings left to climb up to the high plateau that lies between the Zürichsee and Zuger See. It finally skirts the steep flank of the Rossberg, the mountain which produced the landslide of 1806 that overwhelmed Goldau. In a swift descent that loses 305m (1,000ft) in 8km (5 miles) the train reaches Arth-Goldau junction on the main north-south railway axis which lies on the east side of the Rigi mountain. It then crosses onto the Luzern branch of the Gotthard line, first winding its way along the eastern slopes of the Rigi above the Zuger See, then crossing the isthmus to reach Küssnacht on the north-eastern arm of the great neighbouring lake, the Vierwaldstättersee (Lake Luzern). The shore of this lake is skirted before reaching Luzern itself.

Leaving Schwyz on main road No 2 which skirts the idyllic little Lauerzer See, **Goldau** is reached. Near Goldau the landscape, strewn with immense boulders now overgrown with vegetation, bears the scars of a cataclysmic landslide of 1806 which overwhelmed the former village of Goldau. Nowadays this wild landscape is the site of a nature reserve and zoo which is open throughout the year. Twelve kilometres (7½ miles) beyond Goldau is its lakeside 'twin' **Arth**. The joint station Arth-Goldau is an important rail junction on the Gotthard line which conveys the international traffic from Basel and from Zürich south across the Alps into the Ticino canton and then Italy; for Arth-Goldau links Luzern — and through it Bern and Geneva — with that rail artery. Near the Arth-Goldau junction station is the valley station for the Arth-Rigi cogwheel mountain rail to the summit of the Rigi where it meets the other cogwheel Rigi mountain rail that ascends from Vitznau on the shores of Lake Luzern, as the Vierwaldstättersee is usually known in English. Arth lies on the southern corner of the Zuger See and road No 2 now follows the picturesque shore of that lake to **Küssnacht-am-Rigi** (10km, 6 miles). Küssnacht stands on the isthmus that separates the Zuger See from one of the arms of the many-limbed Lake Luzern. Continuing on road No 2 (and passing in 3km [2 miles] from Küssnacht the little chapel by the lake which serves as a memorial to Queen Astrid of Belgium who lost her life nearby in a road accident), **Luzern** is reached 13km (8 miles) further on.

Luzern

A Walk Through Luzern

Luzern, possibly one of the country's greatest tourist attractions, lies at the head of the north-western arm of the lake the Swiss call the Vierwaldstättersee – 'Lake of the Four Forest Cantons'. The reference is to the three cantons (Uri, Schwyz and Unterwalden) that originally got together to form the Swiss Confederation, along with the fourth that soon joined them, Luzern. To add further complication English-speakers rarely give that lake the name used by Swiss, French, Germans and Italians, calling it instead 'Lake Luzern' — a name which the Swiss only apply to one small arm of this many-armed lake, namely, the very arm on which Luzern itself stands.

Luzern developed on a geographic site that is not uncommon among Swiss historic towns — at a place where a river flows out of a substantial lake. Early records are of its being a market town of some local importance. But when the Gotthard Pass route through the Alps to the Mediterranean lands was opened in the thirteenth century by the construction of hair-raising but passable wooden bridges in the gorges near Andermatt, and merchant trade with Italy took off, boat transport of goods on the lake became an indispensable link in the trade route to Northern Europe. Luzern's position as a transhipment and trading depot brought prosperity. It also attracted the covetous attention of the Austrian Habsburgs. So the citizens of Luzern allied themselves with the three neighbouring forest and peasant communities in the defensive League that was principally aimed against Habsburg threats. During the Reformation Luzern stayed loyal to the Catholic faith, as did the other three cantons around the Lake of the Four Forest Cantons.

A stroll through Luzern can begin at the **Bahnhofplatz**, which looks out upon the beautiful lake. Directly facing the rail station across the Bahnhofplatz are the landing stages used by the considerable fleet of lake steamers (including five steam-driven 'paddlers') operated by the *Schiffahrtsgesellschaft des Vierwaldstättersees* (SGV), the Lake Luzern Navigation Company. Cross Pilatus-Strasse, the town's main shopping area, by subway to reach the Seebrücke, the bridge nearest the lake, which carries the main city centre traffic over the River Reuss. The view from the left pavement of the bridge, downstream, gives a good impression of the town's charm with its medieval wooden covered bridges, Renaissance public buildings, churches and merchant mansions, with the city walls and watchtowers behind. In the foreground is the site of what until its destruction by fire on 18/8/1993 was the original medieval Kapellbrücke, a fourteenth-century roofed wooden bridge that crossed the river diagonally. Its roof truss supported more than a hundred early seventeenth-century paintings of local historic and heraldic motifs. The bridge's octagonal defensive *Wasserturm* (water tower) survived the disastrous fire to remain a centre-piece for the reconstructed roofed bridge of 1994. The

Schwyz town hall with its frescoed walls

Opposite: St Martin's Church from the Ital-Reding Haus, Schwyz

Luzern's river front with the town hall and tower

Kapellbrücke's diagonal crossing from South to North offers on the left-hand side an excellent view of the fine Italian Renaissance river frontage of the late sixteenth-century *Rathaus*, typically Swiss.

On the north side of the bridge is the Kapellplatz, one of the old town's many charming squares; the church that stands in it is the town's oldest, St Peter's, built in 1178 but restructured in the eighteenth century. Continuing west parallel to the river one reaches the **Rathaus** with its picturesque fourteenth-century tower attached and typically Swiss hipped roof. The delightful square into which the *Rathaus* faces is the Kornmarkt. From it a flight of steps leads down to the riverside walk and a wide footbridge (Rathaussteg) to the south bank's Bahnhofstrasse. The striking church with twin onion domes is the **Jesuit church** (1669), Switzerland's oldest baroque church.

Retracing steps from the footbridge to the north bank, passing through the flower and vegetable market stalls, ascending the steps and crossing the Kornmarkt, a left turn leads into the picturesque **Weinmarkt** with its Gothic fountain. In late medieval times this was the scene of Passion Play performances that attracted visitors from far and wide. A right and then left turn lead through to the Mühleplatz or Mill Square from which a second wooden bridge crosses the Reuss, the fifteenth-century **Spreuerbrücke** or Mill Bridge: it too has rafter paintings, of a typical medieval subject 'The Dance of Death'. At the south side of the bridge is a very comprehensive **Museum of Natural History** of the region.

By retracing steps again to Mühleplatz and continuing east through Hirschenplatz (with its fine restored burgher houses) into Weggisgasse, a principal shopping area is reached. Ultimately this easterly direction leads through the Hertensteinstrasse to the (on left) Zürichstrasse heading north, from which it is easy to pass through the Löwenplatz to reach the Glacier Garden and the Lion Monument. The **Lion Monument** is hewn out of natural sandstone as a memorial to the Swiss regiment of Life Guards to Louis XVI of France who fell defending the king's palace against revolutionaries in 1792. The **Glacier Garden** is the site of gigantic pot-holes formed by the Reuss Glacier in the Ice Age; there is an associated museum.

From the Lion Monument return south by way of the Löwenstrasse and turn left on the Schweizerhofquai to visit the imposing **Hofkirche**, Cathedral of Luzern's patron St Leodegar, standing on its platform to the east and surrounded by cloisters. Of early date, destroyed in all but its Gothic towers in 1633 by fire, it was rebuilt in Renaissance style.

Return to the Bahnhofplatz by way of the lakeside promenade and Seebrücke. (Instead of returning from Spreuerbrücke via the town streets to the Zürichstrasse, a more extended route would be to proceed north from Spreuerbrücke and walk west to east the length of the Musegg fortification wall of AD1400, with its nine watchtowers one of which, the Clock Tower, is particularly worth visiting and is open for such.)

Finally, one of Luzern's greatest modern attractions is Europe's most

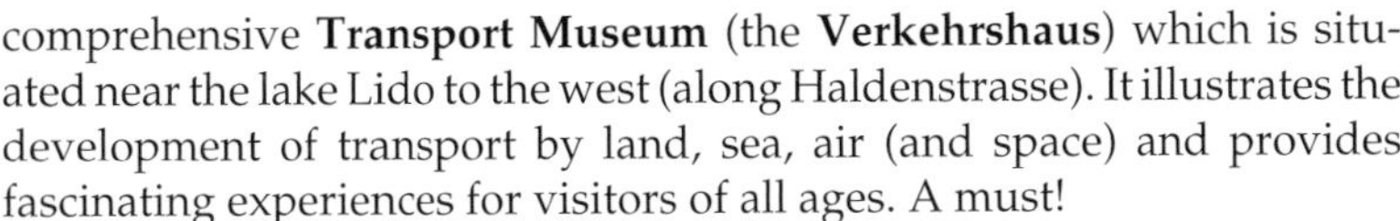

comprehensive **Transport Museum** (the **Verkehrshaus**) which is situated near the lake Lido to the west (along Haldenstrasse). It illustrates the development of transport by land, sea, air (and space) and provides fascinating experiences for visitors of all ages. A must!

The Lake

The lake is arguably Luzern's greatest charm. Its many arms and its very irregular shape, with constrictions here and twists of direction there, contribute much to its fascination providing as they do a series of dramatic changes of vista and interest. Luzern lies at the head of the north-west arm, and the small town of Flüelen, gateway to the Gotthard Pass route, lies 38km (24 miles) away at the end of the long south-east arm which is called the Urner See after the name of the Uri canton in which it lies. Although there are notable mountain peaks within sight of every arm of the lake, the western end — the Luzern end — has more gentle, more settled and more 'tamed' scenery than the more awe-inspiring scenic grandeur that characterises the Urner branch in the south-east.

If visitors wish to gain a reasonable general orientation of the Central Swiss region before they start their particular excursions it is a good idea to begin by taking the 3-hour boat trip from Luzern to Flüelen or vice-versa. (This full-length trip is usually available from the beginning of April to beyond mid-October.) (Timetable 2600: for further information ☎ 041/40 45 40.)

Luzern-Flüelen by Boat

Shortly after leaving the Luzern steamer quays the lakeside Lido can be seen on the northern shore and just behind it the city's camping site. Once clear of the Luzern lake arm the ship enters an open stretch of water that is known locally as the 'Cross Funnel' — it lies in the centre of the cross formed by four branches of the lake: the Luzerner See to the north-west, the Küssnachter See to the north-east, the main body of the lake due east, and the southern basin that leads to the Stansstad narrows and the Alpnacher See beyond. It is called a funnel because it is open to so many wind directions.

From here two famous mountains come into view. The large mass of the Rigi (1,800m, 5,906ft) fills the angle between the Küssnachter See and the main lake body; in the opposite direction to the south-west is the jagged outline of Pilatus (2,120m, 6,956ft), Luzern's 'local' mountain, accessible by cogwheel railway from Alpnachstad. Due south is the Bürgenstock cliff, topped by Europe's highest outdoor elevator lift up to the Hammetschwand (1,128m, 3,701ft), a magnificent viewpoint over the lake.

The ship sails east past the Hertenstein peninsula to call at Weggis, the first of three resort villages that enjoy a mild climate under the shelter of Rigi. The second is the ship's next calling-place, **Vitznau**. Immediately behind the pier is the bottom station of Europe's first-established cog-

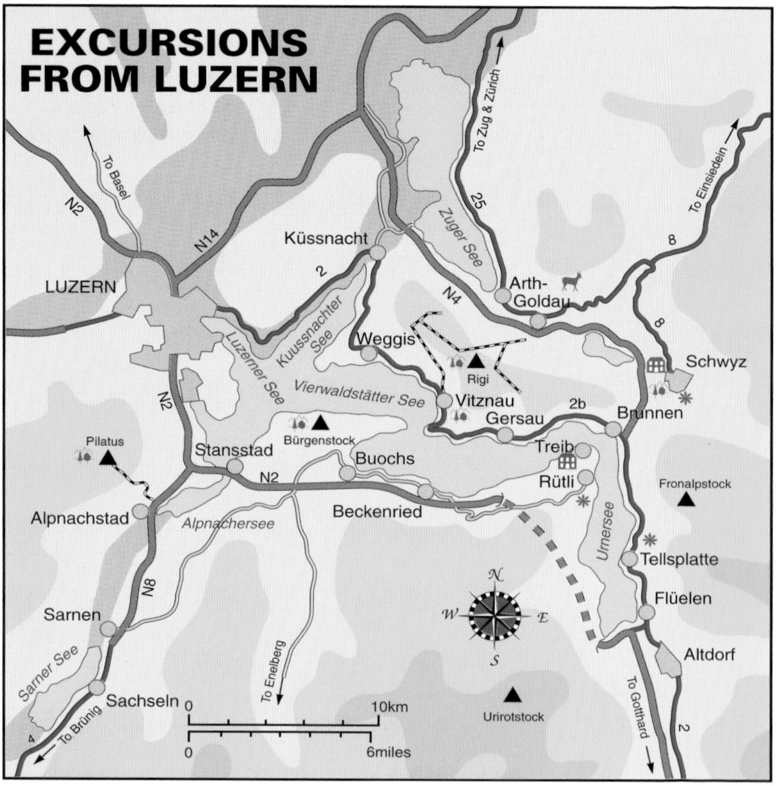

EXCURSIONS FROM LUZERN

To Basel
N2
N14
LUZERN
Küssnacht
2
Kuussnachter See
Luzerner See
Weggis
Zuger See
To Zug & Zürich
25
N4
Arth-Goldau
To Einsiedeln
8
Schwyz
Rigi
Vitznau
Vierwaldstätter See
Gersau
2b
Brunnen
Bürgenstock
Pilatus
Stansstad
Buochs
Treib
Rütli
N2
Beckenried
Fronalpstock
Alpnachstad
Alpnachersee
Urnersee
Tellsplatte
N8
Flüelen
Sarnen
Altdorf
Sarner See
To Enelberg
To Gotthard
Sachseln
To Brünig
4
0
10km
0
6miles
Urirotstock
2

Jesuit church from the Spreuer Sluice, Luzern

Above: The Spreuerbrücke, Luzern's fourteenth-century wooden bridge and its painted ceilings were destroyed by fire in August, 1993. (Below).

wheel railway which climbs via Rigi Kaltbad and Rigi Staffel stations to the mountain summit, Rigi Kulm. From here, instead of a return by the same route, it is possible to descend the mountain's opposite side by taking the other cogwheel railway from the Rigi Kulm to Arth, bottom station near the Arth-Goldau junction-station on the Swiss Federal Railway main line from Luzern, Basel, Zürich and the Gotthard Line.

From Vitznau the ship passes through a narrow channel formed between two promontories from north and south shores called the Upper and Lower Nose, respectively. Beyond this channel there opens out the great main expanse of the lake towards the east. The ship's course normally heads south into the Bay of Beckenried to make calls at Buochs and Beckenried. The mountains immediately ahead are the Klewenalp (1,600m, 5,250ft) on the left and the Buochserhorn on the right. At Beckenried is an aerial railway to the Klewenalp, a winter sports and summer resort on the high plateau.

The ship now heads back to the north shore to call at **Gersau**, the third of the lakeside resorts sheltered by the Rigi massif. (By a curious historical freak this village was an independent republic for four centuries; it was only after the French Revolutionary Wars that it was incorporated in canton Schwyz.) After Gersau the boat crosses diagonally to call at **Treib**, a pier beside a picturesque boatman's timber cottage adjacent to the bottom station of the funicular line that runs to the mountain terrace of **Seelisberg**. Seelisberg lies on top of a buttress cliff which forms the turning corner of the lake's south shore which here swings into a long branch heading south, the Urner See. On the north shore's corresponding corner lies **Brunnen**. Brunnen, situated on the alluvial valley mouth of the Muota stream which enters the lake here, is a long-established resort (former fishing village) well placed for excursions to the most spectacular part of the lake and region, thanks to its position on the main Gotthard railway. Brunnen's centre has a little square with a tiny but particularly charming early baroque *Dorfkirche*, village church. But its greatest charm is the changing panorama of lake and mountain scenery to be enjoyed from its lake-front promenade.

Here on the shores of the Urner See is the very kernel of Switzerland. For it was men of the three original founding cantons, Uri, Schwyz and Unterwalden, who took the first steps to free themselves from external domination and start what was to become an independent Confederation of communities. In their early years they were mostly called simply the Confederates but later became known as the Schweizer after the name of one of the original component areas. The Urner See is William Tell country. Modern historians are quite uncertain whether he really existed and carried out the exploits attributed to him; or whether he is a representative freedom-fighting legend.

The first two landing stages touched by the boat after leaving Brunnen and heading south into the Urner See are part of the story of the struggles. After rounding the imposing sheer cliff face of Seelisberg it is rather surprising when the ship draws inshore to moor at a little pier with no sign of village or community in sight. The landing place is for a meadow lying on a shelf or terrace beneath the cliffs — the **Rütli meadow**, where representatives of the three founding cantons met in AD1307 to take a solemn oath confirming their Everlasting League to defend their liberties against tyrants. 1 August, Switzerland's National Day, is a great occasion here. There is an element of pilgrimage in the crowds of citizens who come here from all parts of the country wearing many varieties of national costume, ferried across from Brunnen by relays of lake steamers.

The next landing stage, this one at a tree-covered spur projecting from the opposite shore of the lake, bears the sign **'Tellsplatte'**; nearby is a memorial chapel to the folk hero who is reputed to have leapt ashore at this spot escaping from an Austrian-manned boat that was carrying him to prison.

The Tellsplatte lies at the base of the Axenberg mount, part of the precipitous east face of the Urner See. More than a century ago tunnels and galleries were cut into the cliffs here by the engineers who constructed the Axenstrasse road which enabled traffic to pass along the lakeside towards the Gotthard and so obviate the need for lake transhipments. Here the view down the Urner See with its many cliff faces and behind them serried mountain peaks, some with perpetual snow and ice, is most dramatic. Ramblers and hikers may be interested in the completion of a new walking trail in this spectacular and also historic landscape. The 700th anniversary of the establishment of the Swiss Confederation was celebrated in 1991. The occasion was marked by the opening of a 'Swiss Path' or 'Swiss Trail' for walkers in the 'Heartland' around the Uri lake. All of the Swiss cantons contributed to the creation of this path, parts of which are entirely new. It starts on the Rütli in canton Uri, runs by way of Seelisberg, Bauen, Isleten, Seedorf, Flüelen, Tellsplate and Sisikon; then entering canton Schwyz it passes through Morschach and ends in Brunnen. Each of the 26 Swiss cantons was responsible for a stretch of the trail, and the beginning of each canton's sectors is marked with a special boundary stone; and these sectors occur in the chronological order in which the individual cantons became part of the Confederation. The length of each sector, too, is proportional to the number of inhabitants in the canton which sponsored it!

In 1992 the Lake Luzern shipping company (the SGV) published descriptions of a number of walks around the lake — including sectors of the new 'Swiss Trail' — that were suitable for passage by young children's push-chairs (or 'baby-buggies') and the initial leaflets proved so popular with parents, grandparents etc that from 1993 they were printed as a collection in the more substantial form of a special illustrated brochure available from the lake shipping company's offices.

At the head of the lake is **Flüelen** on the delta of the River Reuss which enters the lake there after flowing down from the Gotthard. The boat trip described above takes about 3½ hours — the round trip about 7 hours. But

Gersau, for centuries an independent republic

The historic boatman's house at Treib

Cliffs below Seelisberg on the Urner See

The Urner See with Rütli Meadow right foreground

the return journey can be undertaken by Gotthard mainline train (the Flüelen SBB station being adjacent to the ship's landing stage) to Luzern in an hour or less (Timetable 600).

During summer high season (mid-May to late October) a special excursion 'William Tell Express' combines a paddle-steamer trip Luzern-Flüelen (lunch aboard included) with a continuation by first-class train accommodation over the Gotthard line to Lugano in the canton Ticino south of the Alps. A running commentary on board and a special guide during the rail journey are included. Reservations should be made in advance. Further information may be obtained from SGV Central Booking Office, Luzern ☎ 041/40 45 40.

From Northern Europe visitors' routes into Central Switzerland, both road and rail, are via either Basel or Zürich and their first lakeside destinations are often in the neighbourhood of Luzern or Brunnen and its neighbours. Until comparatively recently the Axenstrasse traffic still passed through the streets of Brunnen. Later a bypass was provided for the Gotthard traffic. Since in 1986 the through motorway from Basel to Chiasso (on the Italian frontier) was finally completed, the fast through motorway traffic from Basel no longer passes by way of canton Schwyz and Axenstrasse. The N2 motorway is routed to bypass west of Luzern, run along through canton Unterwalden on the south side of the lake, passing under the Seelisberg in a 9km (5½ miles) tunnel, and beyond Flüelen running parallel with the old Gotthard road (and rail) up the valley of the River Reuss. Among other effects this has freed the 'old Gotthard road' between Flüelen and the Gotthard Pass from much through traffic — and made it more interesting for local tourists.

Exploring Central Switzerland

To the Mountain Viewpoints of Rigi, Bürgenstock and Pilatus

Within the vicinity of Luzern an excursion to one or more of the classic mountain viewpoints is a must. These are the ascents of Rigi, Bürgenstock and Pilatus already mentioned above. The approach to a **Rigi** ascent, whether by road via Goldau or by steamer via Vitznau has already been sketched. More than one option exists also for Luzern's 'local' mountain, **Pilatus**. As with Rigi, perhaps the most exhilarating excursion is a circular tour: first part by either train (Timetable 470) or lake steamer (Timetable 2601) to Alpnachstad; from Alpnachstad by cogwheel railway (the steepest of its kind in Europe) to Pilatus Kulm (2,070m, 6,792ft) (Timetable 473); then return from the Kulm by the suspension cablecar (Timetable 1517) (its station is situated back-to-back with the cogwheel summit station) first to Fräkmüntegg, 651m (2,135ft) lower, and from there by suspended gondola-cabin to Kriens (Timetable 1516). From the nearby trolleybus halt a 10-minute ride to central Luzern completes one of Switzerland's most varied and spectacular excursions. (For motorists who would prefer to drive to Alpnachstad by road and do the excursion from there, it is easily reached by driving south from Luzern's Pilatus Platz to join the N2 motorway, direction Interlaken, for 12km [7 miles].)

The **Bürgenstock** is most easily tackled by taking the Luzern-Alpnachstad steamer (Timetable 2601) to Kehrsiten-Bürgenstock landing stage. Nearby is the lower station of the Bürgenstock funicular rail.

South of the Vierwaldstättersee

The **Titlis** is the highest mountain in Central Switzerland, near the centre of the great massif south of the Vierwaldstättersee. A round trip into this region makes a unique scenic excursion. Leave Luzern southbound either on road No 4 or (if one wishes to avoid suburban villages) by N4 motorway. Crossing the narrows of the Alpnacher lake arm, with, on the left-hand side, Stansstad (the medieval lake port at the foot of the Bürgenstock) take the exit for **Stans**, 13km (8 miles) from Luzern, the principal town of the Nidwalden half-canton, and the place where its *Landsgemeinde* meets annually on the last Sunday of April. (The pyramidical Stanserhorn peak [1,850m, 6,070ft], south-west of the town, is accessible by funicular and cablecar and gives a fine panorama of the Titlis massif to the south.)

Turning south from Stans the road follows the west bank of the Engelberger Aa River for 4km (2½ miles) to **Dallenwil**, a farming village where the lower stations of a group of cablecar lines are sited. The road thereafter crosses to the other side of the stream, rising as the valley narrows, becoming more bare and grim as the road gets steeper until it opens out as **Engelberg** (21km [13 miles] from Stans) comes in sight, having as its impressive backdrop the Titlis with its permanent ice and snow cap. Engelberg lies in a sunny sheltered bowl at just over 1,000m (3,281ft), a perfect example of a mountain climatic resort and centre for winter sports and mountaineering. The village grew round a Benedictine abbey founded about the year 1120 and enjoyed independence until the French Revolutionary invasions. The present abbey buildings are eighteenth century. Today Engelberg is probably best known for the number of cablecars and ski-lifts that give access to the mountains that encircle it, including the chain of aerial suspension railways (of which the final stage actually passes over the very glacier) that conquer the Titlis summit (3,033m, 9,951ft) (Timetable 1535: Engelberg-Trübsee-Kleintitlis). The Titlis cable services now include the new revolutionary 'Rotair' — the world's first aerial cableway with rotating cabins giving a panoramic perspective to the spectacular views over to the great mountains of the Berner Oberland, the Grisons and the Jura. The summit boasts also an ice grotto — and, of course, sun terraces and a restaurant with panoramic outlook.

Returning from Engelberg to Stans, the motorist can make a round trip of his return journey by heading north-east from there (instead of north-west) to **Buochs** (5km, 3 miles) on the southern shore of the

Ochsen Square, Brunnen with the Mythen peaks

Opposite: Brunnen waterfront

P

Vierwaldstättersee and then 4km (2½ miles) along that shore to **Beckenried**, from where a vehicular ferry operates across the lake to **Gersau**, approximately hourly during the season April-mid October. (At Beckenried is the bottom station of the aerial railway to the mountain terrace of the Klewenalp.) From Gersau road No 26 heads east through the two other lake resorts that are sheltered from the north by the great mass of the Rigi, **Vitznau** and **Weggis**, joining road No 2 at Küssnacht to return to Luzern.

Public Transport Option

The Engelberg excursion can be carried out by train on the narrow-gauge railway (cogwheel assisted on steep ascents) that runs along side the road to Engelberg from Luzern (Timetable 480).

Luzern to Canton Uri and the Gotthard

The road from Luzern as far as Schwyz is, in reverse direction, outlined in the route Schwyz-Luzern at the start of this chapter. **Brunnen** lies 5km (3 miles) further south-west on road No 2 from Schwyz. (It can be bypassed by the motorway. However, as it is the principal lakeside alternative to Luzern as a centre for excursions in the region and for accommodation by those who prefer smaller towns, take the road to Brunnen village centre and lakeside.) Brunnen, at one time a fishing village, has long been a principal resort. In the square a few steps from the lake-front is a most

attractive very early baroque chapel (1632). The chestnut-lined lake-front promenade offers a dramatic view across to the Seelisberg cliff and the great mountain massifs of Central Switzerland.

From Brunnen village square or quay head past the Hotel Eden and the Casino on the road which soon joins the bypassing main road from Luzern. This stretch on the Urner See to Flüelen is called the Axenstrasse as it was blasted and tunnelled through the rock faces of the Axenberg. It runs roughly in parallel with the Gotthard railway line. Between tunnels is a view across the lake of Rütli and Seelisberg. At the village of **Sisikon** (camping and caravan site) the road crosses the cantonal boundary from

Schwyz into Uri. After further tunnels comes **Tellsplatte** where parking is possible and a path leads down to the Tell Chapel, with its frescos depicting the Tell story, near the lake steamer quay. The small resort village of **Flüelen** at the end of the lake was for centuries an important lake port and customs station where goods were transshipped from the lake to mule transport for carriage over the Gotthard. As a terminus nowadays of the lake excursion service during the season it is a main stop for many international train services. About 1km (half a mile) further on, the road has a right-hand turn-off for entry to the N2 motorway which has emerged from the Seelisberg 9km (5½ miles) tunnel to run up the Reuss Valley between railway and river for a considerable stretch. Disregard this and continue straight on for 2km (1½ miles) to **Altdorf**, capital of Uri, the canton of mountains and glaciers.

Town and canton rose in importance after the early thirteenth century when the bridging of the Schöllenen Gorge opened up the Gotthard. Of the Old Forest Cantons Uri was always the leader in policies of expansion over the Gotthard into the Ticino. Nowadays it is the centre of the William Tell cult, the place where according to tradition the folk hero shot the apple from his son's head. A huge bronze statue commemorating him stands in the Rathausplatz in front of a thirteenth-century residential tower, renovated and given a dome roof in the early nineteenth century. There is a Tell Theatre too where, every three years, the play *Wilhelm Tell* by Schiller is performed during the season by local players.

The town has many picturesque corners and interesting buildings although it sustained much damage by fire in 1799 when it was fought over by French, Austrian and Russian armies. The town's Capuchin friary was the first founded in Switzerland (1581) to strengthen the Counter-Reformation movement which Uri strongly espoused. A regional Historical Museum is housed in the Gotthardstrasse 18.

Before heading from Altdorf south towards the Gotthard, those who have become intrigued by the William Tell story might be interested to visit a fascinating village only 3km (2 miles) away. Leave Altdorf by the Gotthard road to the south. There is a turn-off to the left almost immediately for road No 17, which within 3km (2 miles) reaches the sizable village of **Bürglen**. This is a very old settlement, as its two sentinel medieval towers suggest. (In AD857 King Ludwig the German placed the village under the protection of the Zürich Fraumünster Abbey, and one of the towers, the Meierturm, is thought to have been the seat of the abbey's bailiff in Bürglen.) Nowadays the other medieval tower houses the William Tell Museum. There is a strong local tradition that Tell was born in Bürglen; and the Tell Chapel, erected in 1582, is reputed to be on the site of Tell's house.

Altdorf to Andermatt on the 'Old Gotthard Road'

The Reuss Valley floor is comparatively wide and level for a considerable stretch south of Altdorf (447m, 1,467ft above sea-level) and only begins to narrow at Erstfeld (472m, 1,549ft), by which point the new N2 motorway has parted company from the 'old Gotthard road' (No 2) as well as the rail, having crossed to the west bank of the river. During this stretch the pyramid of the Bristen mountain (3,072m, 10,079ft) can be seen occupying the valley horizon.

Amsteg (7km, 4½ miles on) lies at the entrance to the Maderaner Valley, another beautiful transverse valley to the east, which the rail crosses on a 53m (175ft) high viaduct. Amsteg's position makes it a well-placed base for climbers and hill walkers. At Amsteg motorists who are in haste to

EVUE
KURSAAL
DANCING BAR

Hilltop church of Wassen known to Gotthard travellers

Opposite: Brunnen waterfront looking southwards

reach a further destination have an opportunity to leave the 'old Gotthard road' in favour of entry to the fast N2 motorway before the old road enters the steepest and most tortuous part of the route. It is at this point that the 'old Gotthard road' and the railway line both cross to the west side of the valley while the modern motorway in galleries and tunnels cuts through the steep rock flank of the massive Bristen. Remain, however, with the old road, passing Gurtnellen rail station.

As the next village, **Wassen**, is approached, it is possible to see from the road the manner in which the railway line (now running on the opposite side of the valley from both roads) climbs the steep 'steps' in the valley floor which give rise to waterfalls. The line bores into the mountainside and tunnels a wide upward spiral in the heart of the mountain so as to emerge again on the same mountain face at a level 35m (115ft) higher. Opposite the village of Wassen the Gotthard line executes two further tunnel loops in succession — almost carrying out a figure-of-eight — while all the time climbing a further height of 122m (400ft) inside the rock. It is the unique experience of rail travellers on the Gotthard to glimpse the same, unmistakable baroque-domed village church three times in a few minutes as the train passes it at different levels above and below. For the motorist on the 'old Gotthard road' now relieved of traffic frenzy the village of Wassen repays a short visit. The church just mentioned above, which is sited on top of a steep hill, was built in 1735 and has beautiful inlaid wooden altars of that era.

Wassen lies at the mouth of the Meien Valley and for the motorist with a day in hand to spare it can be an ideal starting point for the famed **Three Passes Tour** round trip. As it may be a tempting detour for any who have not previously toured the passes of the glacial Alps, here is a brief outline of the circuit:

The Meien Valley road climbs up west from Wassen through varied Alpine landscape including tunnels, through one of which it crosses the Susten Pass summit (2,224m, 7,297ft). It descends into Berner Oberland territory in sweeping bends that present a close view of the Stein Glacier, then along the Gadmen Valley to the gentler scenery of the Aare Valley at Innertkirchen (near Meiringen). Next turning south it ascends the wooded approaches to the attractive Hasli Valley which steadily grows barer and wilder as it rises. It continues to the Grimselsee and then the summit of the Grimsel Pass (at 1,652m, 5,420ft). In the descent from the pass sharp steep bends afford good views of the Rhône Glacier before Gletsch is reached and the junction with the great Upper Rhône Valley road which links Western Switzerland with the eastern cantons. The road, now heading east once more, climbs onward to within a short walking distance from the awesome Rhône Glacier again before tackling the highest pass of the trio, the Furka (2,431m, 7,976ft) — which forms the boundary between cantons Valais and Uri. There are splendid views here to east and west. From the Furka summit the road runs by way of Hospental and Andermatt and so leads back to the Gotthard road and to Wassen.

Note: The Three Passes Tour is usually feasible from mid-June to mid-October. Having so many bends and so much climbing in the thin air, it is quite demanding on vehicle and driver. Depending on the driver's experience of mountain roads, it takes anything from 7 to 9 hours' driving.

Public Transport Option

The route just described from Luzern via Schwyz to Göschenen (excepting of course the Three Passes Tour from Wassen) is paralleled by the Swiss Federal Railways (SBB) Gotthard line (Timetable 600), one of the world's most fascinating rail journeys.

The Three Passes Tour is offered as an excursion by local motor coach transport enterprises, eg, from resorts such as Brunnen; notably too, daily during the season, by the excursion coaches of the Swiss Postbus Service (Timetable 470.69) from Göschenen and Andermatt (with a timetabled train connection from Luzern).

From Wassen the 'old Gotthard road' crosses and recrosses the valley before reaching (in 5km, 3 miles) **Göschenen** in its impressive situation where the River Reuss is joined by a main tributary just as it has emerged from the Schöllenen Gorge. If the Göschenen rail station appears disproportionately large for the size of the village this is due to the control functions here for the traffic through the 15km-long (9 miles) Gotthard railway tunnel which begins here. For very many years the loading of vehicles on to railway trucks here was the only way to get traffic across the Gotthard barrier when the pass road was closed by winter snows. Nowadays the motorway tunnel which also runs from Göschenen through the Gotthard massif into the Ticino canton is the route taken by the overwhelming majority of motorists in summer as well as in winter.

At Göschenen then the motorist has to decide whether to take the tunnel through to Italian-speaking Ticino and southern climes, or to proceed to Andermatt on the 'old Gotthard road' which now climbs sharply up to cross the Reuss tributary and after some hairpin bends enters the forbidding rock walls of the Schöllenen Gorge.

Emerging from the gorge the road crosses the Reuss waterfall on the 'Devil's Bridge' and enters the wide Urseren Valley in which Andermatt lies, occupying the strategic position at the 'crossroads of Switzerland' — or even of Europe — where the main west-east route carved out of the high Alpine massif by the Rhine and Rhône crosses the north-south route gouged out by Rivers Reuss and Ticino. **Andermatt** itself is an attractive town. Many months of snow and a good sunshine record make it a favourite winter sport centre and a multitude of varied excursions and walking trails attract summer visitors.

West from Luzern

The canton bordering Central Switzerland to the west is the Bernerland. Both by train and by road are two routes with very different types of landscape between Luzern and canton Bern; one through the high country by the Brünig Pass (outlined in Chapter 3), the other by way of the valley of the River Emme (the Emmental). The latter makes an interesting contrast to the stark majesty of canton Uri. It passes through landscape which the Swiss call 'Mittelland' (in contrast to 'Oberland', the high country). The concept of Mittelland is very important to the Swiss. In Switzerland there are very few real plains. And the term Mittelland (in which *mittel* means something like 'betwixt and between') is applied to the great areas of pre-Alpine hill country and of rolling plateau country which over many centuries have been settled and cultivated by the ancestors of the Swiss, and on which have grown the great historic centres of agricultural civilisation as well as the civilisation of cities.

From Luzern take the main road north to **Emmenbrücke** and then turn left to head due west (road No 10) towards Wolhusen. In 19½km (12 miles), some 2km (a mile) short of Wolhusen, the road, running alongside

Central Switzerland caters for adventurous watersports

Opposite: Village of Bauen on Lake Uri

the Kleine Emme River (Little Emme) (as does the Luzern-Bern main railway), on a gentle curve passes the strikingly beautiful site of the convent of **Werthenstein**, poised on a high bluff dominating the river bend. It has a lovely pilgrimage early seventeenth-century church and a fine cloister. The setting is idyllic — it is a temptation to find a picnic place. The road then continues to the industrial town of **Wolhusen** on the Kleine Emme. (It is rather confusing that in this area there are two Rivers Emme. The Great Emme — mostly called simply the Emme — rises away to the south on a mountain side north of the Brienzer See and flows north-west to join the Aare (Bern's river). The Kleine Emme rises further east (near the Lungernsee) and flows roughly north and then east to join the Reuss, Luzern's river.

Road No 10 now running south from Wolhusen leads in 8km (5 miles) to the pretty village of **Entlebuch** through what is called the Entlebuch Valley, although the river which actually traverses it is still the Kleine Emme. The valley takes its name from the Entlen torrent, a tributary of the Kleine Emme which races down to join it from the slopes on the left.

From Entlebuch the road continues along the south bank of the Kleine Emme to reach in 7km (4½ miles) the main place of the Entlebuch Valley,

Schüpfheim. Here there is a local history museum, the Entlebucher Heimatmuseum, dealing with the valley; its opening hours are irregular.

The Föhn

Note on Fohn-wind: The Föhn is the name given to the south wind from the Mediterranean which when it meets the Alps precipitates much moisture on their Southern aspect but brings dry warmth to areas immediately to the north of the range. In the spring it has the near miraculous effect of causing accumulated snow to vanish without water-melt. It is usually accompanied with a clarity of distant visibility that is almost eerie at times. When the föhn is channeled through such a 'funnel' as the South-North troughs of the Ticino and Reuss river valleys which form the 'Gotthard Route' it develops at times a violence that is awe-inspiring — and very damaging to buildings and threatening to shipping. It often arrives with dramatic suddenness. Nowadays Alpine lakes such as this one have shore-based warning flashers at strategic points to let navigators know when a storm is imminent. Because the Urner Lake's fjord-like outline continues the South-North 'funnel' this corner is notably vulnerable. (The William Tell story's emphasis on the escape opportunity given to Tell and the disorder caused to the Austrian boat crew by the 'sudden squall' is only too convincing here — where a lake village such as Brunnen has a harbour of refuge which is known as the Föhn-hafen. Treib, across the lake, has for centuries provided just such a refuge for small vessels.

South from Schüpfheim is another attractive village, **Escholzmatt**, still in canton Luzern although hereabout is the watershed between the Entlebuch Valley and the Emmental proper. (Indeed the road here crosses something more than a mere cantonal boundary — what the Swiss recognise as an ancient cultural frontier between the sphere of influence of Bern and that of the Four Original Forest Cantons.)

In a further 3km (2 miles) the road reaches the hamlet of Wiggen, and from there **Trubschachen** is reached in 6km (4 miles). This village has many imposing merchant houses; and in the district are many of the typical timber-built, roofed bridges. Trubschachen has a *Heimatmuseum* where visitors can see traditional pottery crafts at work — at the Hasenlehn Foundation. Following now the Ilfis tributary of the Emme the road arrives at **Langnau** after 6km (4 miles), the principal market town of the Emmental. It has some handsome squares, one of which, the Hirschenplatz, is considered to be one of the finest and most unspoilt in the Bern region. Attractive stone-built houses in the centre of the town have decorated timber surfaces under the gables and half-hipped roofs. A sixteenth-century building with a high saddle roof, the Chuechlihaus, houses the Heimatmuseum which has a collection of old Langnau pottery; it also has exhibits to illustrate the products and tools of the several local timber trades and crafts, particularly appropriate in a district where forestry and the timber trades are of such importance. In the course of this itinerary one will have encountered a fair number of the fifty or so Emmental saw mills and from observation of farms and farmland will be able to appreciate the force of the Emmental saying 'An Emmental farm without woodland is like a bed without a blanket.'

From Langnau road No 10 climbs out of the Ilfis and Emme Valleys and in 21km (13 miles) reaches **Worb**, a town of 11,000 inhabitants. It has a baronial castle which was rebuilt in the early sixteenth century after fire destruction. From Worb Bern is reached in 10km (6 miles).

Public Transport Option

The main railway service on the Emmental route from Luzern to Bern (Timetable 460), has stations at Langnau, Trubschachen, Wiggen, Escholzmatt, Schüpfheim, Entlebuch, Wolhusen, Werthenstein and mostly runs alongside the road described.

Emmental Farming

Motorists travelling in this area at leisure should feel encouraged to make detours and deviations from the itinerary outlined here to visit the beautiful hamlets and the large unitary farmsteads that are so characteristic of this area with its long history of settled agricultural civilisation.

In the Emmental region the local laws of inheritance differed markedly from most of their neighbours'. Farm estates on the death of the owner were not divided up among several offspring but were passed on undi-

HOTEL

vided to a sole heir. This has had the effect that for centuries Emmental farmsteads and lands have had great historical continuity as units of accumulated agricultural wealth and skills; and they have given the landscape very impressive and characteristic features. The majestic farmsteads with enormous double thatched roofs extending like half-folded wings nearly to ground level at the sides encompass under one giant roof not only living quarters but also stables, barns and other ancillary accommodation.

Traditionally pioneers in agriculture, these were the farmers who at the beginning of the nineteenth century concluded that the making of good cheese need not be confined to the high Alpine dairies as was then generally accepted, but could be practised in the rich pasturelands of the Mittelland. The outcome was that 'Emmentaler' became a common European word for Swiss cheese. One important by-product of this style of organisation is that cheese is largely made in the farm villages still instead of in some more or less distant town cheese factory to which milk is conveyed by road. Recently a *Schau-kaserei*, a show- or model-dairy making Emmentaler cheese and butter has been opened to visitors at Affolteren-im-Emmental (lying 9km along the connecting road which runs cross-country from the main road 23 at Hasle, 5km from Burgdorf — which is mentioned in the following Chapter 3)

Additional Information

Places to Visit

Altdorf
Historiches Museum
Gotthardstrasse 18
Art and folklore collections, including textiles, weapons and cultural objects.
Open: Easter to mid-October, Tuesday-Sunday 9-11am, 1-5pm. Closed Mondays.

St Martin's Church.
Priceless museum collection of sixteenth-century gold and silver ecclesiastical treasures (only to be seen by prior appointment through Pastor, ☎ 044/2 11 43).
Guided historical tours of town from Tell Memorial, Wednesdays, June-September 9.30-11am.

Andermatt
Fifteenth-century 'Devil's Bridge' in nearby Schöllenen Gorge.

Bürglen
William Tell Museum
(in a Romanesque tower)
Wattigwiler Tower
CH-6463 Bürglen/Uri
☎ 044/2 41 55 or 2 20 22
Theme is the Tell story and history of Uri.
Open: May-October 10-11.30am, 1.30-5pm daily; July-August 10am-5pm.

Einsiedeln
Famous place of pilgrimage, the Benedictine monastery's eighteenth-century collegiate church.
Great Hall with paintings open Monday-Saturday 1.30-5.30pm.

Engelberg
Benedictine abbey, church treasures and library treasures (twelfth and thirteenth century) guided tour each Wednesday 4-5pm, for men only as library is within monastery.

Goldau
Natur- und Tierpark Goldau
CH-6410 Goldau
☎ 041/82 15 10
Zoo park of Goldau covers area devastated by landslide of 1862: animals mostly native species.
Open: summer 8am-7pm, October 8am-6pm, winter 9am-5pm.

Langnau-im-Emmental
Chuechlihus Heimatmuseum (Emmental Folk Museum)
☎ 035/2 18 19
Open: Tuesday-Sunday 9am-11.30am; 1.30-6pm. Closed December and on public holidays. Includes an Alpine cheese dairy and utensils.

Luzern
Verkehrshaus der Schweiz
(Europe's greatest transport museum)
Lidostrasse 5
☎ 041/31 44 44
Reached by trolleybus No 2 from town. All means of travel, land, sea, air and space represented here. Includes also a planetarium.
Open: March-end October, daily 9am-6pm; November-end February, 10am-4pm.

Kunstmuseum (Museum of Art)
next to Main Rail Station
Permanent exhibition mainly Swiss art, Gothic to present day. For important temporary exhibitions find details in press or Tourist Office publicity.
Open: Monday-Sunday 10am-12noon, 2-5pm, plus Wednesday evening 7.30-9.30pm.

Schweizerisches Trachten- und Heimatmuseum Utenberg
(National Costume Museum at Utenberg)
☎ 041/36 80 58
Outward journey by bus No 12 to Gundoldingerplatz, then on foot to Utenberg Estate. About 100 life-size figures display national costumes still in use. Also antique rural furniture.
Open: Easter-November, daily 9am-5.30pm (July-mid-September until 6pm).

Gletschergarten
(Glacier Garden) near Lion Monument
Denkmalstrasse 4
☎ 041/51 43 40
Reached by bus No 1 to Löwenplatz (Lion Square), then on foot. Glacier mills formed millennia ago. Also other items.
Open: March-end April daily 9am-5pm; May-mid-October daily 8am-6pm.

Schüpfheim
Entlebucher Heimatmuseum
(Folk Museum of Entlebuch Valley)
Farming way of life; agricultural and allied implements and crafts.
Open: first Sunday each month 2-5pm. By arrangement for groups (☎ 041/76 15 42).

Schwyz
Bundesbriefarchiv
(Swiss Federal Archives)
Originals of federal documents AD1291-1513, also historic flags, banners.
☎ 043/24 20 64
Open: daily, 9.30-11.30am, 2-5pm.

Turm-Museum
Medieval tower house which formerly housed federal archives (see above), now holds a local museum collection mostly on pre- and early history.
Open: mid-April-mid-October, Wed, Friday, Saturday, Sunday 10am-12noon, 2-5pm. In July-August also Tuesday and Thursday 2-5pm.

Ital-Reding Haus
Seventeenth-century residence and garden estate, now museum.
Open: May-October Tuesday-Friday 2-5pm, Saturday-Sunday 10am-12noon.

Sport and Recreation

Altdorf
Indoor swimming pool
☎ 044/2 58 25

Amsteg
Mountaineering; hill walking; touring.

Andermatt
Mountaineering schools. Guided mountaineering. Horse riding:
☎ 044/6 71 30

Brunnen
Swimming: modern indoor pool adjacent to Lido beach:
☎ 043/31 18 87

Engelberg
Mountaineering; tours with guides from Kletterschule (Climbing School):
☎ 041/94 34 04
Swimming and sauna at indoor pools. Fitness (jogging) track at Gerschniwald (2km, about a mile).
Sport centre 'Erlen':
☎ 041/94 34 94

Flüelen
Swimming, boating and sailing, windsurfing.

Gersau
Swimming, sailing (☎ 041/84 17 40) and Tennis.

Göschenen
Swimming pool. Fitness circuit (jogging). Cross-country ski circuit.

Langnau
Indoor swimming school; sport centre.

Luzern
Sailing, windsurfing, swimming and tennis available at several centres, full details from local Tourist Office.
Golf (18 holes) at Dietschiberg; Further information from ☎ 041/23 12 16. List of sauna centres also from Tourist Office.
Fitness (jogging) track at Bireggwalk (1½km, 1 mile).

Schwyz
Tennis, sauna, squash, fitness circuit. Swimming at nearby Brunnen.

Sisikon
Sailing, windsurfing:
☎ 043/31 30 23. Centre for hill walking.

Vitznau
Swimming, waterski (Park Hotel:
☎ 041/83 13 22), camping Vitznau:
☎ 041/83 12 80.

Worb
Open-air swimming pool.

Tourist Information Offices

The *regional office* for the tourist region of Central Switzerland is:
Verkehrsverband-Zentralschweiz
Alpenstrasse 1
CH-6002 Luzern
☎ 041/51 18 91

Canton Uri also has an Information Office in a Gotthard Motorway Rest Area which also deals with postal and telephone enquiries:
Information Uri
Gotthard Raststätte
CH-6467 Schattdorf-Uri
☎ 044/2 53 53

NB, the 4-figure number in a Swiss address — usually preceded by the initials CH *(Confoederatio Helvetica, ie, Switzerland)* is the postcode of the place name following it.

Local Offices (usually open 8am-5.30pm but vary)

Altdorf (Capital of Canton Uri)
Verkehrsverein
CH-6460 Altdorf
☎ 044/2 28 88

Andermatt
Verkehrsbüro
CH-6490 Andermatt
☎ 044/6 74 54

Brunnen
Verkehrsbüro
CH-6440 Brunnen
☎ 043/31 17 77 (during July-Aug open also on Sun 10am-12noon).

Einsiedeln
Verkehrsbüro
CH-8840 Einsiedeln
☎ 055/53 44 88

Flüelen
Verkehrsbüro
CH-6454 Flüelen/Uri
☎ 044/2 42 23

Gersau
Verkehrsbüro
CH-6442 Gersau
☎ 041/84 12 20

Goldau
Verkehrsbüro
CH-6410 Goldau
☎ 041/82 11 29

Langnau
Verkehrsbüro
CH-3550 Langnau-im-Emmental
☎ 035 2 34 34

Luzern
Schweizerhofquai 2
CH-6002 Luzern
☎ 041/51 71 71
Open: Monday to Friday 8.30am–6pm, closes 5pm Saturday and 12 noon Sunday.

Schwyz
(cantonal capital)
Verkehrsbüro, Postplatz 9
CH-6430 Schwyz
☎ 043/22 19 91

Vitznau
Verkehrsbüro
CH-6354 Vitznau
☎ 041/83 13 55

Public Transport

The Lake Luzern shipping timetable is to be found in the Swiss Official Timetable, 2600 to 2605; the ships are operated by: Schiffahrtsgesellschaft des Vierwaldstättersees (SGV)
Postfach 4265
CH-6002 Luzern
☎ 041/40 45 40

Alpnachstad Valley station of cogwheel railway to Mt Pilatus summit (Timetable 473). Does not operate in winter (☎ 041/96 11 30).

Beckenried Valley station of Klewenalp cablecar (Timetable 1556) ☎ 041/64 12 64: car ferry service across lake to Gersau
☎ 041/64 14 07 (Beckenried side) and
☎ 041/84 13 75 (Gersau).
Flüelen Lake steamer excursion terminus at head of lake. Major Postbus office point of departure for the Alpine passes: Klausen, Gotthard, Susten, Furka and Oberalp (☎ 044/2 21 36).

3

Bern, Oberland and Mittelland

3.1 Bern

As capital cities go, Bern, with about 133,000 inhabitants (400,000, if conurbation is included), is not a big city. Indeed its inhabitants take rather a pride in having a city where 'man is the measure' of things and where reminders of past glories and achievements are present as a stimulus to the present. The city was founded in 1191 by the last of the Dukes of Zähringen, for sound strategic considerations, on the peninsula formed by a loop in the River Aare. A century later it was enlarged and developing as an independent city having a protective alliance with Savoy against acquisitive Burgundian magnates. Its survival in independence had to be fought for against the Burgundian nobility and won at the battle of Laupen in 1339.

The city followed up this victory by obtaining admission to the Swiss Confederation in 1353. For many centuries it exercised a vigorous and expansionist policy in a westerly direction (in the era when Uri and the other Forest Cantons were equally active in penetrating southwards). Large territories along Lake Geneva became subject to Bernese rule. Indeed, it is largely because of Bernese influence and energy that a large part of modern French-speaking Switzerland came within the Confederation. It was only after the upheavals of the French Revolutionary and Napoleonic Wars that Bern lost control of wide dependencies that were formed into new cantons in 1815. In 1848 when Bern was chosen to be the whole country's capital it was a matter of great satisfaction to the people of Bern that their former subject lands were supporters of that choice.

A Walk through the Heart of Bern

Leave the *Bahnhof* concourse by the escalator nearest to the Tourist Information Office and emerge into the Spitalgasse, one of the sections of a long, continuous thoroughfare down the spine of the peninsula within a river loop which is the site of the Bern *Altstadt*. At the corner opposite the escalator exit is the restrained baroque reformed Church of the Holy Spirit, dating from 1726-9. Walk east to the next corner, where the street name now becomes Marktgasse and the first place of interest is the **Käfigturm** or Prison Tower (*Käfig* means a cage!). This was erected 1641-43 on the site of the city's second West Gate of 1256 and served as a prison until 1897.

All these main streets in the old city are impressive, built as they are of weathered sandstone, all arcaded with the arcades forming the street level façades of all buildings 6km (4 miles) of them! so that no matter what the weather Berners are accustomed to stroll, leisurely engaged in window-shopping, beneath their arcades' wide shelter. At intervals the centre of the street is enlivened by one of a series of medieval fountains (many of which were erected about 1550 in place of earlier wooden ones) with magnificently sculpted and vividly coloured representative figures such as a bag-piper and an ogre; street traffic, including trams, circumnavigates them as best it can. Everywhere balcony rails and window boxes are profuse with flowers which set off the ancient sandstone.

At the next intersection, where Marktgasse continues into Kramgasse, is the city's famed **Zytgloggeturm** or Clock Tower, which was the first West Gate of the city, erected about 1131. It is renowned for the precision of its mechanical clock, constructed four-and-a-half centuries ago. In high summer season visitors often impede trams and buses here by thronging both pavement and roadway, with cameras at the ready, as the final four minutes of each hour approach when the clock puts on its mechanised puppet-show parade of jester, bears with drums and fifes, armoured knight, crowing cockerel and Father Time himself with sceptre and hour-glass. (A one-hour guided tour of the Clock Tower, including demonstration of the mechanism, is available at 4.30pm daily, May to October, for a limited number. Tickets from the Tourist Office in advance.)

Where the Kramgasse ends, before entering Gerechtigkeitsgasse (Justice Street) it is worth while turning left into the intersecting street, Kreuzgasse. A few paces lead into the Rathausgasse, and — diagonally across on the right — the beautiful Gothic **Town Hall** (dating from 1405-17) with its characteristic and impressive external staircase to the Council Chamber.

Returning to the Gerechtigkeitsgasse, with one of the most handsome fountains in the form of a figure of blindfolded Justice (1543), the street leads gently downhill as it approaches the Nydegg Bridge (Nydegg Brücke) over the River Aare. Across the bridge, to the right, is the **Bear Pit** where brown bears, live exemplars of the omnipresent flag emblem of the city, play to the gallery of spectators. But many may prefer before visiting the bears, to cross the avenue beyond Nydegg Bridge and take the lane up to the **Rose Garden** on the hill to the left. From it there is a classic view over the Old City which gives an exceptionally illuminating understanding of its strategic position and of its strikingly symmetrical layout.

Return to the Bear Pit. Its entertaining occupants are a reminder of the

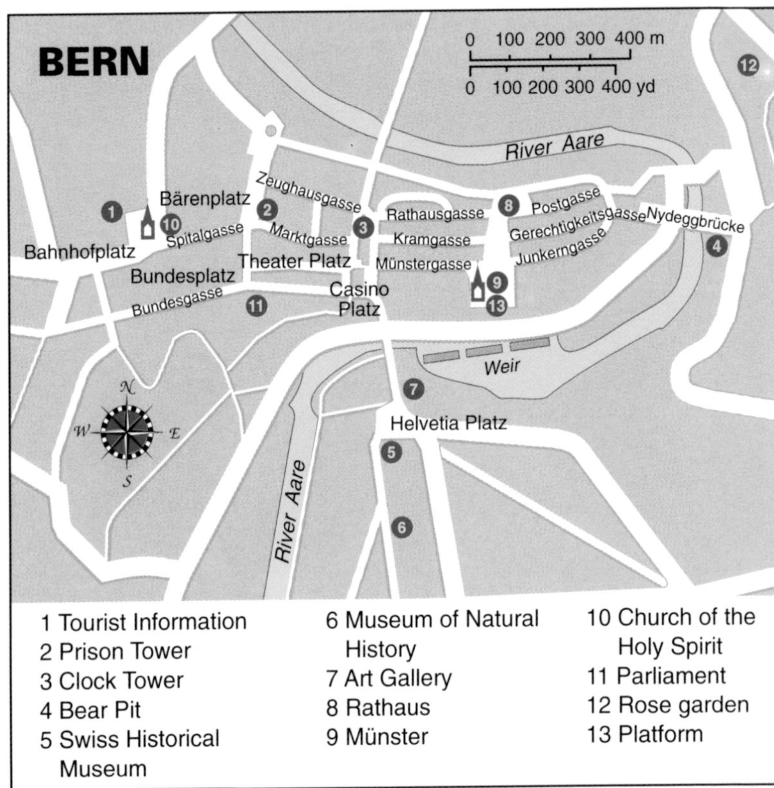

legend that Bern's founding Duke of Zähringen named his city after the first animal hunted on the banks of the Aare. The German word *Bären*, English 'bears', sounds very like the name of the city and is popularly believed to be its derivation. Certainly the oldest surviving civic seal features a bear. And the flags in city and canton do not permit the legend to be easily forgotten.

Recrossing the Nydegg Bridge turn half-left into Junkerngasse which curves round to run parallel with Gerechtigkeitsgasse. Standing on the left is the fifteenth-century **Minster**, Switzerland's masterpiece of late Gothic architecture. Prominent among its treasures are the sculpted figures (1490-95) of the *Last Judgment* group in the main portal, the mid-fifteenth-century stained glass, and the Renaissance carved choir-stalls (1523-25).

To the south of the Minster is a massive stone platform overhanging the River Aare, giving a fine prospect of the river weirs opposite, and, below, of the picturesque waterside precinct on the near bank in the direction of the Nydegg Bridge. There is also a view over the river to the Helvetia Platz beyond the Kirchenfeldbrücke. Around and beyond that square is a cluster of important museums: the Swiss Alpine Museum, the Swiss Post

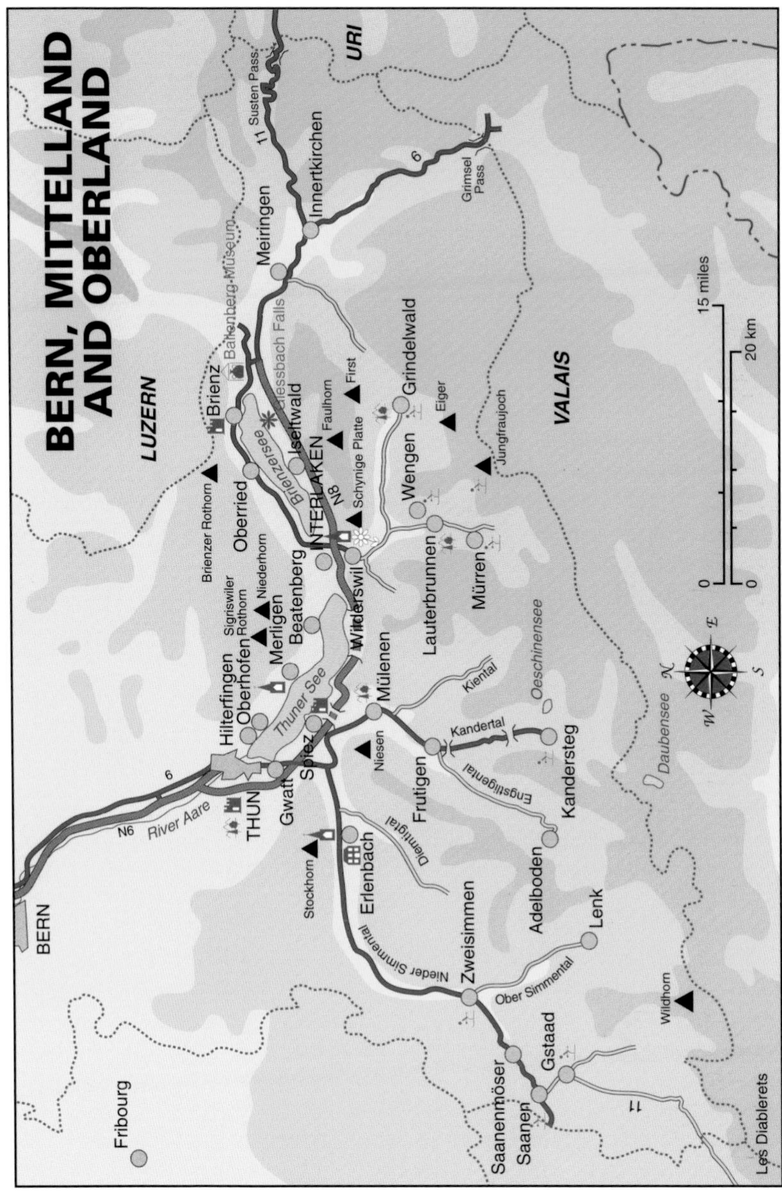

and Telegraph (PTT) Museum, the Art Gallery, the great Berner Historical Museum, the Museum of Natural History and the Swiss Rifle Museum. (All of these can be reached via the Münstergasse and by crossing the Kirchenfeldbrücke).

From the Münstergasse continue west across the Casino Platz into the Amtshausgasse to arrive at the **Bundesplatz**. This square faces onto the front of the Parliament Building. (Behind it, too, is a garden terrace with attractive views toward the river.) It is specially interesting to take this walk on one of the weekly market days when the two squares, Bundesplatz and **Bärenplatz**, are occupied with colourful market stalls and housewives are purchasing vegetables and fruit direct from the growers. One of the great traditional festival days of the Bern year is the fourth Monday of November when the *Zibelemarit*, the Onion Market, takes over the city centre from daybreak.

The Bärenplatz leads directly into the Spitalgasse and Marktgasse where this walk through the heart of Bern began.

Illuminations: from dusk until midnight daily during the season from Easter until the end of October most of the notable buildings of this old centre part of the city are flood-lit.

Local Excursions

1 A sight-seeing tour of the old city is available by coach with a multilingual guide, 10am-2pm daily May to October (in April Monday to Saturday 2pm and in March Saturdays 2pm only). Tickets from the Tourist Office at the Main Station, from where the tours also depart.

2 The favourite excursion for a panoramic view is to the Gurten belvedere hill (858m, 2,815ft) on the city outskirts (suburb Wabern). Take a No 9 tram from the Main Station; alight at the stop for the funicular that runs to the Gurten summit. Good views of the city and the Berner Oberland.

Major Excursions from Bern to the Mittelland

Bern, half-way between Zürich and Geneva, is well-placed as a starting point for a wide range of major excursions. Some to places of special interest in the region the Swiss call Mittelland are listed below.

1 Bern to Burgdorf

From Bern take the N1 motorway to the north, heading for Olten/Basel. Leave the N1 after 19km (12 miles) turning right (east) for Burgdorf. The nucleus of this historic town occupies a striking strategic position on a hill commanding the River Emme. It has a long tradition of settlement, the hill having been a fortified place since the mid-tenth century. From 1127 onward the Zähringer Dukes extended the castle which is one of Switzerland's earliest brick buildings; and the town alongside it on the ridge grew in proportion to its strategic importance and was in fact included in the walled defences by the Kyburg dynasty which followed the Zähringers. When the Kyburgers sold Burgdorf to Bern in 1384 the townsfolk had by then acquired burgher rights. Until the French Revolutionary wars (which had quite momentous impact on Switzerland) the castle was occupied by a Bernese governor. The triple-towered castle which is today so prominent a landmark now serves as a historical museum. The late fifteenth-century parish church (Reformed) is a fine example of late

Gothic and possesses a notable rood screen of 1512. The residential part of the castle has a Romanesque hall and a chapel with fourteenth-century frescos. There is much of the old town that is well worth seeing, with its handsome Gothic and baroque-style merchant houses in the Höhengasse and Kronenplatz.

Public Transport Option

Burgdorf has a principal SBB station on the main railway from Bern to Olten/Basel/Zürich.

2 Bern to Murten

There is a broad tract of rolling plateau country which lies between Bern and the shores of Lake Geneva. In the past it was often the corridor crossed by migrating peoples or invading armies. So it is perhaps not surprising that in this region cantonal frontiers are rather irregular in their outline, reflecting many historical changes. The interesting small town of Murten, which preserves so intact its medieval fortified walls, exemplifies this. Murten does not lie in Berner Mittelland today but in the neighbouring canton of Fribourg. But it was once Bernese. And for centuries it was under the joint rule of Bern and Fribourg.

Murten is conveniently reached from Bern, whether by road or rail. By road take the N1 motorway heading west from Bern taking care in 12km (7½ miles) not to take the exit for Kerzers and Neuchâtel but to continue on the motorway as it curves south and becomes an ordinary national road a short distance from Murten.

Murten lies beside the lake which bears its name. The little town was founded in its present form in the second half of the twelfth century by the Dukes of Zähringen. It has preserved its architectural setting and character and its medieval town walls (twelfth and fifteenth century) are exceptionally well-preserved and maintained. The rampart walks are freely accessible and provide an atmospheric experience with interesting views into the town and out over the surrounding countryside — including the town moat that now holds orchard gardens. One of two original gates, the Berner Gate, survives in its eighteenth-century baroque form. The wide main street which the Berner Gate bounds, and which forms a market place, has sixteenth-century arcaded pavements and houses with seventeenth- and eighteenth-century façades. It is a delightful place to stroll through, as it is sufficiently small (population under 5,000) for a visitor to explore its layout and enjoy its relaxed atmosphere.

Murten has considerable significance in Swiss history as it gave its name to a critical battle fought close by in 1476. At Murten in 1476 the Confederates won their first victory over Charles the Bold's Burgundian army. And to this present day the historic linguistic frontier separating French-speaking and German-speaking Switzerland passes close to Murten (the

Rampart walk at the walled town of Mürten

Opposite: Fribourg

French form of its name being Morat).

In the summer season an interesting boat excursion can be made from Murten, by boat on the Murten See and the Lac de Neuchâtel with which it is linked by canal, to **Neuchâtel**, capital of the French-speaking canton of the same name further west (Timetable 2212). Return to Bern can be made swiftly from Neuchâtel by train, of course.

Public Transport Option

Although the rail journey involves a change of trains, the timetable of services is so well co-ordinated that the change is no great inconvenience. The best route with a Bern-Murten rail ticket is to take from Bern Main Station a train on the frequent Bern-Neuchâtel service (Timetable 220), alight at Kerzers and change platform for a train to Murten on the line to Payerne (Timetable 251).

3 Bern to Fribourg

Fribourg, city of some 33,000 inhabitants, is the historic capital of the canton of the same name which lies on the great 'corridor' of rolling plateau that stretches from Bern in the direction of Lake Geneva. It is only 31km (19 miles) distant from Bern on road No 12 or by the N12 motorway and its station is a principal stop for Intercity trains to Lausanne and Geneva (Timetable 290). It occupies a most striking position on the River Sarine (the linguistic and ethnic boundary between French- and German-speaking communities, villages of the former being on the left bank, and of the latter on the right bank of the river which in German is called the Saane).

Founded by the Duke of Zähringen in 1157 as a stronghold at a strategic river crossing, the medieval city grew on its craggy ridge situated on a deeply sculpted curve of the river, its limestone buildings nestling in layers between the ridge and the river's left bank. It was eminently defensible in its cliff-like environment and in addition acquired important fortifications. Although parts of the town wall were removed to allow expansion in the nineteenth century, the walls and towers that still survive are Switzerland's most important medieval defensive system and contribute greatly to the unique atmosphere of the city.

The city defences were important in the early medieval period when Fribourg was often at loggerheads with Bern. But during Bern's wars with the Burgundians Fribourg supported the Swiss Confederates and in 1481 became a member of the Confederation.

The Reformation failed to take hold here and indeed Fribourg in 1580 invited the Jesuits to establish themselves in the city, so making it a centre of the Counter-Reformation. In the seventeenth century it provided a home to many other Catholic religious orders. It became seat of the Catholic bishopric of Lausanne, Geneva and Fribourg. Its renowned

Catholic university was founded towards the end of the nineteenth century.

That history is reflected in the variety of its architecture which includes around 200 'protected' Gothic houses, many patrician mansions exemplifying baroque and French classicist styles, as well as the great churches. A place of steep streets, it nonetheless repays the effort of a walkabout, because the irregularities of its site present many charming, some really impressive and frequently unexpected viewpoints: in particular the panoramas of the old town from the great stone Zähringen Bridge across the Sarine, and from the modern Gotteron Bridge 500m further on.

Places to visit above all include the St Nicholas Cathedral; its splendid fifteenth-century Gothic tower dominates the rooftops of the old quarter, called the *Bourg*; and its interior contains many treasures of religious art such as the sculpted *Entombment* (1433) in its Chapel of the Holy Sepulchre. In the upper town is the College and Church of St Michel (with its rococo decorated interior) founded by the Jesuits, the Eglise des Cordeliers (Franciscan Church) with its many ecclesiastical treasures, and the Art and History Museum which houses the richest collection of medieval and religious sculptures in Switzerland.

4 Bern to Langnau-im-Emmental

Langnau, readily accessible from Bern, was briefly described in Chapter 2 'West from Luzern'.

Bern to Thun and Interlaken

A favourite choice of the Berner for an excursion is in the direction of their 'own' Thuner See (Lake Thun) 28km (17 miles) to the south-south-west. Nothing so enhances the majesty of the Oberland peaks as their reflections in the mirror of the lake. And a high proportion of these excursionists, whether travelling through the green Mittelland by train (Timetable 290), by highway No 6, or its parallel modern motorway, choose to alight at Thun to continue the approach to the mountain massif by lake steamer.

Visitors who wish to get an idea of the layout of the Oberland before they start their particular excursions could take the 2-hour boat trip from Thun to Interlaken or vice-versa. The full-length trip is available from early April to beyond mid-November in most years (Timetable 2310: for further information ☎ 033/36 02 58). But before taking the boat trip it is worth while taking a look at Thun.

Thun lies at the opposite end of the Thuner See from Interlaken. In terms of political and administrative boundaries, Thun is counted as part of the Oberland. (Indeed long before the clusters of nineteenth-century hotels arose in Interlaken, Thun was the gateway to the Oberland for the earliest Alpine travellers.) Yet in geographical and historical terms Thun could almost serve as the model of a Mittelland town, a main urban centre for the extensive pastoral and agricultural hinterland. Today Thun might

The Rathausplatz, Thun

Opposite: Thun's church and castle overlooking the river Aare

equally well be described as a gateway to the Mittelland; it faces both ways.

Some might think of the two towns, Thun and Interlaken at the opposite ends of the lake, as rivals. However, they serve such different functions. In Interlaken one is always conscious of being in a town that is almost entirely taken up with its function as a centre of tourism — for which it is so well placed, almost a base camp for the approach by rail, road and cable to the giants of the Oberland rearing up immediately behind. Thun, on the other hand, is mainly concerned with its long-established business of serving as a market town and centre of services and administration for a wide area, and a garrison town now providing the Swiss Army's major training centre for light and mechanized troops. Associated factory units to the north of the town produce high-tech equipment. Its hotels accommodate only a fraction of the number of visitors that Interlaken can take.

A Walk through the Heart of Thun

Thun is another of the Swiss towns which is strategically situated, like Luzern and Zürich, at the outflow of a river, in this case the Aare, from its lake. Its picturesque site is a defensive one: the old town nucleus was partly tucked into an island formed by the river dividing into two almost equal arms as it leaves the lake; and partly on the north-east bank facing the island, in the shelter of the protective ridge on which the Duke of Zähringen built the present Thun Castle about 1190. (There had been previous strongholds on the site going back even to prehistoric times; scholars derive the name of Thun from the Celtic root *dun* as in Dundalk and Dunbarton meaning a hillfort.)

A walk can start conveniently from the Bahnhofplatz (Station Square), across which lie the lake steamer berths to the right, and to their left the bus termini for the surrounding lake- and countryside. The Bahnhofstrasse ahead leads out of the square to a main bridge across the Aussere Aare, the outer river arm, and continues as the Freienhofgasse, with picturesque arcaded shops reminiscent of Bern. The first street on the left, known as the Bälliz, runs straight down the island site, has the Main Post Office, the site of the Wednesday and Saturday street market and many principal shops and banks. From it two alleys to the right lead to footbridges across the Innere Aare arm. Both offer colourful views of the old town, parish church and castle on the facing hill.

Cross the second footbridge to find your way through to the **Rathausplatz**, one of the most charming town hall squares in Switzerland, dating from the Middle Ages. Enclosed by the Town Hall, guild halls and the attractive eighteenth-century hospital that now serves as police headquarters, it is the spacious summertime venue for open-air concerts, folklore presentations and similar events. From it, parallel to the river, the **Hauptstrasse** (Main Street) runs to the right. This remarkable street gives the impression of having two layers of shops. The pavements of its middle section are raised house-high on the top of what were built as projecting basements. These flower-adorned and railinged walkways give an almost theatrical effect to the street.

Near the top of the Obere Hauptgasse (Upper Main Street) on the left is the roofed stone stairway that leads up steeply to the church on the right and the castle on the left. The **parish church** (Reformed) is a typical early eighteenth-century baroque 'preaching' church, but has a strikingly attractive fourteenth-century polygonal tower which somehow fits in well with the neighbouring castle. The frescos in the vestibule date to the fifteenth century.

Thun Castle has an impressive square-built keep with corner towers. Its typically Bernese steep-hipped roof was a later addition when the castle became the residence of Bernese governors. For the past century it has housed a historical museum of which the centrepiece is the Knights' Hall magnificently furnished (partly with booty from the Burgundian war of 1476). Among other exhibits is a unique collection of the colourful ceramic ware, so popular at the turn of the century, called Thuner majolica.

From castle and church there are splendid views over river and lake to the nearer Oberland mountains, notably the Stockhorn (2,190m, 7,185ft) group and the Niesen (2,362m, 7,750ft). Complete the walk by leaving the church grounds by the main descent to the east, leading down to the Lauitor and there taking the passage at the Savings Bank to reach the Aare Quay promenade. Just beyond the river frontage of the handsome Beau Rivage hotel is a pedestrian bridge that leads to the upstream point of the island from which stretches the roofed timber bridge and the main outflow control sluice for the Aussere Aare; a most picturesque corner with views that change with every few paces. An avenue then leads straight to the Bahnhofplatz.

The Thuner See

The lake steamer berths lie on a canalised extension of the lake. Near the outer end of this the steamer passes a tiny church on the right-hand side among tall trees. The **Scherzligen Church** is reckoned to be about a thousand years old, its nave dating from around AD1000 although the chancel and steeple are Gothic. It contains notable frescos. This church borders upon a green, wooded promontory — the Schadau parkland and mansion which serve as a recreational and cultural centre.

On the north shore of the lake — along which runs the road linking Thun to Interlaken with a good bus service (Timetable 310.60) — is a near continuous chain of attractive residential villages with sunlit chalets set up the hillside, while attractive villas and houses on the lakeside have boathouses as their basements.

Hilterfingen, nestling in parkland, has a thriving sailing school. Its nineteenth-century Hunegg Castle houses a museum of furnishings representing the Jugendstil (art nouveau) period. Its neighbour, **Oberhofen**, has perhaps the most spectacular of the landing stages called at; for its

Schloss Oberhofen on the Thuner See

steamer pier is but a stone's throw from the medieval castle with its twelfth-century keep. This one-time Habsburg possession, since the mid-twentieth century, has housed a branch of the Bern historical museum. Oberhofen almost merges into the next resort, **Gunten**, the water-skiing centre for the lake. From Gunten the ship turns at right-angles to cross the lake to Spiez on the southern shore, facing all the while the near symmetrical cone of the Niesen (2,362m, 7,750ft).

Spiez sits in a natural amphitheatre, surrounded by vines and orchards, with a charming, sheltered bay at lake level with a bluff promontory to the north on which stands Spiez Castle and its attendant early Romanesque church, thought to date from the turn of the millennium. The lower level of the castle keep also goes back to that era, the remainder being fifteenth to sixteenth century. It is worth while alighting at Spiez (and carrying on the journey by a later steamer) if for no other reason than to ascend the road from the pier to the 'amphitheatre' where the upper town and the railway station lie; there is a fine panorama of Spiez itself from here and of the lake's north shore dominated by the Sigriswiler Rothorn (2,050m, 6,726ft) opposite, and the Niederhorn's pinnacle (1,950m, 6,398ft) further to the right.

The Spiez railway station has an importance out of all proportion to the size of the town because of its function as a junction. The Niesen 'cone' that dominates the Spiez section of the lake stands like a sentinel between the mouths of two Oberland valleys whose streams (running roughly south-north) join to enter the lake near Spiez. The eastern valley is the

Spiez

The alpine plateau lying below the Jungfrau massif

Kandertal along which runs the Loetschberg railway line to tunnel ultimately through to Brig, Simplon and Italy; the western valley is the Simmental, and the Simmental line runs south to Zweisimmen where it meets the Montreux-Oberland railway that has twisted and turned its ascent from Lake Geneva. The third line to thread through Spiez is the lakeside main line bringing international traffic via Bern to Interlaken. Spiez is the key to the international rail timetable in the Oberland!

From Spiez pier the steamer usually makes for the neighbouring bay to call at Faulensee before recrossing the lake to **Merligen** on the north shore with its sheltered sunny slopes at the mouth of the Justis Valley. Next is the pier at **Beatenbucht** from which a cable railway rises to the high terrace of Beatenberg. Four kilometres (2½ miles) further on is the stop for the **Beatushöhlen** (stalactite caves, former place of pilgrimage associated with eighth-century St Beatus). After a further stop at **Neuhaus** with its lido and sailing school the ship curves round the lake end to reverse up the canal to its berth below the Interlaken West railway station.

3.3 Interlaken and the Oberland

The significance of the name Interlaken almost speaks for itself. Its position on the alluvial flat built up between the Thuner See and Brienzer See by silt and deposits carried down by Oberland streams made it an ideal starting place for the nineteenth-century pioneers of mountain railways to penetrate into the great massif of the Berner Oberland. The original small village grew in the neighbourhood of an Augustinian monastery; but the scant relics of its past have been swamped by this century's development of a well-equipped tourist centre. It has its own atmosphere of exhilaration and expectancy fostered by the visitor's first sight of the famed view of the Jungfrau mountain group seen from the town's main promenade, the Höheweg. The Höheweg runs from west to east through one of Interlaken's most attractive assets, the Höhematte, a great open space of some 35 acres of green parkland adorned with flower gardens.

The Berner Oberland is the mountainous terrain in the south of the canton, bounded to the north by the Simmental and the Thuner See and Brienzer See, and to the south by the great Alpine barrier that forms the border with the valley of the River Rhône (in effect, canton Valais). Lines of access to this great massif mostly penetrate from the north. Interlaken lies very nearly at their hub.

Interlaken has two main-line stations: Interlaken West, one level above where the Thuner See steamer docked and near the town's main centre; and, 3km (nearly 2 miles) further on, Interlaken Ost, which is a junction station for Oberland mountain rails to Grindelwald, Lauterbrunnen, Mürren, Wengen and Jungfraujoch. Nearby too are the landing stages for steamers on Brienzer See which is reached by a canalised waterway.

One of the railways which terminates at Interlaken Ost is the Brünig line from Luzern which was referred to in Chapter 2 as a contrasting alternative to the Emmental route from Luzern to Bern by road or rail. This is a suitable point at which to give a brief description of the Brünig route. Once again the rail route (Timetable 470) and road No 4 run very closely parallel.

Luzern to Interlaken via Brünig by Rail

Most of the rail tracks at the platforms of Luzern station are of the usual standard gauge: the Brünig line platform is an exception, being 'narrow-gauge' (1m wide). For the first stretch of the journey as far as **Hergiswil** the train runs alongside the Vierwaldstättersee (Lake Luzern) allowing a fine direct view across the lake from the left-hand window to the Rigi (1,798m, 5,899ft) and the Bürgenstock (1,128m, 3,701ft) heights.

At Hergiswil a branch of the line goes off to the left to Stans and Engelberg (see the Luzern-Engelberg route described in Chapter 2) while the Brünig line continues south, through a longish tunnel into the half-canton of Obwalden. (Unterwalden, one of the Four Original Forest Cantons, has for long been administered as two half-cantons, Nidwalden and Obwalden, the names suggesting a Lower Forest district and an Upper Forest district.) The westernmost arm of the lake alongside is now known as the Alpnacher See. At **Alpnachstad** station some passengers alight to change to the steep cogwheel railway to Pilatus (2,129m, 6,985ft).

The rail now runs in the broad valley of the Sarner Aa River. The town of **Sarnen**, capital of Obwalden, has some historic buildings of such merit as to warrant a visit here; each year on the last Sunday of April the town is the scene of another open-air *Landsgemeinde* (see Chapter 1). The placid lake to be seen next from the right window is the Sarner See. Beyond the upper end of the lake is **Giswil**. The slight clanking noise during the minute or two of the train's stop here is the rack-and-pinion ('cogwheel') traction gearing being brought into play for the one-in-ten climb from this point to the next station, **Kaiserstuhl**.

The Lungernsee that next appears on the right is really an artificial lake dammed as a reservoir. It reflects the impressive peak of the Giswilerstock (2,014m, 6,608ft) beyond to the west. The stretch beyond Lungern twists through hilly country, thickly overgrown with bush and trees over the Brünig Pass summit of 1,002m (3,288ft), still requiring rack-and-pinion gearing on leaving the Brünig-Hasliberg station, but now to control the twisting descent which presents tantalizing glimpses through the trees of the distant valley floor, Brienzer See and the Wetterhorn (3,708m, 12,166ft). Now the train is over the boundary and in Berner Oberland.

During the descent towards Meiringen the traveller sometimes glimpses or hears an aeroplane. The Aare Valley floor is astonishingly wide between its steep, lowering walls, and flat — suitable for military and emergency aircraft to use.

The train abandons rack-and-pinion gearing well before curving round to the left to enter **Meiringen**, a town of some antiquity with an interesting church, rebuilt in the seventeenth century but with some fourteenth-

Lauterbrunnen with the Staubbach Falls

Opposite: The north face of the Eiger seen from above Beatenberg

century wall paintings and a fourteenth-century Romanesque tower capped by a wooden spire. The town is now quite a tourist centre: there is a cablecar to the Hasliberg ski-field up near the Brünig. Also, from 1 July to mid-September a bus service runs the 4km (2½ miles) to the famed **Aareschlucht**, the gorge with overhanging limestone cliff walls, where a mile-long (1½km) passable walkway above the stream has become a very popular excursion. The same bus service has a stop (2km [about a mile] from Meiringen) at the Reichenbach cablecar bottom station to the viewpoint terrace for the **Reichenbach Falls** (of Sherlock Holmes' fame). It is also a principal starting point for the summer (late June to mid-October) day tours taking in the three Alpine passes of Grimsel, Susten and Furka, and the four passes of Grimsel, Nufenen, Gotthard and Susten (Timetable 470.69 in each case).

Meiringen is one of those stations where the engine has to change ends and bring the train back out onto the same track as it entered on. The train soon reaches **Brienz**, main village on the lakeside, and an attractive and colourful one, too, with its chalet-style houses bedecked with bright window boxes, nestling between lake shore and hillside. The village is famed for its traditional crafts of wood-carving and violin-making and arrangements can be made locally to visit one of the wood-carving workshops.

A short distance behind the railway station (which lies on the lakeside) is the bottom station of the Brienz-Rothorn mountain railway (Timetable 475, operating early June to mid-October), which still uses steam engines (as well as diesel locomotives) for the ascent to the 2,353m-high (7,720ft) peak that dominates the region between the Brienzer See and Lungernsee. The summit view takes in the Bernese, Valais and Urner Alps, and from the summit an aerial cablecar operates to the opposite (north) side of the mountain, the pre-Alpine country that lies between Oberland and Emmental.

The Swiss rightly set great store by their heritage and traditions, national and local and this is reflected in the number and variety of their museums. Near Brienz is a unique and magnificent open-air museum, so important that at Brienz station square each hourly train from Bern/ Interlaken and also from Luzern is met by a bus to convey visitors to the museum 6km (3¾ miles) away at **Ballenberg** (Timetable 470.92). The museum deals with rural architecture and living styles — which differ markedly from region to region — and is lively enough to warrant a full day's visit. Grouped according to region it consists of genuine traditional rural homes and farm buildings, many of them fully equipped with implements, that have been transported from their original sites in all regions of the country and re-erected here complete in an appropriate setting. Demonstrations of rural crafts of all kinds go on, from the baking of bread to the operation of lime-kilns for the production of fertiliser. From May to October Swiss Rail conduct 'package' excursions from main centres such as Bern and Luzern to Ballenberg inclusive of entry ticket and lunch at one of the museum's inns (enquire at main railway stations).

From the stretch of main line after leaving Brienz the traveller has a glimpse, across the lake, of the **Giessbach Falls**, with their seven steps, the final one being a sheer cascade into the lake itself. This is another favourite excursion best approached by way of the lake steamer's calling-place at the Giessbach lake station from which a funicular railway runs between May and September (Timetable 1470. Further information ☎ 036/51 3535). Seventeen kilometres (10½ miles) further on, after a lakeside run with charming views across towards Iseltwald, the train enters **Interlaken Ost**, its junction with the main line (Bern-Loetschberg-Simplon Rail [BLS] from Thun and Bern, and the Berner-Oberland-Bahn [BOB]) the other narrow-gauge rail that runs to Grindelwald and Lauterbrunnen.

Note for Users of Private Transport

As indicated above, the Brünig route from Luzern can be carried out by the road which substantially follows the same route as the train. Descending from the Brünig Pass into the Aare Valley, however, the route provides drivers with the option of turning right direct for Brienz, without visiting Meiringen. Parking places are available at Ballenberg, Aare Gorge and Reichenbach cable station. It should be recalled that the Brünig road links the two most popular Swiss destinations for English-speaking tourists, Luzern and Interlaken. During the 'season' the big problem for many years has been the congestion of the narrow and serpentine road through Brienz and satellite villages. A solution is now offered by a new motorway extension of the N8, opened some years ago, which bypasses Brienz quite drastically by going from Interlaken along the south side of the lake to Brienzwiler. The new road passes near Iseltwald — and perhaps in future may rob it of some of its picturesque seclusion on its romantic peninsula. This road greatly speeds up the connection of Interlaken with Meiringen and the Susten Pass.

Schynige Platte by rail

To get a perspective of the Jungfrau region the tourist could make a short preliminary excursion to Schynige Platte by cogwheel rail (Timetable 314). The bottom station of the line is at Wilderswil, only 3½km (2 miles) from Interlaken, which can be reached by motorway, by walking on the level meadow paths, or from Interlaken Ost main station by the Berner Oberland narrow-gauge railway, on which Wilderswil is the first stop. The ascent takes less than an hour, giving good views of the lakes on the climb. From the upper station (1,987m, 6,519ft) it pays best to do the easy ascent to the higher terrace known as the Daube (2,076m, 6,811ft) for one of the finest all-round views. It also gives an excellent bird's-eye view of the routes taken by the much more ambitious Berner Oberland mountain railways that penetrate the Jungfrau region by way of Grindelwald and Lauterbrunnen (described below). There is an Alpine garden too that can be visited to brush up on Alpine flowers before coming across them in their natural situation. On the return to **Wilderswil**, the pleasant village with some fine traditional chalets makes an enjoyable place for a walk around; cross the roofed wooden bridge to the other bank of the Lütschine stream to visit the baroque church of St Michael.

Interlaken to Grindelwald

In the Jungfrau region Grindelwald is unique among the great resorts in that the private motorist can reach it by road all the way. In high season, winter or summer, this can make it very busy — but the bustle makes for a stimulating atmosphere. Beyond Wilderswil the Lütschine Valley (Lütschental) is pleasantly wooded. At the village of Zweilütschinen the Weisse Lütschine River is joined by its Schwarze Lütschine tributary, and

the road forks. Take the left turn. (The other road goes on to Lauterbrunnen.) Beyond Lütschental there is quite a steep gradient with one or two sharp bends and the Wetterhorn (3,708m, 12,166ft) comes into sight half-left. The road and the narrow-gauge cogwheel rail tracks criss-cross one another at several points on the way; as the valley opens out the rail keeps position to the left of the road and so they enter **Grindelwald** which lies on a gentle, sheltered sloping site.

On passing the station and centre of the straggling town towards the church, the view of the mountains from the main street is breathtaking: the Wetterhorn, the Schreckhorn ridge with its glaciers, and, most striking because of its close position parallel to the village street, the eerie, chisel-like north face of the Eiger (3,974m, 13,039ft); a spectacular and memorable sight to admire from the comfort of one of the café balconies.

Grindelwald is possibly the favourite Oberland resort, and provides a great range of sports facilities and a variety of cableways and chairlifts. Notable is the Firstbahn cableway with its comfortable new six-seater cabins plying to the First sun terrace where the panoramas are splendid and there is access to the fine skiing terrain of the Grindelalp. Grindelwald's two glaciers (issuing between Wetterhorn and Schreckhorn, and between Schreckhorn and Eiger respectively) are a fascinating attraction for a visit by hill walkers adequately shod and equipped.

Public Transport Option

The BOB narrow-gauge rail from Interlaken Ost (Timetable 312) takes substantially the same path as the road to Grindelwald. Grindelwald station also serves as the junction with another cog-wheel railway, the Wengernalpbahn which turns down into the Lütschine Valley at Grindelwald Grund before climbing up steeply to the dominating ridge of Kleine Scheidegg.

Interlaken to Lauterbrunnen and Wengen

The road to Lauterbrunnen is the same as to Grindelwald as far as Zweilütschinen (where the 'Black' and 'White' branches of the River Lütschine meet). For Lauterbrunnen, however, go straight on at the fork. As you ascend the left (ie, west) bank of the stream, the valley floor widens, walled in by the sheer rock faces of limestone (averaging heights of 400m, 1,312ft) that are typical of a valley formed by glacial action. They are made all the more impressive by the frequent waterfalls that plunge from clifftop water courses. Behind **Lauterbrunnen** itself are the **Staubbach Falls** tumbling from a rocky spout 300m (984ft) above on the terrace where the resort of Mürren is sited; as it falls it turns into a cloud of fine spray. Most visitors find it worth while to cross the Lütschine and proceed 4km ($2^1/_2$ miles) further up the valley in the Stechelberg direction to visit the even more notable **Trümmelbach Falls**. Here there is a car park; the stream called the Trümmelbach has carved a gorge for itself in the left-hand wall of the valley, cascading through five 'steps'; access is simplified by a lift, by stepped paths and by flood-lighting.

Motorists intending to proceed beyond Lauterbrunnen to Wengen should return to the village and use the appropriate car park before taking the Wengernalp Rail for the cogwheel ascent. **Wengen** (1,275m, 4,183ft) is one of the car-free summer and winter resorts of this region, in a beautiful situation on a sunny, sheltered terrace high above the Lauterbrunnen Valley at the foot of the Jungfrau (4,149m, 13,646ft) and protected from the east by the ridge linking the Männlichen (2,343m, 7,687ft), Tschungen (2,520m, 8,268ft) and Lauberhorn (2,472m, 8,111ft) peaks. In Wengen every January the international Lauberhorn ski race (World Cup) is held. The village is also an excellent base for climbs and walks; there is a cableway to the Männlichen, a magnificent viewpoint (Timetable 1455).

Mürren is another traffic-free village. It too is perched on a sunny terrace — a ledge of Alpine pastureland — high (1,650m, 5,414ft) above the Lauterbrunnen Valley, on the opposite side from Wengen. Many claim it has the most magnificent views of the Jungfrau massif which it faces. Always a favourite with British skiers for the challenging quality of its ski-runs, it was here that the Kandahar Ski Club and the prestigious Arlberg-Kandahar competition were set up. To reach Mürren, motorists start from Lauterbrunnen, driving up the valley beyond Trümmelbach on the road to Stechelberg. After 6km (nearly 4 miles), and about 1km before the village, a side road goes to the right, leading to the bottom station of the Schildhornbahn, the cablecar (Timetable 1460) which rises to the Schildhorn (2,967m, 9,735ft) with Mürren as an intermediate station. (The Schildhorn with magnificent panoramas and with a revolving restaurant 'Piz Gloria' at the summit station of the cablecar is a favourite excursion from Mürren.)

Public Transport Option

There is a regular Postbus service (Timetable 311.15) from Lauterbrunnen to Stechelberg, with stops at the Trümmelbach Falls and the Schildhornbahn. But for most users of public transport, the journey to Mürren would most likely be made by starting from Interlaken Ost (Timetable 311) to Lauterbrunnen, then Lauterbrunnen (Timetable 313) to Grütschalp by cablecar and Grütschalp to Mürren by narrow-gauge rail.

To the Jungfraujoch by rail

The epitome of all mountain railway journeys is to the highest rail station in Europe, situated well above the permanent ice- and snowline even in

Alpine pastureland above Lauterbrunnen

Opposite: Iseltwald on the Brienzer See

summer. The Jungfraujoch is the ridge or saddle at 3,454m (11,333ft) which links the crests of the Mönch (4,105m, 13,469ft) and the Jungfrau (4,159m, 13,646ft).

The first section of the route (Timetable 311 or 312) is from **Interlaken Ost** either to **Grindelwald** or to **Lauterbrunnen**; many tourists take the opportunity of travelling outward by the one and return by the other. Assume an outward route via Lauterbrunnen; the Jungfrau destination can be seen ahead, beckoning to the traveller, during the journey up the Lauterbrunnen Valley. From Lauterbrunnen the Wengen plateau is reached by the Wengernalp Railway through a steep climb that uses a series of tunnels.

From **Wengen** the train continues over Alpine pastures first to the south then gradually rounds the shoulder towards the east to reach Wengernalp. The view of Eiger, Mönch and Jungfrau from here is breathtaking and so formidable do the giant snow-peaks appear that the proposition of reaching the Jungfraujoch by train seems hardly possible. From Wengernalp the train proceeds to **Kleine Scheidegg**, a resort poised on the ledge between the deep Grindelwald and Lauterbrunnen Valleys. It is here the journey is taken over on the Jungfraubahn proper, travellers from both Grindelwald and Lauterbrunnen having met at this point. The rail now heads apparently direct for the mountain wall and the Eiger glacier, entering a tunnel at Eigergletscher and, boring upwards at ascent rates up to one-in-four, reaches **Eigerwand** in 17 minutes, a station carved out of the rock, offering views through windows in the rock down to

Grindelwald and Interlaken's green valleys.

The next section is to the **Eismeer** station from where the views are over permanent snow and ice. The final station is the **Jungfraujoch** — an almost incredible mini 'resort' amid eternal snows, offering ice-palaces, rides over snowfields on sleighs drawn by husky dogs from July to September, views to the south of the most extensive glacier in the Alps as well as, to the north, the distant green and blue world of the lakeland far below. The wise tourist should be well-shod, well-clad and provided with sun-glasses to protect his eyes from the snowfields' reflection.

Having started the Jungfraujoch expedition via Lauterbrunnen, a 'round trip' element can be built into it by making the final stage of the return trip from the Kleine Scheidegg junction by way of Grindelwald to Interlaken Ost.

Beatenberg and Niederhorn

Many enthusiasts have found a favourite viewpoint of that trio of great snow peaks, the Eiger, Mönch and Jungfrau by taking a comparatively inexpensive half-day trip from Thun or Interlaken. **Beatenberg** is a charming village which straggles along a sheltered ledge at a height of 1,121m (3,678ft) on the mountainside on the north side of the Thuner See only 10km (6.2 miles) from Interlaken. As indicated earlier in this chapter, it can be reached by funicular rail from Beatenbucht, a lake steamer station and also bus stop on the Thun-Interlaken service (Timetable 310.60). There is also a Postbus service hourly from Interlaken West (Timetable 310.75). Motorists from Interlaken Station Square cross the railway and the Aare to the northern suburb of Unterseen; the well-engineered hill road to Beatenberg goes off the Thun road on the right.

As well as being a delightfully unsophisticated climatic resort in itself, it has one of the most interesting chairlifts in the region that ascends through pine woods to the **Niederhorn** (1,949m, 6,395ft). It is an unforgettable experience, as the twin-chair carries you up in silence broken only by the hiss and faint hum of the cable, to see the great ice-capped giants of the Oberland framed by the tall green conifers and the blue waters of the lake. The Niederhorn offers incomparable views over the lake to the whole Oberland range.

The Kandertal

Just as the Lütschental pokes southward into the great massif from Interlaken, so does the Kandertal from near Spiez. The motorist turns off the Thun road to the south to reach Spiezwiler where there is a fork: the Simmental road continues ahead, but the Kandertal road goes off to the left. In 7km (4½ miles) it reaches **Mülenen**. Here is the bottom station for the steep funicular that ascends the Niesen, the conical peak that dominates the middle section of the Thuner See. This is a worth while excursion

(Timetable 1405) for its astonishing panorama of the Bernese Alps, the Thuner See and Brienzer See and the distant Jura.

About 8km (5 miles) beyond Mülenen is the main pre-Alpine resort village of the valley, **Frutigen**, at the junction of the Kander with its tributary the Engstligen which flows down from **Adelboden**, a fashionable high resort in a sunny bowl at its valley head. From Frutigen to Kandersteg is a very interesting road of some 6.4km (4 miles), crossed at a halfway point by the BLS railway line as it enters its remarkable double loops to spiral up to the higher level of the valley. A good minor road links Frutigen also to Adelboden, 20km (12.4 miles).

Nearby, set in forest surroundings, is the appropriately-named **Blausee**, the Blue Lake, a picturesque excursion spot, with a trout hatchery close by.

Kandersteg itself is finally reached after two serpentine loops in a steep climb; the famous mountaineering and winter sports centre, which straggles in a long ribbon across floral Alpine meadows embraced by great mountain rock faces, has many outdoor attractions for summer visitors too, including the excursion by chairlift (Timetable 1410) to the **Oeschinensee** in its formidable cliff-girt setting. Kandersteg rail station is the loading point for car transport by the Loetschberg rail tunnel through the mountain barrier lying between the Oberland and the Rhône Valley.

Public Transport Option

The Kandertal is seen to great effect from the Bern-Loetschberg-Simplon railway which penetrates the massif to reach the Rhône Valley from canton Bern, Kandersteg itself being the last station before the Loetschberg tunnel which gave its name to the line (Timetable 300). Bus service 300.20 connects Frutigen with Adelboden, and service 300.23 with Kandesteg, in each case about hourly.

The Simmental

From Spiez both road and rail also go to the valley of the River Simme, the Simmental. The Simmental road (road No 11), goes off south-west at Spiezwiler after looping to cross the River Kander and skirting the foot of the Niesen. Administratively the Lower Simmental is included in the Oberland, although the rich pasturelands and woods of this pleasant valley have fairly typical pre-Alpine 'Mittelland' character, and are the home of the widely-famed Simmental breed of cattle.

Road and rail gently ascend the valley of this river which with its attractive pools and swift 'runs', crossed by several handsome timber-roofed bridges, cannot fail to attract the angler's eye. **Erlenbach**, 16km (10 miles) from Spiez, on a rise above the stream, is fairly characteristic of the valley. It has cattle markets of regional importance and its history is

Lenk in the Simmental

Children revel in a boat trip in Alpine lakeland

attested by its Reformed tenth- to thirteenth-century parish church with interior early fifteenth-century wall paintings. Its main street timber buildings with Bernese saddleback roofs are of later date, subsequent to an eighteenth-century fire. From Erlenbach a two-section cablecar (Timetable 1370) runs up to the Stockhorn (2,146m, 7,041ft) whose unmistakeable silhouette faces Thun across its lake.

Eleven kilometres (7 miles) further lies Boltigen where the valley now heads more truly south. (Shortly afterwards a very steep road turns off to the right to zigzag up to the Jaun Pass which gives a spectacular route through to Bulle and Gruyères in canton Fribourg and to Lausanne in Vaud.) **Zweisimmen**, charming main village of the Upper Simmental, set in wide Alpine pastures (popular for cross-country *langlauf* skiing in winter), is reached in 10km (6 miles) more. The rail station here is important as the junction where one can change to the spectacular narrow-gauge Montreux-Oberland Bahn (generally known as MOB) which with rack-and-pinion facilities twists and turns its way through the Bernese and Vaudoise Alpine borders to Lake Geneva, by way of Gstaad and Château d'Oex (Timetable 120). One can also change to the other, shorter, narrow-gauge line that runs to the winter and summer resort, and medicinal spa, of **Lenk**, encompassed by mountains in its sunny basin.

From Zweisimmen road No 11 continues to the last main area of Berner Oberland resorts before the cantonal and language frontier, an area with a great variety of winter sports facilities and scores of skilifts giving access to a wide choice of ski-runs. **Saanen** is a popular resort on the main road, on the language border, equally accessible from French-speaking Switzerland as from the Bernerland. Only a short distance (3km, 2 miles) to the south-west, however, lies perhaps the most fashionable and interational of all these resorts, **Gstaad**, in the upper valley of the River Saane which, under its French name of Sarine, was mentioned as the river of the city of Fribourg much further downstream. The Gstaad area abounds in possibilities for walkers, climbers and other sports-lovers in summer as well as for skiers, curlers and skaters in winter.

Public Transport Option

From Bern, Thun and Interlaken the BLS division of Swiss Rail's main lines connect at Spiez with the BLS line to Zweisimmen, road and rail running practically in parallel up the valley. From Zweisimmen the MOB narrow-gauge line does not always take the same course as the road, but in its own way links Zweisimmen, Saanenmöser and Saanen with Château d'Oex and places beyond on the way to Montreux. It does not provide the fastest connection between Bern, Thun or Interlaken with Lake Geneva (which is achieved by Intercity expresses Lausanne-Bern) but is certainly the most spectacular tourist route.

Additional Information

Places to Visit

Ballenberg
Schweizerisches Freilichtmuseum fur ländliche Bau- u. Wohnkultur
Ballenberg, CH-3855 Brienz
☎ 036/51 14 42
Open-air museum of Swiss houses, farms, settlements.
Life-size, grouped by regions.
Open: April, May, October 10am-5pm daily, June-end September 9am-5.30pm.

Beatushöhlen (Beatus Caves)
Between Beatenbucht and Sundlauenen.
Open: Palm Sunday to October, daily 9.30am to 5.30pm. Guided tours approx every 30 minutes. Information from Beatushöhlen Genossenschaft.
CH-3801 Sundlauenen
☎ 036/41 16 43

Bern
Kunstmuseum
(Museum of Fine Arts)
Hodlerstrasse 12

☎ 031/311 09 44
Bus No 11 or 20/21 to Bollwerk stop. Paul Klee foundation of international repute. Also Italian masters of fourteenth, fifteenth, sixteenth century. Open: Tuesday 10am-9pm, Wednesday-Sunday 10am-5pm. Closed Monday.

Kunsthalle Bern
Helvetiaplatz 1
☎ 031/351 00 31
Tram No 3 or 5 to Helvetia P. Special exhibitions of contemporary art.
Open: Tuesday 10am-9pm, Wednesday-Sunday 10am-5pm. Closed Monday.

Historisches Museum
Helvetiaplatz 5
☎ 031/351 18 11
Tram No 3 or 5 to Helvetia P. Prehistoric, historic, ethnographical collections. Booty of the Burgundian War of 1476.
Open: Tuesday-Sunday 10am-5pm. Closed Monday.

Käfigturm
Marktgasse 67
☎ 031/311 23 06
Historic prison tower, documentation centre of Bernese economy and culture. Open: Tuesday-Sunday 10am-1pm and 2-6pm (Thursday until 9pm).

Schweizerisches Schützenmuseum
(Swiss Rifle Museum)
Bernastrasse 5
☎ 031/351 01 27
Tram No 3 or 5 to Helvetia P. Development of firearms etc.
Open: Tuesday-Saturday 2-4pm, Sunday 10am-12noon, 2-4pm. Closed Monday.

Schweizerisches Alpines Museum
(Alpine Museum)
Helvetiaplatz 4
☎ 031/351 04 34
Tram No 3 or 5 to Helvetia P. Development of Alpinism. Alpine rescue service. Topographical models. Open: Monday 2-5pm, Tuesday-Sunday 10am-5pm. Winter closed 12noon-2pm lunch.

Schweizerisches PTT Museum
(Postal Museum)
Helvetiastrasse 16
☎ 031/338 7777
Tram No 3 or 5 to Helvetia P.
One of largest stamp collections in world open to public. Other postal exhibits. Open: Monday 2-5pm, Tuesday-Sunday 10am-5pm. Winter closed 12noon-2pm lunch.

Burgdorf
Schloss Burgdorf Museum
☎ 034/21 61 31
Exhibits illustrate Emmental culture, including ceramics.
Open: April-October, Monday-Saturday 2-5pm, Sunday 9.30-11.30am, 2-5pm.

Emmental Cheese Dairies
For visits consult separate pamphlet obtainable from Verkehrsverband Emmental,
CH-3550 Langnau, ☎ 035/2 42 52.

Fribourg
Schweizer Figurentheater-museum
(Puppet Theatre Museum)
Derrière les Jardins 2 (Old Town)
☎ 037/22 85 13
Museum is extension of puppet theatre. Open: July-August, Friday, Saturday, Sunday 2-5pm, September-June only Sunday 2-5pm.

Langnau
Chuechlihus Heimatmuseum
(Emmental Museum)
Includes local ceramics and an Alpine cheese dairy and utensils.
Open: Tuesday-Sunday, 9-11.30am; 1.30-6pm. Closed December and on public holidays.

Meiringen
Aare Gorge
Open: daily Easter to October 9.30am-6pm.

Merligen
For the Beatus Caves see entry above under Beatus.

Murten
Historical Museum
Opening times from Verkehrsbüro
☎ 037/71 31 00

Oberhofen
Historical Museum
in castle on lake front.
☎ 033/43 12 35
Open: from mid-May to mid-October, 10am-12noon; 2-5pm. (Closed Monday forenoons.)

Sarnen
Heimatmuseum
(Local Museum)
Open: April-end October 10-11am, 2-5pm daily except Sunday (when only opened by request).

Thun
Historic Castle Museum
☎ 033/22 15 12
Exhibits include weapons, ceramics, folk art. Fine parish church adjacent, well worth a visit.
Open: April, May, October from 10am to 5pm. June, July, August, September from 9am to 6pm.

Sport and Recreation

Gunten
Instruction in sailing, water-ski and windsurfing available from:
Sailing School RASMUS
CH-3654 Gunten
☎ 033/51 31 77 or 033/51 19 35
Water-ski School Gunten
☎ 033/51 22 66
Windsurfing School Gunten
CH-3653 Oberhofen
☎ 033/43 29 77

Interlaken
Information obtainable from Verkehrsbüro on: sailing and surfing school; 18-hole golf course; tennis; swimming; archery; clay-pigeon shooting; artificial ice-rink
☎ 036/22 37 19

Langnau
Indoor and open-air swimming pools with sauna; sport centre. Ice rink with curling.

Murten
Swimming pools, both indoor and open-air.

Oberhofen
Indoor swimming pool combined with regional 'Fitness Centre'.
Open: 10am to 9pm. (Saturday/Sunday 10am to 6pm.)

Sarnen
Windsurfing, tennis; fitness (jogging) track at Ennetriederwald (3km, 2 miles).

Thun
Swimming from biggest lake strand in Switzerland, with heated inner pool. Horse riding (including indoor provision). Curling and ice-skating indoor rinks. 'Fitness' trail.
Windsurfing school beside the lake strand bathing station. Thun Rowing Club (☎ 033/22 82 47). Windsurf Club Thun (☎ 033/22 82 82). Swiss Sailing Schools Thunersee: contact Sekretariat Verkehrsbüro.

Worb
Open-air swimming pool.

Hiking and Rambling
The Mittelland regions are renowned for rambling and walking facilities, with well laid-out and signposted paths. Useful information and maps available from:
Sekretariat
Berner Wanderwege
Postfach 263
CH-3000 Bern
☎ 031/42 37 66
The REKA ramblers' pass for use of public transport is also worth considering.

Other Activities
Information (including leaflets and brochures) on camping, cycling trails, weekend stays on farmsteadings, four-day tours by horse-drawn cart, etc may be had *gratis* from the appropriate Tourist Association (Verkehrsverband) Office, address given below.

Tourist Information Offices

Regional Offices
Verkehrsverband Berner-Mittelland
Geschäftsstelle Verkehrsbüro Bern
Im Bahnhof
Postfach 2700
CH-3001 Bern
☎ 031/311 12 12

Verkehrsverein Berner-Oberland
Jungfraustrasse 38
CH-3800 Interlaken
☎ 036/22 26 21

Verkehrsverband Thunersee
Thunstrasse 4
Postfach 355
CH-3700 Spiez
☎ 033/54 72 56

Verkehrsverband Emmental
Geschäftsstelle, Mühlegässli 2
CH-3550 Langnau-im-Emmental
☎ 035/2 42 52

For individual resorts information may be obtained from:
Bern City
Offizielles Verkehrsbüro
Im Bahnhof
CH-3001 Bern
☎ 031/311 66 11

Beatenberg
Verkehrsbüro
CH-3803 Beatenberg
☎ 036/41 12 86

Brienz
Verkehrsbüro Brienz-am-See
Bahnhofplatz, Postfach 59
CH-3855 Brienz
☎ 036/51 32 42

Fribourg
Office du Tourisme
Square des Places 1
CH-1700 Fribourg
☎ 037/81 31 75

Grindelwald
Verkehrsbüro
Sportzentrum
CH-3818 Grindelwald
☎ 036/53 12 12

Gstaad
Verkehrsbüro
CH-3780 Gstaad
☎ 030/4 71 71

Interlaken
Verkehrsbüro
Höheweg 37
CH-3800 Interlaken
☎ 036/22 21 21

Langnau
Verkehrsbüro
CH-3550 Langnau-im-Emmental
☎ 035 2 34 34

Meiringen
Verkehrsbüro
CH-3860 Meiringen
☎ 036/71 43 22

Mürren
Verkehrsbüro
Sportzentrum
CH-3825 Mürren
☎ 036/55 16 16

Murten
Verkehrsbüro
Kirchgasse 6
CH-3280 Murten
☎ 037/71 51 12

Neuchâtel
Office Neuchâtelois du Tourisme
Rue Place d'Armes
CH-2001 Neuchâtel
☎ 038/25 42 42

Oberhofen
Verkehrsbüro
CH-3653 Oberhofen
☎ 033/43 14 19

Spiez
Verkehrsbüro
CH-3700 Spiez
☎ 033/54 21 38

Thun
Verkehrsbüro
Bahnhofstrasse 2
CH-3600 Thun
☎ 033/22 23 40

Wengen
Verkehrsbüro
CH-3823 Wengen
☎ 036/55 14 14

Wilderswil
Verkehrsbüro
CH-3812 Wilderswil
☎ 036/22 84 55

Zweisimmen
Verkehrsbüro
CH-3770 Zweisimmen
☎ 030/2 11 33

Public Transport

The shipping services on Lakes Thun and Brienz are carried out by:
Schiffsbetrieb Thuner- und Brienzersee
CH-3604 Thun
☎ 033/36 02 58 (Timetable 2310 and 2470)

4

The Valais

From Canton Bern to Brig by rail

Interlaken and the Oberland in the previous chapter dealt with the route up the Kandertal from Spiez to Kandersteg. Beyond Kandersteg the valley floor rises in a high 'step' which presents a formidable barrier to further progress south in the form of a virtual mountain wall. Early this century the railway engineers conquered the barrier by boring a 9-mile-long tunnel through the heart of the mountain massif from Kandersteg in the Kandertal to **Goppenstein** in the high valley of the River Lonza, a tributary of the Rhône. This short-cut from the Oberland to the canton Valais, passing through the watershed between the river systems draining to the North Sea and those draining to the Mediterranean, is solely a railway tunnel. But between the stations of Kandersteg and Goppenstein it provides rail transport of cars in all seasons.

The section beyond Goppenstein is one of Europe's spectacular rail journeys, both in its headlong descent of the Lonza ravine and when it wins through to the north wall of the Rhône Valley. The track runs high along the mountainside in galleries that tunnel through rock buttresses and over viaducts bridging the rugged gorges which score the northern wall of the Rhône Valley. On the way the right-hand windows reveal breathtaking views of the valley below and the mountains on the southern side; including, above the Rhône Valley market town of Visp, the narrow ravine that reveals the valley leading up to Saas-Fee and to Zermatt. In just over 19km (12 miles), the train has to descend 447m (1,465ft) to reach the valley floor, cross the Rhône and, on the south bank, join the main line that comes up the Rhône Valley from Lake Geneva and distant Paris. The two railways run alongside into the main station at Brig.

Brig (the French spell it Brigue) is the capital of the Oberwallis, the German-speaking upper section of the canton which in French is named Valais (in German Wallis). The canton is comprised entirely of the valley of the Rhône from its source to where it enters Lake Geneva. Understand-

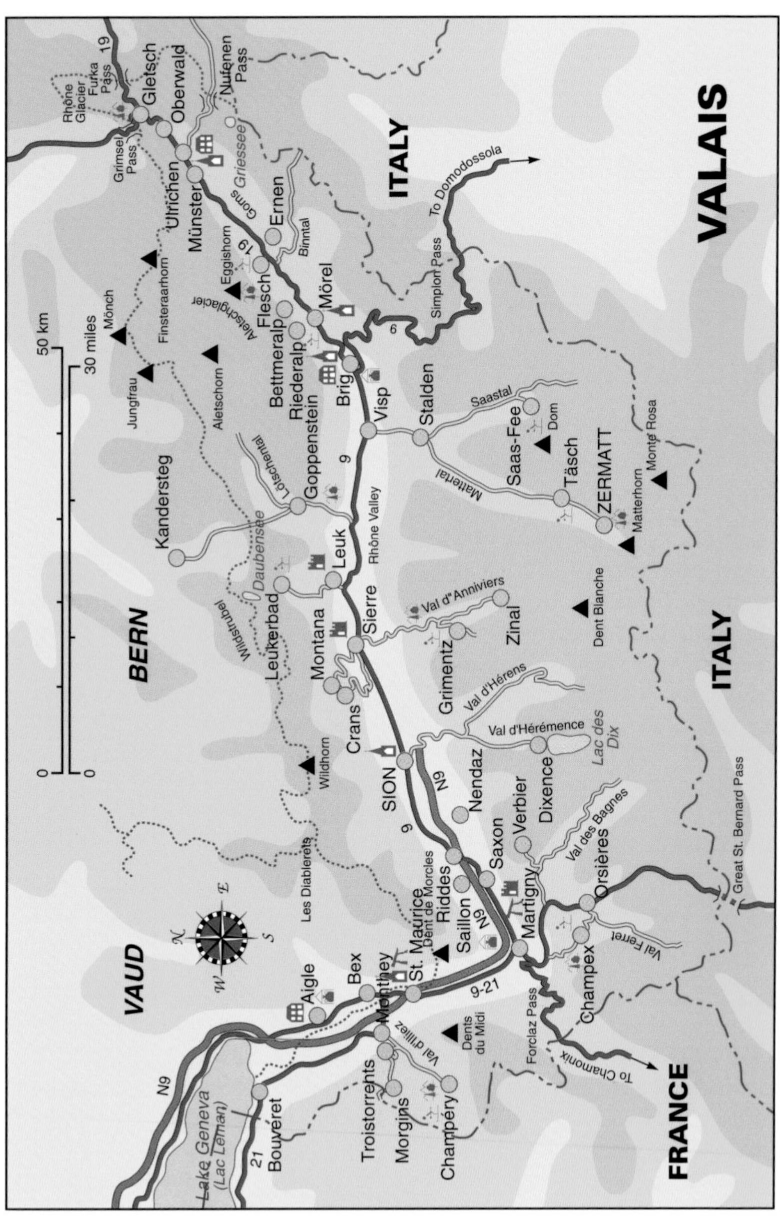

ably, it is commonly believed that the canton's name derives from the Latin word for a valley, *vallis*. Scholars find this a bit simplistic and suggest another derivation. There is much evidence that in the Iron Age the valley was peopled with Celtic tribes who became, to varying degrees, Romanised under Roman occupation. In the post-Roman era people of

The Stockalper Palace, Brig

Germanic race pushed into the valley from the north, and it is now thought they gave the region its name; for in many Germanic languages (including Anglo-Saxon branches) exists an adjective with slight variations in spelling but obviously the same root: *walsch, waelsch, welsh, welsch* meaning 'Celtic', or 'Roman' or 'derived from Roman' (such as French, Italian) and even 'southern'. This is now viewed as the source of Wallis, Valais and the adjectives Walliser and Walser.

Brig is a historic town, although nowadays perhaps best known to tourists as the key junction town of the region; for here meet rail from Berner Oberland, road and rail from the French-speaking Lower Valais and Lake Geneva, road and rail from Andermatt and from Switzerland's further easterly canton of Graubünden or Grisons; it also lies at the north end of the Simplon tunnel, the world's longest rail-tunnel (19km, 12 miles), which with the Simplon Pass highway penetrates south into Italy by way of Stresa and Milan; and is also the terminus of the narrow-gauge line to Zermatt. Its history reflects its position on international trading crossroads. The bulk of today's visitors are passing through; but many appreciate it as a base for exploration and become acquainted with its

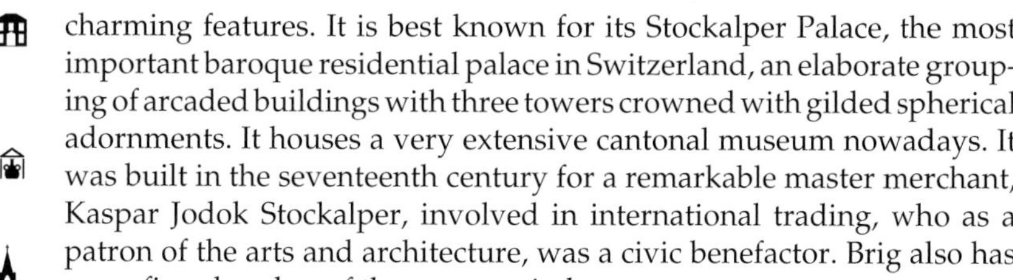
charming features. It is best known for its Stockalper Palace, the most important baroque residential palace in Switzerland, an elaborate grouping of arcaded buildings with three towers crowned with gilded spherical adornments. It houses a very extensive cantonal museum nowadays. It was built in the seventeenth century for a remarkable master merchant, Kaspar Jodok Stockalper, involved in international trading, who as a patron of the arts and architecture, was a civic benefactor. Brig also has some fine churches of the same period.

From Brig to Zermatt

Only 9km (5½ miles) by road or by rail from Brig is **Visp**, the little market town in the valley which was seen from the Loetschberg train as it made its way down from the crags and cliffs of the valley's north wall. Visp, a village of fair antiquity, acquired importance in modern times from becoming the valley junction for two mountain resorts of international fame: Zermatt and Saas-Fee. Both road and narrow-gauge railway line run south from Visp into the narrow, steep ravine that is the valley of the Vispa and climb in 7km (4½ miles) to **Stalden**, which stands just above where two component tributaries of the river meet, the Saaser Vispa and Matter Vispa. Roads follow the line of each stream: a steep one climbing to the south-east reaches the resort of **Saas-Fee** in its imposing setting among the heights; while the right-hand road and the rail climb to the south-west on either side of a craggy gorge, to the village of St Niklaus, then by a winding ascent to **Täsch**, 30km (19 miles) from Visp. Beyond Täsch the road is not open to motor vehicles; there is a giant car park near the Täsch station from which a shuttle service is operated by train to **Zermatt**, where local transport is horse-drawn. On this final section of the railway line is the first view of the great crooked peak of the Matterhorn (4,478m, 14,692ft) which lies on the frontier with Italy where it is known as Monte Cervino.

Zermatt's traffic-free situation makes even the crowded village street of this international, leading winter sports and climbing resort of the Valais seem comparatively relaxing. Its setting, in extensive Alpine pastoral meadows (*matten*, from which the name derives), with its emblematic Matterhorn towering behind, is beautiful; and in part of the village typical Valais-style brown timber chalets are still to be seen. There is lavish provision of sports facilities, cable railways, ski-lifts, ice-rinks, and above all splendid long ski-runs.

The most popular, indeed almost traditional, local excursion from Zermatt is carried out by the cogwheel narrow-gauge rail (Timetable 142; its station faces the main rail station) to the Gornergrat (3,089m, 10,135ft) where there is a belvedere with extensive views over glacial fields and ice-capped peaks such as the famed Monte Rosa group lying further east on the Italian border. From the Gornergrat an aerial cablecar (Timetable 1296) ascends still higher in two sections to the Stockhorn (3,413m, 11,198ft).

Public Transport Option

In view of the fact that Zermatt is not open to motor vehicles, there is much to be said for making the whole journey by rail from Visp or from Brig (Timetable 140).

The Rhône Valley: Brig to Martigny

Canton Valais takes the form of a long trough, the valley of the Rhône together with its side valleys that pierce the mountain walls which fence it in on either side. The width of the trough varies, being much narrower upstream. As road and rail travel further downstream the valley widens, becomes increasingly fertile and cultivation increases. Twenty kilometres on from Visp, on the sunny right side of the valley is the interesting little market town of **Leuk**, one-time summer residence of the Bishop of Sion whose sixteenth-century castle tower is its landmark. From Leuk a lateral road runs up in 14km (8½ miles) to **Leukerbad**, a spa of some antiquity going back to Roman times and fashionable in Mark Twain's day. It is now up-dated with a sports centre and the inevitable cablecars and is popular for winter sports and summer activities too in its sun-trap of Alpine meadows.

On the same sunny side of the valley in 7km (4½ miles) is **Sierre**. Just before reaching it the road has crossed an ancient but unmarked boundary — from the German-speaking Wallis to French-speaking Valais. Sierre, surrounded by hilly vineyards, has some old mansions of merit, some fine churches, and in its main street the restored castle of the bailiffs who once held it for the Bishop of Sion. From Sierre serpentine roads, and a funicular rail (Timetable 1225) ascend to the two modern resorts of **Montana** and **Crans** on the upper slopes with fine panoramas across the valley to the great Valais Alps in the south. Facing Sierre across the Rhône is the impressive entrance to one of the most interesting of its side valleys, the Val d'Anniviers. Nearby are two pleasant villages that have become popular skiing centres, Grimentz and Zinal, the latter also being a climbing base in quite a splendid setting.

The main road down the valley reaches, in 15km (9 miles), the capital of the Valais, **Sion** (in German, Sitten). This ancient episcopal see is in a magnificent situation distinguished by two prominent hills set in its midst, each crowned with a castle. The old centre is very interesting. The town plays a further important role as a renowned market centre both for the wine trade and for the fruit and vegetables of the valley.

Of Sion's two hills, the Valeria is the one to the left, seen from the river (or the railway as it heads up the valley); on it stand the castle and the collegiate church of Nôtre-Dame de Valère. There is evidence that Sion — and indeed the Lower Valais — was Celtic in the Iron Age, and it is thought that the Valeria was a Celtic defensive hill town. The castle was

Valeria Castle, Sion

The Matterhorn from Gürner Grad

Typical Upper Rhône village

in existence by the eleventh century and the hilltop had continued as an extended fortification with church and habitations inside the walls, the church bell-tower serving as a keep. The church dates to twelfth and thirteenth century, in part Romanesque and in part early Gothic. It contains many fine carvings, wall paintings, fabrics and sculptures; the fourteenth-century organ is held to be the oldest in the world still playable. Near the church the Musée de Valère is housed in castle buildings; it has interesting Roman and medieval exhibits. Its hall has fine fifteenth-century wall paintings.

The Tourbillon hill, slightly further away from the centre, is also thought to have once been a Celtic fortified settlement. The castle there is dated to the end of the thirteenth century during a period when Sion was a target of Savoyard expansionism. It was used as an episcopal residence during troubled times.

The town's Cathédrale de Nôtre-Dame-du-Glarier is a fifteenth-century rebuilding, the massive Romanesque bell-tower being the only surviving part of the earlier twelfth-century church which was otherwise destroyed by fire in 1418. The cathedral treasury holds priceless medieval gold plate. In the town are numerous secular buildings and patrician houses of great distinction, such as the richly decorated Supersaxo House built in 1505. A prominent bulbous tower, the Tour des Sorcières (Witches' Tower) is the only surviving part of the town's twelfth-century fortifications. Do not allow the modern extensions of the town to put you off the fascinating heart of old Sion.

There is a good range of fascinating excursions from Sion, especially into the series of side valleys which penetrate the mountain masses on the southern side of the Rhône Valley; for instance, into the Val de Hérens and the parallel Val de Hérémence which ends in the great dam known as the Barrage de la Grande Dixence which seals in the artificial Lac des Dix, reached from the road end by aerial cablecar (Timetable 1190).

Twenty-eight kilometres (17 miles) further down the main valley from Sion is **Martigny**, a small industrial town. Set pleasantly among vineyards, however, it occupies a strategic position at the meeting of routes from the Simplon Pass (from Lake Maggiore), the Great St Bernard Pass (from Aosta) and the Forclaz Pass (from Chamonix). Here too there was once a Celtic hill settlement, and a Roman market town named *Octodurus*. There is a Gallo-Roman museum in the town's Pierre Gianadda Foundation cultural centre in the Rue du Forum at the site of the ruins of a first-

Public Transport Option

It is possible to travel all the way to Champex by public transport from Martigny. Orsières can be reached by bus as well as by train, being a main stop on the route to the Great St Bernard (Timetable 100.46). From Orsières rail station is one of the famed Swiss mountain Postbus services to Champex (Timetable 133.20). The little resort is not merely a climbing and skiing base; it has sports facilities and an Alpine botanical garden.

Public transport options also exist for the excursions from Sierre and Sion. It should first be made clear that excellent services are maintained by the main railway line linking Martigny, Sion, Sierre with Brig to the east and Lake Geneva resorts to the west (Timetable 100). Zinal is reached from Sierre by another Postbus mountain route (Timetable 100.78); and Grimentz also by Postbus mountain service (Timetable 100.77). From Sion rail station in summer (mid-June to mid-October) a motor coach excursion service runs to Dixence via Hérémence (Timetable 135.66); from Dixence (Le Chargeur) there is an aerial cablecar to Lac des Dix (Timetable 1190).

Verbier, lying on its sunny plateau facing south has become a favoured skiing centre especially for the skilled and experienced and is reached from Martigny by using the branch line (Timetable 133) to Le Chable village and thence by Postbus mountain route (Timetable 133.35) or by using the cable-cabin (Timetable 1160).

century Roman temple which was excavated recently. Martigny's landmark and emblem is the impressive ruined medieval castle, Château de la Batiaz, which dominates the valley of the Drance, the tributary which here joins the Rhône. At this point, Martigny marks the place at which the Rhône, after so long and so consistent a straight-line course down its valley, abruptly takes a right-angled turn north, to pour ultimately into Lake Geneva (Lac Léman).

Martigny's position still makes it a base for major excursions. Many motorists make an excursion over the Great St Bernard Pass to Aosta in Italy, using perhaps for the outward journey the modern tunnel (which has made the route an all-year-round one) and returning by the Pass, visiting the famed Hospice where dogs are still bred although the demand for their life-saving services is not what it once was.

Slightly more adventurous is an excursion of shorter distance in the same southerly direction. Almost half-way from Martigny to the Great St Bernard tunnel is the village of **Orsières**. It is also the terminus of a branch rail line (Timetable 133) from Martigny. From Orsières a mountain road runs west for 13km (8 miles) to a tiny winter and summer resort called **Champex** (1,472m, 4,830ft), by a small lake of the same name considered the little jewel of the Valais, set into the Mont Blanc massif, and well worth seeking out.

Martigny to Lake Geneva (Lac Léman)

Take highway No 9 rather than the bypassing motorway N9 north from Martigny (or using the main rail line) and in 15km (9 miles) **St Maurice** is reached. It is a little town but a very historic one largely because of its ancient Augustinian abbey, on a picturesque site in a narrow section of the valley framed by the Dents du Midi (3,257m, 10,682ft) on one side and the Dent de Morcles (2,969m, 9,741ft) on the other. On the occupation of the Valais by the Romans it became the first capital. Its name derives from a Roman commander of about the end of the third century who according to local tradition was martyred along with his legion by order of the Emperor Maximian for refusing to act against fellow Christians in Gaul.

As a memorial to the martyrs, two centuries later the Burgundian King Sigismund founded an abbey, Switzerland's oldest Christian site. (For several centuries the Burgundian kings also made the little town their main residence.) The abbey church, originally eleventh century, has seen many alterations and reconstructions. The entrance tower has survived, however, in Romanesque style. It is most noted for the wealth of its ecclesiastical treasury, its medieval gold work being among the most prized in Europe, including a water jug given by Charlemagne. Recent excavations below the nearby cliff have revealed remains of a much earlier series of sacred buildings erected over fifteen centuries.

Shortly beyond St Maurice road number 9 crosses the Rhone and reaches **Bex** (a small spa that was fashionable in the nineteenth century).

The Wines of the Valais

Swiss wines are rarely found outside Switzerland. The reason for this is simple. The supply of Swiss wines (and white wines predominate) hardly meets more than one-third of the home demand. Wines are made in many parts of Switzerland. But the most important areas both for the quality and the quantity of white wines produced are the Valais and its neighbouring large canton on the shores of Lake Geneva, the Vaud. And in all parts of Switzerland people disagree on whether Valais wines are superior to Vaud or vice-versa.

The two Valais white wines most in demand are known by generic names. Fendant is the Valais name for the fairly prolific grape variety known as Chasselas in France and Gutedel in Germany. A well made Valais Fendant, especially if it also bears the name of the village from

which it comes, eg Fendant de Sion, has more distinction of flavour than products of the same grape variety in the neighbouring countries. Johannisberg is the name given in the Valais to the Sylvaner grape variety which here can make a very full-flavoured dry white wine which also finds favour as an aperitif. Dole is the appellation of the favourite red wine made from a blend of Pinot Noir and Gamay grape varieties which goes well with meats and cheese. Swiss wines are never inexpensive but those grown on the well-sheltered and sunny northern face of the Rhone valley have a ripe distinction of flavour that wins them devotees.

Château at Aigle with its extensive vineyards

Bex is in Canton Vaud, for by this point the river, running in a more northerly direction, has become the boundary between canton Valais and canton Vaud. All the way now to where the Rhone enters Lac Leman its right bank is in canton Vaud while the left continues to be in Valais. This historic boundary for many centuries had the added significance that the prevailing religion on the left bank was Catholic and on the right Protestant.

Before road 9 from St Maurice crosses river and boundary, however, a left-hand fork gives motorists from St Maurice an opportunity for a detour of **Champéry**, a famous resort some 18km (11 miles) distant to the south-west. The left bank route to Champéry is by way of the lively little industrial town of Monthey at the mouth of the Val d'Illiez. The road ascends that valley in steep turns as far as Troistorrents and then more gently to Champéry, running up the attractive valley on a parallel course to the cog-wheel railway. (At Troistorrents another branch of the road goes off to the right, climbing in steep zigzags to Morgins which is almost on the French frontier, and which has magnificent views of the Dents du Midi group). Champéry is another one-street village facing the jagged Dents du Midi, and is a climatic resort that has a great name for winter sports.

The last town of significance on the right-hand, canton Vaud, bank of the river before it enters the lake, some 13km (8 miles) beyond Bex, is **Aigle**, another pleasant little market town, wine centre of another distinguished region of vineyards, Le Chablais (not to be confused with the Chablis of Burgundy).

The Romans knew it as *Aquilea*. For most of its early history it was subject to Savoy, was captured by the Bernese in their fifteenth-century expansionist period and was ruled from Bern until the French Revolutionary Wars. Its medieval *château* is quite significant, occupied in turn by bailiffs of the House of Savoy and by Bernese governors. Today it houses a Museum of Wine and Salt, the commodities which were of much importance to the economic life of the town for so long.

From Brig through the Upper Rhone Valley

The Upper Rhône Valley which lies between Brig and the river's source in the great Rhône Glacier is an entirely different landscape from the Lake Geneva end, but one that certainly does not lack grandeur and an element of the spectacular. Because of the confines of the valley walls, the courses of the road and the Furka-Oberalp metre-gauge railway to Andermatt and Disentis do not greatly diverge. Incidentally, from here on, this upper region of the Valais is known as the 'Goms'.

Leaving Brig, the motorist crosses the Rhône (or as it is known in the upper valley by its German form, the Rotten) and turns right to travel upstream on road No 19. Very shortly, look across the rail and river on the right, and view the massive portals of the Simplon tunnel.

The first section of road, running up the valley close to the briskly flowing river in quite a narrow, winding trench, is fairly straightforward, with small villages spaced fairly frequently. Before reaching **Mörel** it is a surprise to pass a large baroque church standing in isolation, the early eighteenth-century Virgin of Hohenfluh chapel. Mörel itself provides the valley stations of two cablecar services to the Riederalp (Timetables 1330 and 1331).

Riederalp is a favourite holiday resort, situated at 1,930m (6,332ft) on a sunny plateau above the Goms Valley; two chairlifts (Timetable 1333) from Riederalp take you higher to Moosfluh (2,394m, 7,855ft) from where there is a magnificent view of the Aletsch Glacier, the greatest in the Alps. Bettmeralp, on the same high plateau, can be reached by cable car from the next village Betten (Timetable 1337-9).

The road soon starts a steeper rate of climb and the railway, crossing a viaduct, enters a tunnel in the rock wall to gain height by a spiral climb. In 18km (11 miles) from Brig the road reaches **Fiesch**, another village resort with chalets typical of the Goms. From Fiesch, too, cablecar (Timetable 1343) operates to a level below the summit of the Eggishorn (2,878m, 9,443ft) with exceptional panoramas of the great glacier.

Beyond Fiesch there is a stiff climb again for the road to breast another 'step' in the valley. The main village of the Goms, **Münster**, is reached in 15km (9 miles). It has some interesting dark fifteenth- and sixteenth-century timber houses and a parish church with a thirteenth-century Romanesque bell-tower, a Gothic high altar and some fine baroque altars and carved wood. A further 4km (2½ miles) on is **Ulrichen**, nowadays perhaps best known for the road to the south, opened up only in the past two decades, over the Nufenen Pass (2,478m, 8,133ft) to reach the Bedretto Valley in the Ticino and along it to Airolo the first important town of canton Ticino south of the Gotthard Pass. Nowadays many tourists in the central Alpine area take the opportunity of taking the Three Alpine Passes excursion comprising the Nufenen, Gotthard and Furka Passes or the Four Passes Tour comprising Grimsel, Nufenen, Gotthard and Susten Passes, both organised in the season late June to mid-October by the Swiss Postbus services (Timetable 470.69 for special excursions). Further information ☎ 036/71 32 05 (Meiringen); 044/6 71 88 (Andermatt); and 028/73 11 41 (Oberwald).

In 5km the road reaches **Oberwald**, the highest village in the Goms at 1,368m (4,488ft). The Oberwald railway station is the loading point for motor vehicles using the car-carrying facilities through the Furka tunnel when the Pass road is impassable. The Furka tunnel, opened in 1982, is the longest narrow-gauge rail tunnel in the world (14½ km, 9 miles long).

Beyond Oberwald the road has to resort to extensive zigzags (passing the Rhône Falls) to climb the ascent which finally brings the Rhône Glacier into sight. It reaches **Gletsch** in 6km (3¾ miles) where it meets the Grimsel route (from Innertkirchen) and the Furka route (from Andermatt). The Furka road, which is joined here, embarks on a further series of giant

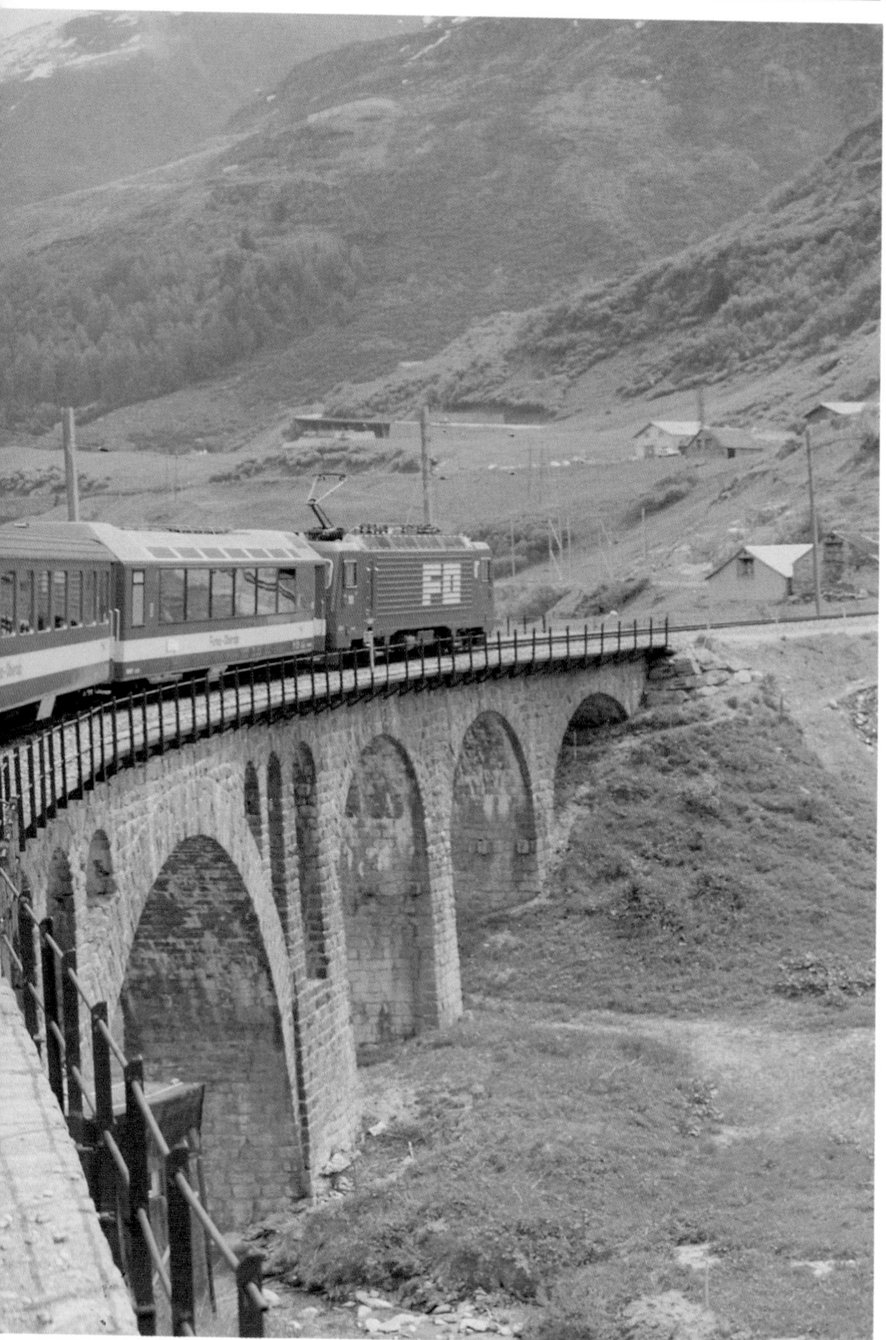

Above the tree-line in the Upper Rhône valley

Opposite: High pasture land in the Upper Rhône valley

zigzags to arrive in 11km (7 miles) at the Furka Pass summit (2,431m, 7,976ft). From the extensive belvedere just before the pass there is an impressive, unforgettable view over the Rhône Glacier with its fascinating ice falls at the base of which the river originates.

Beyond the pass the road winds down for 12km, 7½ miles to the village of **Realp** in its eerie, barren situation beneath its avalanche defences. **Hospental** is reached after a further 6km (3¾ miles) where the road from the St Gotthard also comes down. **Andermatt** is only 2km (1¼ miles) away, at what may be well described as the crossroads of the Alps — and in some ways, it can be said, of Europe. For visitors who have just toured in the Valais, the choices include an excursion south into the Ticino — or a continuation along the west-east Alpine axis via the Upper Rhine into canton Graubünden (sometimes called Grisons).

Public Transport Option

The route from Brig to Andermatt can easily be taken by public transport. The Goms villages are well served by the Furka-Oberalp railway from Brig (Timetable 610) to Andermatt. Also the Swiss Postbus services have a cover of the lateral valleys, operating from the village rail stations on the Furka-Oberalp line, Fiesch and Ernen (Timetable 610.15 and 610.18).

Indeed one of the most fascinating railway journeys in Europe takes in the Brig-Andermatt section as only part of its complete journey which begins in Zermatt, and, having run via Brig to Andermatt, continues its journey east by climbing the Oberalp Pass into the neighbouring canton of Graubünden and travelling down the course of the Upper Rhine to the Graubünden capital of Chur. From there it continues south through the spectacular Schin Gorge and over the Albula Pass to St Moritz. The trains which cover this journey in both directions are called the Glacier Express and (because of the mountain passes they climb) are billed proudly if paradoxically as 'The Slowest Express in the World'.

Additional Information

Places to Visit

Aigle
Musée de la Vigne et du Vin
(Museum of Viticulture and Wine)
Château
CH-1860 Aigle
☎ 025/26 21 30
Open: April to October daily
9am-12 noon, 2-6pm.

Leuk
Ausstellungspavillon der Satelliten-Bodenstation Leuk, CH-3953 Leuk-Stadt
☎ 027/63 19 22
Satellite centre's exhibition to illustrate its function and the principles of space communication with models and slide show.
Open: May to September daily 9am-8pm; October to April daily
9am-4.30pm.

Bishop's Palace
Leuk-Stadt
Medieval stronghold now used as small museum. For current opening times since renovation ask at tourist office ☎ 027/61 14 13.

Martigny
Foundation Pierre Gianadda Musée
Rue du Forum, CH-1920 Martigny
☎ 026/22 39 78
1. Museum of Gallo-Roman relics
2. Car museum, thirty veterans built 1883-1932.
Open: April to October daily 10am-7pm, November to March Tuesday to Sunday 1.30-6pm, or by arrangement.

Riederalp
Chalet Museum
Open: June to mid October, Tuesday/ Thursday/Sunday only 2-5pm.

St Maurice
Trésor de l'Abbaye
CH-1890 St Maurice
☎ 025/65 11 81
Medieval items of gold.
Guided tours: November to April daily at 3 and 4.30pm. May/June/September/October Monday to Sat urday at 10.30am, 3pm, 4pm, Sunday at 3pm, 4.30pm; July to August Monday to Saturday at 9.30am, 10.30am, 2.30pm, 3.30pm, 4.30pm, Sunday at 2.30pm, 3.30pm, 4.30pm or by arrangement.

Castle and Military Museum
Open: Tuesday to Sunday 10am-12noon and 2-5pm (until 7pm, June to September).

Sion
Archaeological Museum
Open: Tuesday to Sunday 10am-12noon and 2-6pm. July to August also Monday.

Art Gallery
Open: May to October Tuesday to Sunday 10am-12noon and 2-6pm.

Musée de Valère
Historical Museum in castle grounds
Open: April to November Tuesday to Sunday 10am-12noon and 2-5pm; July to August, also Monday.

Museum of Natural History
All year open Sunday 10am-12noon and 2-6pm; mid-July/August daily 2-6pm.

Zermatt
Alpine Museum
Open: daily 10am-12noon, 4-6pm.

Sport and Recreation

Winter Sports
The following Valais resorts provide winter sports facilities; details of these facilities — including paragliding — should be sought from the local tourist offices listed below:
Bettmeralp, Champéry, Crans-Montana, Fiesch, Grimentz, Leukerbad, Morgins, Riederalp, Saas-Fee, Val-d'Illiez, Verbier, Zermatt, Zinal.
Guided Hiking Excursions
Organised in June/July-September by almost all the local tourist offices in the list given below.
Hot Air Ballooning
Organised by a club in Crans-Montana: Club Aerostatique de Crans-Montana, Hôtel du Golf, CH-3963 Crans-Montana ☎ 027/41 42 42

Tourist Information Offices

Cantonal Office
Union Valaisanne du Tourisme/
Walliser Verkehrsverband
rue Pré-Fleuri 6
CH-1951 Sion/Sitten
☎ 027/22 31 61

LOCAL OFFICES
Aigle
Office du Tourisme d'Aigle
Ave de la Gare 4
CH-1860 Aigle
☎ 025/26 12 12

Bettmeralp
Verkehrsbüro
CH-3992 Bettmeralp
☎ 028/27 12 91

Brig
Verkehrsverein
Bahnhof
CH-3900 Brig-am-Simplon
☎ 028/23 19 01

Champéry
Office du Tourisme
CH-1874 Champéry
☎ 025/79 11 41

Crans-Montana
Office du Tourisme Crans sur Sierre
CH-3963 Crans
☎ 027/41 21 32
and
Office du Tourisme Montana-Vermala
CH-3962 Montana
☎ 027/41 30 41

Fiesch
Verkehrsbüro
CH-3984 Fiesch
☎ 028/71 14 66

Grimentz
Office du Tourisme
CH-3961 Grimentz
☎ 027/65 14 93

Leukerbad
Verkehrsverein
CH-3954 Leukerbad
☎ 027/62 11 11

Martigny
Office Régional du Tourisme
Place Centrale 1
CH-1920 Martigny
☎ 026/22 10 18

Morgins
Office du Tourisme
CH-1875 Morgins
☎ 025/77 23 61

Riederalp
Verkehrsbüro
CH-3987 Riederalp
☎ 028//27 13 65

St Maurice
Office du Tourisme
Place Val-de-Marne
CH-1890 St Maurice
☎ 025/3 77 77

Saas-Fee
Verkehrsbüro
CH-3906 Saas-Fee
☎ 028/59 11 11

Sierre
Verkehrsbüro
Place de la Gare 10
CH-3960 Sierre
☎ 027/55 85 35

Sion
Office du Tourisme de Sion et environs
15 rue de Lausanne
CH-1950 Sion
☎ 027/22 85 86

Val d'Illiez
Office du Tourisme
CH-1873 Val d'Illiez
☎ 025/77 20 77

Verbier
Office du Tourisme
CH-1936 Verbier
☎ 026/31 62 22

Zermatt
Offizielles Verkehrsbüro
CH-3920 Zermatt
☎ 028/66 11 81

Zinal
Office du Tourisme
CH-3961 Zinal
☎ 027/65 32 63

5

The Ticino

Only one Swiss canton lies entirely on the south side of the Alps — the Ticino. The canton takes its name from its main river, which has its origin in the great Alpine watershed and then flows south from near the St Gotthard Pass. The name Ticino is an Italian word. The German and French form of the name is spelled Tessin. The inhabitants of the canton, the Ticinesi, are Italian-speaking and share with Italian Lombardy not only their language but also much of their cultural heritage and their daily customs.

Indeed, up to the thirteenth century the Ticino shared its history with the rest of Lombardy. When the Gotthard Pass was reopened to use about the mid-twelfth century, the men of the Central Swiss valleys developed trade contacts with their southern neighbours. And from the earliest days of the independent Confederation of the Original Four Forest Cantons the

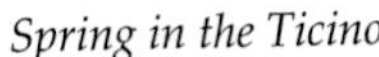

Spring in the Ticino

route across the Alps as a corridor to the world of Mediterranean trade and culture was a magnet for the Swiss Confederates. They pursued with great tenacity what was called 'the Gotthard policy'. It led in three stages to the incorporation into Swiss territory of, firstly, the region as far as Bellinzona, then of the Locarno area and finally the area beyond the barrier of Monte Ceneri that lies north and south of Lake Lugano. After many centuries under the dominion of the northern cantons, the Ticino finally, in 1803, became a constituent canton of the Swiss Confederation.

The canton's southerly orientation gives it its unique character. Its climate, its flora and fauna reflect this, especially in the southern part, yet, having its highest point over 3,400m (11,155ft) above sea level and its lowest less than 200m (656ft) it exhibits considerable extremes. On the map the canton's shape reminds one roughly of a primitive arrowhead, with the point facing south to the Mediterranean. There is something appropriate about that, for the Ticino has always had a key position on historic trade and cultural transit-routes across the Alps. For centuries the St Gotthard route down the valley of the River Ticino has linked Italy and the Mediterranean not merely with Northern Switzerland but with much of Northern Europe.

The River Ticino rises high up in the Alps not so far from where the Rhône and the Rhine also rise; it carves its way with turbulent force through granite and gneiss in a very rapid descent over a comparatively short distance on its upper course and ultimately flows into Lake Maggiore near Locarno. The region is particularly interesting to botanists because in many places Alpine plants co-exist with Mediterranean ones. The streams have brought Alpine flora down to the foothills of the lake districts where they flourish alongside Mediterranean flora which can survive there because of the mild winters. Hours of sunshine are much greater throughout the year than in the zones immediately north or south, notably so in winter. Rainfall is in aggregate higher than in these neighbouring zones, but the number of rainy days is notably fewer than on the north side of the Alps.

Although it is quite practicable to travel to the Ticino via Milan, the great majority of visitors prefer the traditional route from Northern Europe, and enter Switzerland via Zürich (by plane) or via Basel (by road or rail). From Zürich, Geneva and Bern air travellers can find daily plane connections on internal services to Lugano. The railway or road journey from Northern Switzerland through Central Switzerland and over the Gotthard is not only a direct route but is also one of the most interesting and spectacular journeys in Europe.

One of the most dramatic climatic changes that can be experienced by a traveller in Europe is to pass through the Gotthard tunnel (whether road or rail) after climbing up the valley of the Reuss from Central Switzerland on, say, an overcast spring day when snow is piling high in Göschenen — to emerge twenty minutes later into sunlight and blue skies. (Once in a while the reverse can happen: when the warm, moisture-laden wind from the Mediterranean brings rain south of the Alpine barrier but reaches

Central Switzerland as the 'Föhn' that brings almost unseasonable warmth and clear horizons.)

It often surprises travellers to find that the southern side of the Alpine crossing involves an even more headlong descent and even more precipitous rocky surroundings than the northern. The human settlements merge into the landscape for the typical Central Swiss wood-framed 'chalet' gives way to grey stone-built houses, roofed with stone slabs. The boundaries of gardens and plots of land are neither formed of fences, hedges, nor of walls but are made of up-ended split-slabs of granite set edge to edge. The Ticino has been called a land of gneiss and granite! Villages are characteristically set wherever terraces or ledges offer a bit of level ground, however high, above the channel carved by the river. Side roads branching off from the main road zigzag up to the inhabited terraces at many levels. Often the first obvious sign of human settlement is a glimpse of the slim square stone tower with tent-shaped stone campanile of the village church.

The Val Leventina

Airolo is the first town in the Ticino the traveller meets when he or she emerges from the 16km-long (10 miles) Gotthard rail or road tunnel from the north. It stands 1,154m (3,786ft) above sea level, and, set in a ring of mountain scenery, is an important winter and summer resort, starting point for excursions, particularly high pass walks and ski-tours. As well as being gateway to the south, it is also gateway to the upper valley of the River Ticino which flows from the west down the Bedretto Valley until it reaches Airolo. There it swings round into its southerly course down the Val Leventina.

Very many of those who travel over the Gotthard and down the Val Leventina are bound either for the popular lakeside resorts on Lake Maggiore and Lake Lugano or beyond into Italy. For them it is probably advantageous to use the Basel-Chiasso motorway (N2) which enables through-traffic to bypass towns and villages. In compensation, the transfer of the through-traffic to the motorway has relieved the 'old Gotthard road' of congestion and made it more interesting for tourists with time to spare for the unique features of the Leventina.

Six kilometres (4 miles) south of Airolo on the 'old Gotthard road' lie two villages in an open space in the valley, **Piotta** and **Ambrì**, sharing a rail station, Ambrì-Piotta. On the left, beyond the motorway and the river is a large electric power station which supplies current for the railway. Close by it is the valley station of a funicular railway, the country's steepest, rising 785m (2,576ft) in 23 minutes (Timetable 1603). The funicular serves more than one station at upper levels but from the topmost one, **Piora**, a 15-20-minute walk enables one to reach Lago Ritom, an artificial lake supplying the hydro-electric station at Piotta below: to the south of the lake extends the Piora Alpine Park, an area of Alpine pasture famed for its flora.

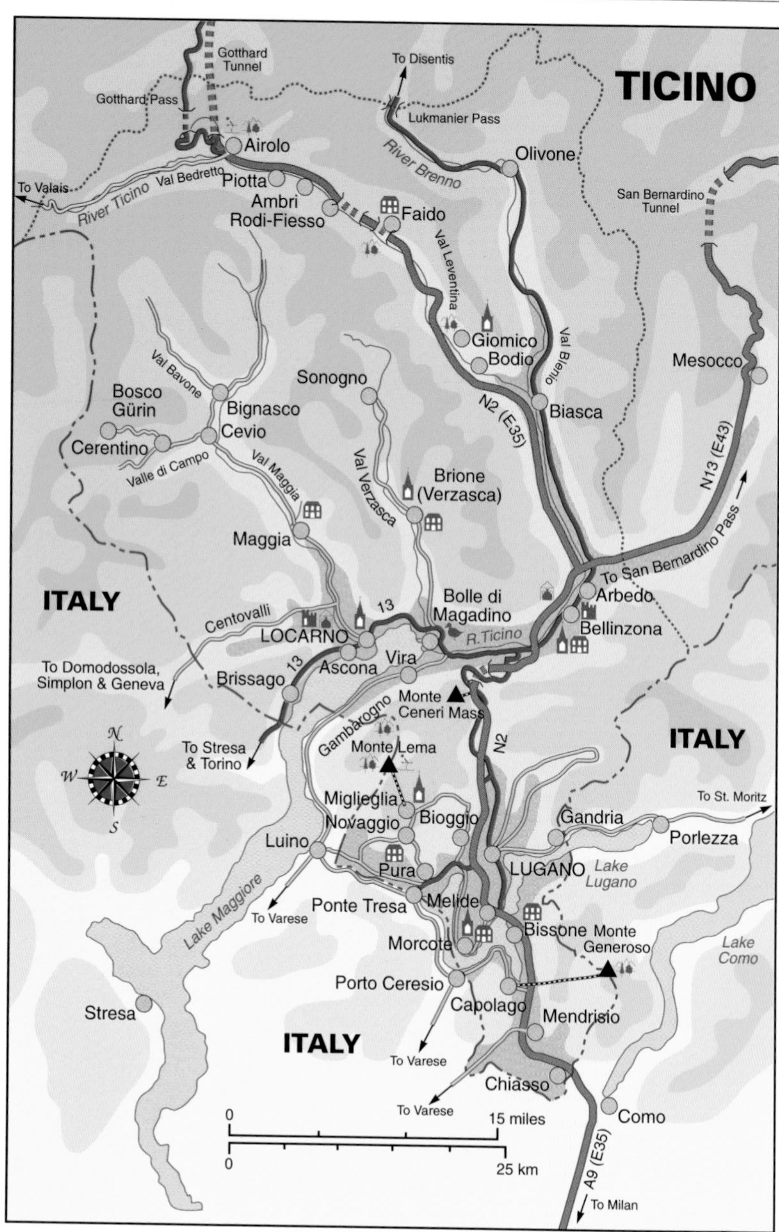

The most spectacular part of the Val Leventina for road or rail travellers lies between the villages of **Rodi** (rail station Rodi-Fiesso) and Giornico. The River Ticino forces its passage down through two narrow gorges involving a huge drop in the valley floor. To cope with this drop the railway uses four spiral tunnels boring into the rock faces of the gorges in order to climb down. In this section are some striking glimpses of waterfalls.

South of Rodi-Fiesso, after plunging through another spectacular gorge, the river reaches **Faido**, principal town of Val Leventina, at the much lower level of 725m (2,379ft). Faido is picturesque, for alongside the typical Ticinese stone-built houses, it has conserved some handsome sixteenth-century wooden residences with decorative carvings. For more than three centuries this was the seat of the North Swiss representative governors of the valley, and an important transit centre for Gotthard trade. It is here, too, that the first definite signs of a 'southern landscape' show themselves in the form of vines, mulberries and sweet chestnuts. To the west is an impressive view of three waterfalls of the River Piumogna as it drops to join the Ticino.

Other waterfalls can be seen from the cantonal road in the course of the 11km (7 miles) between Faido and Giornico. Half-way the road enters the last of the great 'steps' downward of the valley floor, the Biaschina Gorge, dropping 225m (738ft) in 5½km (3½ miles), just before reaching Giornico. (The rate of headlong descent of the Leventina valley floor — a total fall of 974m [3,196ft] in the 37km [23 miles] from Airolo to Biasca — is unique in all Europe.)

The village of **Giornico** lies on both sides of the river. Indeed, it owed its early importance to the fact that this was the place where the historic Gotthard trade road crossed over to the other side of the valley; a lovely old arched bridge is said to mark the crossing place. Giornico is best known, however, for possessing what is regarded as the finest Romanesque ecclesiastical building in a canton which abounds in architectural treasures. The twelfth-century church of San Nicolao is reached in 5 minutes from the rail station by crossing the bridge. Epitomising pure Lombardy-Romanesque style, it probably originally belonged to a monastery. Sculpted beasts guard the portal and uniquely carved capitals adorn the columns in the crypt.

A 15-minute walk uphill to the site of a former castle leads to another church, the chapel of St Maria of the Castle, noted for its fifteenth-century wall paintings. Back across the river in the other part of the village is the Casa Stanga, sixteenth-century residence of a noble family, with exterior walls bearing painted coats of arms of its period; for a long time an inn, it now houses the Folk Museum of the Val Leventina. Just at the northern entrance to the village, on the left is the memorial to a decisive battle that took place in 1478 when a small force of Swiss Confederates defeated a well-equipped Milanese army of the House of Sforza.

Nine kilometres (5½ miles) farther on is **Biasca**, town of 6,000 inhabitants where the valley has opened out into a broad, fertile basin which stretches almost to Bellinzona, the cantonal capital 17km (10½ miles) farther south; this wide valley floor is known as the Riviera. At Biasca the River Ticino has been joined from the north-east by the River Brenno which flows down the Blenio Valley. The fertile Riviera also produces mulberries, vines, figs and walnuts. Historically Biasca has been a place of strategic and commercial importance as the gateway to not just one but two of the medieval pass routes: the Gotthard route coming down the Val Leventina, and the Lukmanier (Lucomagno) Pass route down the Blenio.

Biasca is the main town of the mountain region of the Three Valleys — Leventina, Blenio and the Riviera, the latter being the luxuriant, fertile section of the River Ticino's valley lying between Biasca and Bellinzona. It is also the centre of the Ticino's stone quarrying industry, for in this region the natural stone is a slatey gneiss. Biasca itself has a modern look, having a variety of industries which originated from the coming of the Gotthard railway last century and its electrification in the twentieth. It is also the long-established ecclesiastical centre of the Three Valleys. Its collegiate church of St Peter and St Paul (Santi Pietro e Paolo) has a dominating site. It is a Romanesque basilica, probably twelfth-century, though restored in mid-twentieth-century, and it has a great art treasure of thirteenth- to seventeenth-century frescos.

Exploring the Leventina by Cycle and Rail

Before leaving Biasca and the Val Leventina it is worth noting an interesting initiative there, promoted by Swiss Rail (known in German as SBB, in Italian as FFS, in French as CFF). As was mentioned earlier the completion of the Basel-Chiasso motorway freed the cantonal road down the valley from through-traffic. Among activities that can profit from this is cycling, which in Switzerland has become popular as part of the current movement for promoting 'fitness'. (They have adopted the English word into their language in this context!) The SBB/FFS scheme provides a new and interesting way of exploring the historic towns and villages of the Leventina by cycle.

The scheme is based on Airolo and Biasca rail stations. At any time up to the day before travel, phone Airolo station and reserve a cycle for hire. On the day agreed, travel to Airolo by rail on a special round-journey ticket, pick up the reserved cycle at Airolo, and set off downhill on the old cantonal road, taking as long as you like, with whatever halts and detours. At journey's end in Biasca, say, the cycle is returned to the FFS station and the round-ticket by rail covers the return journey to home or wherever. A similar arrangement exists on the northern side of the Gotthard between Göschenen and Flüelen, and in other suitable regions. A range of cycle models is available.

The Blenio Valley

The Blenio Valley, incidentally, makes a striking contrast to its near parallel neighbour, the Leventina. Compared to the rocky, precipitate, 'shut in' aspects of the Leventina, the Blenio is wider, sunnier and more kindly. Because it is more open, the sun's rays seem to penetrate every corner — while its neighbour has many zones of all-year shadow beneath lowering mountains. The Blenio has a long history of settlement and a long history of providing a through route between north and south. There is evidence that the Lukmanier Pass — which is the lowest of the Alpine passes and more flat in contour than the Gotthard — was favoured by the Romans. It was also an invasion route into Italy of early medieval German Emperors such as Otto I and the great Barbarossa. However, the nineteenth- and twentieth-century rail and road engineers applied themselves to the more direct, if more challenging, route by the Gotthard. So nowadays the Lukmanier-Blenio route has no railway, no motorway and escapes the full flood of modern tourism. Yet it has many treasures that make it well worth exploring. For those without independent transport, it is excellently served by the local bus lines from Biasca (Timetable 600.72-76).

Bellinzona

Only 17km (10½ miles) separate Biasca from the Ticino's cantonal capital, Bellinzona, lying at the southern end of the Riviera. Before reaching it the cantonal road crosses the N13 motorway coming in on the left from the Mesolcina (or Misox) Valley and the San Bernardino Pass; and passes the small town of Arbedo which gave its name to a battle in 1422 when the Swiss Confederates suffered a disastrous defeat at the hands of a greatly superior Milanese force.

Bellinzona, a modern industrial city, administrative and route centre, and historic cultural centre, has been a key strategic point for centuries yet the majority of tourists scarcely think of it as anything more than a junction town. Here three of the main routes from Alpine passes meet, from Gotthard, Lukmanier, and San Bernardino, as do two other routes from the opposite direction, ie, from Italy and the south via Lakes Maggiore and Lugano.

The one-time frontier fortress city which controlled passage between Lombardy and Central Switzerland has three impressive castles which are among the most important medieval fortifications in the whole country. Although they have more formal names they are commonly called after three Original Forest Cantons of Central Switzerland which made the Ticino Swiss: Uri, Schwyz and Unterwalden.

A city tour best starts at the FFS station, along the Viale Stazione to the Piazza Collegiata with its charming eighteenth-century baroque buildings. The picturesque heart of the 'old town' that has retained its original character is concentrated between this square and its neighbour to the south, Piazza Nosetto, with the lovely arcades in the Lombardy tradition. The Piazza Collegiata takes its name from the very fine collegiate church of St Peter and St Stephen (Santi Pietro e Stefano), a building of Renaissance period with baroque interior features. Beside the church is the

Visconti Castle, Locarno

stepped pedestrian alley that climbs to the impressive Castello Montebello (Castle Schwyz) standing some 90m (295ft) above the city. Today it houses the Civic Museum, largely archaeological and historical. From its high keep is a fine panorama of the city, the Ticino Valley and Lake Maggiore in the distance.

Returning to the triangular Piazza Nosetto (Tourist Information Office) a short walk leads through to the eighteenth-century Palazzo del Governo, and from there to the avenue which ascends past vineyards to the Castello Grande (Uri) dominated by its two thirteenth-century towers, which were restored in 1991 and house the archaeological museum. The third castle, Sasso Corbaro (Unterwalden) lies further from the 'old town' centre. Sited south-east of Castello Montebello, it is best reached either from there by Via Artore, or the Via Lugano, Via Ospedale and then by serpentine Via Sasso Corbaro to its height above the city. This castle is said to have been built by the Milanese forces in only six months in 1479 after the Confederates' victory at Giornico, in order to block further Swiss advance south. It houses a museum of folk art and traditions. On Saturday mornings a very picturesque open-air market is held in the centre of Bellinzona.

About 3km (2 miles) south of Bellinzona is industrial Giubiasco (also a rail junction) where one can join the motorway south to Lugano; or, by staying on the cantonal road, one can continue straight south or turn east to Locarno and its valleys.

Locarno

Locarno is beautifully situated on a bay near the head of Lake Maggiore, sheltered from the north. Along with its satellite resort, one-time fishing village Ascona, it is one of the two main tourist centres in the Ticino, with a pronounced southern climate and character that is particularly colourful in spring with the luxuriant growth of magnolias, camellias, mimosa, oleander and palm trees.

One of the charms of this small city is that although it is famous as the chosen location in 1925 of a meeting of world statesmen who agreed a Locarno Pact to prevent any renewal of World War I enmities, and as the modern location of an International Film Festival, it also still maintains the air of the market town and rendezvous of country folk. Its arcaded Piazza Grande is not merely the centre of ceremonies for the town but of a whole region, and in that role is truly impressive.

Locarno's fifteenth-century Castello Visconti survives from much more extensive medieval fortifications. The Castello now houses a Civic Museum which among other things holds Roman artefacts found in the course of local excavations. Past the Castello one ascends to the narrow, picturesque old world streets leading to the heart of the old town, signposted as 'Citta Vecchia'.

The Piazza Grande to the east leads to the Debarcadero, the landing stage for the lake steamers which ply Lake Maggiore; and also to the extensive lakeside gardens which make so appealing and informal a natural promenade.

On a wooded spur above Locarno is a little plateau on which stands the pilgrimage church of the Madonna del Sasso, associated with its Capuchin friary. (It was founded in 1480 and rebuilt in the early seventeenth century.) The trip to it is best taken by funicular line from the town centre. It is quite the most popular excursion in Locarno, many making pilgrimages, many being interested in art. The church contains, for instance, the painting by Bramantino, *Flight to Egypt* (1520), and fine Gothic carvings. Many come simply to enjoy the splendid view over Locarno and Lake Maggiore from the cloisters.

Ascona is only 4km (2½ miles) from Locarno, round the corner on the other side of the 'delta' of the River Maggia, and faces south. Once a very small fishing port, its picturesque and colourful setting and favourable clime made it a magnet for artists and writers, such as Paul Klee and Hermann Hesse. In more recent times it has come to rival its older and bigger neighbour as a prime destination for tourists and has inevitably expanded out of recognition in many ways. Yet the core of old Ascona around the picturesque stone-built harbour, with its surrounding palms, flowers, colourful boutiques, cafés, antique and craft shops, still has a lot of character. This is especially so in spring when the colour contrast is most marked between the immediate subtropical foreground and the background of the blue lake and snow-capped Gambarogno.

As a resort it is well provided nowadays with all the expected sports and other facilities including a Lido. It also has some historic buildings of artistic and architectural merit well worth seeking out, such as the Collegio Pontificio Papio, founded by Bartolomeo Papio of Ascona towards the end of the sixteenth century, with its elegant two-storey arcaded Renaissance courtyard. Next to the college is the church of Santa Maria della Misericordia built at the turn of fourteenth and fifteenth century, with important wall frescos from the fifteenth and sixteenth centuries.

Excursions from Ascona and Locarno

For the two resorts placed back to back at the mouth of the River Maggia, the same excursions are popular.

1 Lake Maggiore

Lake steamer excursions on Maggiore are a great favourite. After Garda it is the second largest of the North Italian lakes, 64km (40 miles) in length. Barely one-fifth of its extent lies in Swiss territory, the rest being in Italy. (On voyages other than very local, remember to carry your passport.) Popular Italian destinations are **Stresa** and its nearby **Borromean Islands** with their beautiful formal gardens; more local are the **Islands of Brissago** (Swiss part of lake) with their subtropical Botanical Garden, and also, on the lake shore the small Swiss resort with the Italian atmosphere, **Brissago** itself.

2 The Gambarogno

The district on the opposite shore of the lake from Locarno, the Gambarogno, is very charming and unspoiled. The countryside is lush and fertile, abundant in vineyards and cherry orchards. Apricots, peaches and figs testify to the sub-tropical climate of the terraces on the gentle slopes of Monte Gambarogno. The colourful little village of Vira with its harbour and pleasant lake front makes an enjoyable destination for an afternoon excursion. It can be reached in 20 minutes by lake steamer (Timetable 2630). By car it is reached by crossing the flat Magadino plain through which the River Ticino's final course flows; then by turning right on to the road following the lake's south shore. Lying almost on the corner of the lake head is the village of **Magadino** which was for centuries a transhipment point for trade goods crossing the Alps via the Gotthard. **Vira** is the next village. On either the outward or return journey it is worth visiting the Nature Conservancy Zone, known as the **Bolle di Magadino** which lies on the delta between the outfalls of the Rivers Ticino and Verzasca. The vegetation and the rare birdlife are unique in Europe.

3 By Train to the Gambarogno

The visitor can get a good impression of the Gambarogno by local train from Locarno to the immense weekly Wednesday market held in the streets and squares of the Italian town of **Luino** on the south shore of the lake 22km (13½ miles) beyond Vira (Timetable 631, involving a scheduled change of trains at Cadenazzo).

4 Locarno's Valleys

Locarno has a hinterland of lateral valleys to the west which present a striking contrast to the large lakeside resorts. Because of the half-circle of towering mountains to the west, these valleys are short and steep-sided, with precipitate water courses. Valley populations for centuries lived a hard life on grudging soil. Depopulation in the present century has been headlong and many specialised crafts — such as straw-weaving — have died out. Some villages have been partly repopulated by townspeople taking over or converting rural cottages into holiday homes. In the areas nearer to Locarno improved roads have brought in commuter residents.

Of the valleys the most secluded and the one which has, to a considerable extent, kept its wild original character is the **Val Verzasca**. The route up the valley to Sonogno, the mountain village where the post road ends, is only 25km (15½ miles) in length but is both varied and picturesque. The main village, Brione-Verzasca, about two-thirds of the way up the valley, is known for its granite quarries and has a parish church that goes back to the thirteenth century; its façade has a larger-than-life fresco of St Christopher and inside are important fourteenth- and fifteenth-century frescos in the style of Giotto. In the village square stands a most picturesque seventeenth-century fortified residence with corner towers and walls, now a restaurant.

The **Val Maggia** further west is longer than the Verzasca and its approach road is less steep to tackle. Its principal village, Cevio, 21km (13 miles) up the valley has much of interest, having been the valley administrative centre both under Milanese rule and later under the Landvogts, the Swiss Confederate governors. In the village square is a three-storey *Casa Pretoria*, Court House, displaying the coats of arms of the Maggia villages as well as of Landvogts. Nearby is the former residence of eighteenth-century governors and other houses of prominent citizens of the same era, with wall paintings and handsome gardens.

From the Maggia a favourite extended excursion is into the picturesque side valley, **Valle di Campo**, by the spectacular road that corkscrews up

The Piazza Grande, Locarno

Opposite: Ascona, on Lake Maggiore

to it from Cevio and, after some 5km, after Cerentino at a road fork takes the right-hand branch to climb to the head of a tributary valley to Bosco Gurin. This is Ticino's highest village (at 1,506m, 4,941ft), the road having climbed 915m (3,000ft) in 16km (10 miles). The village is unusual in other respects. The inhabitants speak a dialect of German, not Italian. Their ancestors in the thirteenth century crossed the mountains from canton Valais (or Wallis, one should perhaps say) and, settling here, maintained not only their language to the present day but also their customs, manners and even their style of building.

The **Centovalli** differs from those above in that it runs in an east-west direction. *Cento valli* means literally 'a hundred valleys' and the reference is to the numerous side valleys that run at right angles, usually headlong at that, into the valley of the main River Melezza. It also differs by having a good service by narrow-gauge electric railway run from Locarno up the valley, continuing beyond Camedo, the last Swiss station on the line, into Italy and ultimately to Domodossola, main line station on the international Milan-Stresa-Simplon line into Switzerland by way of Brig (with further connections to Geneva and Bern).

The trip by Centovalli railway from Locarno to Domodossola takes

about 1¾ hours in a through train (Timetable 620). Thanks to the many side valley gorges which the line must cross, the railway exhibits some daring and spectacular bridge-building feats which makes the trip fascinating. A road runs along the same valley all the way, providing motorists with an interesting, very picturesque and fairly demanding route through to link with the Simplon Pass road either for Italy or for cantons Valais, Vaud, Bern or Geneva.

Public Transport Option

Verzasca and Maggia can be explored by Swiss Postbus services from Locarno. The appropriate lines are:

Val Verzasca, Locarno to Sonogno (Timetable 630.55).

Val Maggia, Locarno to Cevio (Timetable 630.60). Cevio to Bosco Gurin (Timetable 630.65).

Grotti in the Ticino

The *grotto* is a great institution in the Ticino valleys. Understandably in a land of 'granite and gneiss', as the valleys have been described, there are difficulties in the way of excavating domestic underground cellars in the normal sense of the term. It was much easier to find a suitable place to start a *grotto* or cave. So what was originally the word for a cave came to be used commonly for a storage place dug out in a rock face in which to keep wine and cheeses at cellar temperature. They were mostly just outside the village and in tree shade. They became favourite spots for the men of the village to meet on Sundays or holidays to play a game or two of *boccia* (bowls) and to talk over a glass of local wine. Often someone cooked up a snack of some local dish, perhaps locally-shot game, setting up a granite slab as a rough table. This caught on.

Some *grotti* became favourite rendezvous for wider circles and began to cater as a regular enterprise for local customers and even for visitors or strangers of the right sort. Needless to say, nowadays especially in urban or near-urban settings where commercial temptations are hard to resist the term *grotto* is not infrequently borrowed for establishments that are simply ordinary eating places. But if you can be fortunate enough to learn the favourite *grotto* of a local Ticinese citizen, that is where to find homely local food and wine — often with entertainment, too. In short, the genuine *grotto* has something of a club atmosphere and visitors are most likely to be welcome if they show they recognise that.

Lugano and its Lake

Lugano and the lake which in English bears its name (though the locals know it as Lago Ceresio) lie south of a natural barrier, Monte Ceneri, which lies between them and the River Ticino's valley floor. Through the ages a very clear distinction was made between the Northern Ticino, or Sopra-Ceneri, as they call it, and the Southern Ticino, or Sotto-Ceneri. The barrier mass of Ceneri presents its steep rock face to the north and shows a more gradual slope taking the form of a long trough to the south — the Val Vedeggio.

For centuries the Ceneri Pass was the scene of tales of robber bands who preyed on wayfarers. (In the eighteenth century when a famous market was sited at Lugano, the Ceneri Pass was posted with soldiers to protect the passage of traders during the market period.) Today, although Lugano, one of Europe's most sophisticated small cities, is probably Switzerland's most popular resort for well-off Northerners it is also a centre from which one can easily reach the 'little old-style world' places described in the great Italian nineteenth-century novel *Il Piccolo Mondo Antico* written by Fogazzaro.

For a period of 75 years last century the role of cantonal capital of the Ticino circulated by rota between the cities of Bellinzona, Locarno and Lugano until practical considerations finally anchored it in Bellinzona. Though no longer the administrative capital, Lugano has continued to be the major town and cultural centre of the canton. Its site is a splendid one, extending along a crescent-shaped bay of the lake, flanked by its two sentinel peaks, Monte Bré to the east and Monte San Salvatore to the south. Mountains of moderate height shield it from northerly winds. Its situation and climate are very sunny; its boast is of 2,248 hours of sunshine per year — with an especially generous ration in the winter months when it is scarce elsewhere.

As a health resort it has a great asset in its attractive lakeside promenade, level, paved and tree-shaded the whole length of the bay, with steadily changing viewpoints of the lake and of the gardens, flower beds and flowering shrubs of the shoreline.

Behind the lake front in the town centre is the main square, Piazza Riforma, where traditional markets take place on Tuesdays and Fridays and which on any day is set with apparently countless café tables inviting you to drop into a chair facing the sun. Further behind, traffic-free cobbled alleys wind to colourful window displays of delicatessen, exotic fruits and vegetables, confectionery and craftwork, everything very Italian. From the further end of the Piazza, however, the tone becomes cosmopolitan as one strolls past the great banking premises and saunters in the shade of the arcaded Via Nassa to window shop outside elegant establishments, boutiques, jewellers and antique dealers with displays that could compete with Zürich's Bahnhofstrasse.

At the far end of Via Nassa is a church with a fairly austere exterior. The Santa Maria degli Angioli was built 1499-1515 as the church of a former Franciscan monastery. Inside, its rood screen, separating choir from nave, is decorated with a truly monumental wall painting by Bernardino Luini, early sixteenth century, depicting the Passion and Crucifixion; it is regarded as one of the finest works of the Lombardy High Renaissance.

Piazza Riforma, Lugano

Opposite: Morcote, on Lake Lugano

RISTORANTE DELLA POSTA
ORANTE DELLA POSTA

Other frescos appear on other walls. The total impact of this interior is memorable.

To find the cathedral it is necessary to retrace one's steps to the cobbled streets behind the Piazza Riforma, and mount the slope to the little square from which a funicular lifts pedestrians to the main railway station on its hillside 'shelf'. Pass the funicular station and ascend the steps of the Via Cattedrale (with its gay boutiques and craft shops), turn a corner at the top and a second flight leads to the impressive façade of the Cathedral of San Lorenzo — a masterpiece of the Lombardy Renaissance, dating from 1500-17. Interior decoration is baroque but there are also fine thirteenth- to fifteenth-century wall paintings and many other treasures. The cathedral's bell tower is a city landmark.

Walking east on the lakeside promenade from near Piazza Riforma one passes the Ufficio Turistico (Tourist Office) and then the Casino, before reaching the entrance to the delightful Parco Civico. Within the park grounds are a civic museum, a cantonal library and the Palazzo dei Congressi with its convention facilities.

Further east still, beyond the outflow of the Cassarate stream, is a swimming pool and Lido. Beyond that the shore road leads to the eastern residential suburb of Castagnola. Here is the famed Villa Favorita, where the Pinacoteca (gallery) houses a world-renowned private collection of paintings, the property of Baron Thyssen.

Excursions from Lugano

Few visitors miss the opportunity to ascend the town's two hills, Monte Bré and Monte San Salvatore, both of which have funicular railways.

1 Monte Bré (Timetable 1653)

The ascent is from Cassarate, which is readily reached from the town centre by trolley-bus. The Monte Bré is reputed to be Switzerland's sunniest mountain. From the summit terrace there are views of the Valais and Bernese Alps and a bird's-eye view of Lugano and its lake.

2 Monte San Salvatore (Timetable 1652)

The bottom station is in the southern lakeside suburb of Paradiso. Again, the summit offers great panoramas of Swiss and French Alps as well as the arms of Lake Lugano. Walking paths to Carona and Melide also offer the chance of circular excursions with a return by boat from Melide (see 'Swissminiatur' below) to the Paradiso boat station.

3 Swissminiatur

At Melide, near where the road and rail causeway crosses the lake, is an exhibit representing 'Switzerland in Miniature' — consisting of small-scale replicas of real scenes from all parts of the country, including working model layouts (to an extent of 3km, 2 miles) of railways and cablecars. Probably in theory planned for children, in practice adults find it absorbing. It can be reached by bus, train or especially by lake steamer (calling at the special Swissminiatur boat station).

4 Morcote

One of the most picturesque villages of the lakeside lies 11km (7 miles) from Lugano at the end of the peninsula stretching south from Monte San Salvatore. The tall medieval bell-tower of its Madonna del Sasso church, standing on a bluff, is a landmark of the southern arm of the lake. Church and village, with handsomely ornamented and arcaded lakeside houses reflected in the lake make a compelling picture. It is easily reached by private transport, by bus from Lugano (Timetable 633.64) or by lake steamer (Timetable 2606, 2609).

Lake Excursions

A well-developed programme of boat excursions is operated by the modern vessels of the Societa Navigazione Lago di Lugano (SNL). Lake Lugano is shared by Italy and Switzerland; of its surface area very slightly over half is Swiss, the rest Italian. When customs officers board the vessel at the first landing stage after a passage from one country to the other it adds to the atmosphere of the cruise. And any circular tour on dry land that takes in a fair circuit of the lake inevitably crosses frontiers. For landing in, or transit through, Italian territory passports are of course required.

Regular round-trip tours of the lake are available, some longer than others. Among favourite short trips is one to the typical old fishing village of **Gandria** (Timetable 2608). Gandria lies on the eastern arm of the lake, 5km (3 miles) away. Its colourful houses and taverns cling picturesquely to the steep hillside and terraces, while the villagers' boats swing, hoisted on davits, above the deep water inshore — a favourite subject with artists and photographers. Another destination for a short excursion is Campione d'Italia directly across the lake from Lugano.

Major afternoon boat excursions include:

1 Porlezza

This Italian town lies on an isthmus separating Lake Lugano from Lake Como. The shores of this arm of the lake are impressively stern and girt by steep mountain faces. There are interesting Italian ports of call on both shores.

2 To Ponte Tresa (Timetable 2606)

The vessel sails under the bridge in the causeway which carries rail and road over the lake south of Monte San Salvatore into the gentler southern lake arm. It calls, after Morcote, at the little Italian township of Porto Ceresio, and sails past shores which abound in subtropical flora to the western lake arm's head at Ponte Tresa. This frontier town has long been

Arcaded residence, Morcote

Opposite: Campione d'Italia across the lake from Lugano

an important transit point. The River Tresa flowing out of the lake divides the town into two parts. The original 'old town', lying on the south, ie, Italian side, is linked to the Swiss side by a modern bridge which is an important customs station.

From Ponte Tresa two roads run west, one on the Italian, one on the Swiss bank of the river, to Luino (12km, 7 miles), an Italian town on Lake Maggiore into which the River Tresa flows. **Luino** is famed for its weekly Wednesday market.

From Ponte Tresa one can return to Lugano by the Lugano-Ponte Tresa narrow-gauge railway through the mellow hinterland via Agno and the little Laghetto di Muzzano (Timetable 635).

Monte Lema via Miglieglia

A favourite excursion by road is via Laghetto di Muzzano and Agno (6km, 4 miles) then following the Ponte Tresa road as far as Magliaso. Once through Magliaso take the first minor road on the right which leads into the district known as the **Malcantone**, held by many to be the most beautiful in the canton for its landscape and rural architecture. It occupies roughly the rectangle between the western arm of Lake Lugano and the mountain ridge which forms the Italian boundary on the west.

Proceed through **Pura**, 1km (half a mile) from the road turn-off, a particularly pretty resort with lots of attractive country walks and rare flowers. Next, **Novaggio**, with vineyards and typical loggias and porticos to the houses. From Novaggio continue north to **Miglieglia**. This pleasant village, interesting for the excellent condition of the late Gothic wall paintings in its upper church, is also the station for a chairlift (Timetable 1660) to the peak of **Monte Lema** (1,621m, 5,319ft). The top of Monte Lema is a wide grass-covered plateau, a good skiing area. This, the Ticino's best viewpoint, provides an impressive panorama of Valais, Bernese and Grisons Alps as well as of the Malcantone and Lake Lugano and Lake Maggiore.

Public Transport Option

A Postbus service from Lugano caters for this route to Miglieglia (Timetable 635.20).

Mendrisiotto and Monte Generoso

South-east of Lugano and its lake is the **Mendrisiotto** district which forms the 'tip' of the Ticino's 'arrowhead' on the map outline. A broad, fertile basin, it is the most industrialised region of Ticino and the most productive in terms of agriculture. At one time the centre of mulberry culture for the silk industry, it now specialises in textiles, tobacco and the food industry and is the great home of the Merlot wine grape. In climate, architecture and vegetation it is like part of Lombardy.

From Lugano it is approached by the route which carries the heaviest tourist traffic in the country — the great *ponte diga* or causeway, first built 1844-7, now fortified to carry main railway, national road and also motorway across Lake Lugano. (The national road leaves Lugano via the suburb of Paradiso for the causeway. The motorway, having bypassed the city to the west, tunnels under the ridge of Monte Salvatore — Lugano's southern 'sentinel' — to reach the causeway.) Roads and rail swing south after Bissone on the far bank. **Bissone** — despite such road and rail neighbours — has managed to preserve its stylish old arcaded centre and its showpiece patrician mansion Tencalla (AD1600), furnished in period style, still lived in but open in the afternoon to the public.

Capolago is reached 6km (3¾miles) further on, lying at the head of the south-east 'horn' of the lake. Here is the bottom station of the cogwheel railway (Timetable 636) which climbs in about forty minutes to the summit of **Monte Generoso** (1,594m, 5,530ft) which affords a splendid panorama over the lake to the great chain of the Alps, and over the Plain of Lombardy to Milan. A kilometre west of Capolago is **Riva San Vitale** (with which it shares the main line railway station). Just off its main square is a unique treasure, Switzerland's oldest ecclesiastical building, an early Christian baptistry of around AD500; in the centre of the original floor is an octagonal basin for baptismal immersion.

Public Transport Option

Bissone and Capolago are easily reached both by regional trains from Lugano (Timetable 300) and by certain of the lake steamers (see Timetables 3606 and 3609).

Additional Information

Places to Visit

Ascona
Museo Comunale
Via Borgo 34
Fine art collection.
Open: March to December.

Bellinzona
Castello Grande
Greatly renovated
Open: daily except Monday.

Castello di Montebello
(Civic Museum of Local History and Archaeology)
Open: daily except Monday, 9.30am-12noon, 2-5.30pm.

Castello di Sasso Corbaro
Ticino Museum of Arts, Crafts and Folk Traditions
Open: Easter to end October Tuesday to Sunday 9am-12noon and 2-5pm.

Bissone
Casa Tencalla
☎ 091/68 73 42
Museum in patrician mansion shows patrician lifestyle in baroque period.
Open: mid-March to mid-October

10.30am-12noon, 2-5pm. Closed Saturday.

Bolle di Magadino
Nature Conservancy Area on delta of River Ticino. Rare plants and birds. Guided boat trips Monday and Thursday mornings. Enquire details Ente Turistico Gambarogno, address and telephone as listed below.

Bosco-Gurin
Museum Walserhaus
☎ 093/96 15 80
Exhibits illustrate customs and history of unique community.
Open: May to October daily except Mon day 9-11am and 2-5pm; Sunday 2-5pm.

Cevio
Former administrative centre of Maggia Valley.
Antica Casa Franzoni
Maggia Museum
Open: April to October, daily except Monday, 9.30am-12noon, 2-6pm; Sundays 2-6pm.

Gandria
Customs Museum
Cantine di Gandria (on opposite side of lake from village and only accessible by steamer).
Exhibits of smuggling devices and counter-methods.
Open: April to end September, daily 2.30-5.30pm.
☎ 091/23 98 43.

Giornico
Casa Stanga
Leventine Valley Museum
☎ 092/74 24 01
Open: Easter Monday to end October, Saturday and holidays.

Locarno
Museo Civico Archeologico
In the Castello Visconteo
Piazza Castello
☎ 093/31 59 72
Rich collection of Roman objects from local excavations, especially glass.

Museo dell' Arte Moderna
Also in the Castello Viconteo (west wing), based on the Jean and Margherita Arp collections of modern works. Closed Monday. For current opening hours consult Tourist Office or telephone inquiry.

Lugano
Picture Gallery Villa Favorita
Castagnola
Masterpieces from thirteenth- to eighteenth-century Europe. Also frequent special exhibits from Thyssen-Bornemisza Collection. For times and prices of admission seek information from.
☎ 091/52 17 41

Municipal Art Museum
Villa Ciani (in Municipal Park)
Open: Tuesday to Sunday 10am-12noon, 2-6pm. Closed Monday.

Santa Maria degli Angioli
Church in Piazza B. Luini, has famous frescoes by Bernardini Luini, the *Crucifixion* and *The Lord's Supper*.

Melide
Swissminiatur
Exhibition of Swiss city and resort scenes reproduced in 1:25 scale.
Open: mid-March-end October daily 8.30am-6pm, mid-July-August 8am-10pm.

Morcote
Parco Scherrer
☎ 091/69 21 25
Garden park of rare plants and buildings based on exotic models.
Open: March to October: only conducted tours, Tuesday, Thursday at 10am, 1.30pm and 3.30pm; other days open 9am-5pm.

Sonogno
Casa Genardini
Local Museum
☎ 093/31 85 46
Open: July to September 1.30-4.30pm daily. Exhibits on local crafts and agriculture, utensils, costumes.

Sport and Recreation

Ascona
All water sports on Lake Maggiore. Golf.

Airolo
Climbing, angling (permits from local authority office), *boccia* bowls. Several ski-lifts for winter sports locally. Starting point for hiking and hill walking excursions in Bedretto, Leventina and Blenio Valley trails. Details from Ente Turistico Faido. For cycle hire for the special cycling project on the old Gotthard road between Airolo and Biasca contact Airolo mainline SBB-FFS station:
☎ 094/88 12 22.

Bellinzona
Rock-climbing practice near Arbedo; fishing; tennis; horse riding; ice rink in winter. Details from Ente Turistico Bellinzona.

Biasca
Fishing, horse riding, *boccia* bowls, canoeing; two well-situated camping places. In September: Rivera Gymkhana. For Swiss Rail cyclist's special Gotthard Road scheme, Airolo-Biasca, see entry under Airolo.

Locarno
Golf at Ascona. Fishing, tennis, sailing, water-skiing. Ice rink.

Lugano
All water sports on lake. Swimming (bathing beach, heated pools and indoor pools). Golf (*Magliaso*).
Tennis, keep-fit track, *boccia*, judo, flying (Agno aerodrome).

Miglieglia
Skiing, hill walking (well marked trails).

Morcote
Water sports in lake, angling.
Windsurfing courses.

Sonogno
Angling, mountaineering, winter ice-skating.

Tourist Information Offices

The *cantonal office* for the Ticino is
Ente Ticinese per il Turismo
Villa Turrita
CH-6501 Bellinzona
☎ 092/25 70 56
The addresses and telephone numbers of the *district tourist boards* for the districts of Ticino covered in the text follow. (In each case, ET means Ente Turistico.)

ET Bellinzona e dintorni
CH-6500 Bellinzona
☎ 092/25 21 31

ET Biasca e Riviera
CH-6710 Biasca
☎ 092/72 33 27

ET Ceresio
CH-6815 Melide
☎ 091/68 63 83

ET Gambarogno
CH-6574 Vira
☎ 093/61 18 66

ET Leventina
CH-6760 Faido
☎ 094/38 16 16

ET Locarno
CH-6600 Locarno
Teatro Kursaal
☎ 093/31 03 33

ET Lugano e dintorni
CH-6901 Lugano
Riva Abertolli 5
☎ 091/21 46 64

ET Malcantone
CH-6987 Caslano
☎ 091/71 29 86

ET Mendrisiotto
CH-6850 Mendrisio
☎ 091/46 57 61

ET Tenero e Valle Verzasca
CH-6598 Tenero
☎ 093/67 16 61

ET Vallemaggia
CH-6673 Maggia
☎ 093/87 18 85

ET Valli di Lugano
CH-6950 Tesserete
☎ 091/91 18 88

Public Transport

The shipping services on Lake Lugano are conducted by the Societa Navigazione Lago di Lugano (☎ 091/51 52 23).
Timetable 2606-9.

Ambri-Piotta Station on Gotthard line. Piotta is also the valley station of funicular rail to Piora for Lake Ritom reservoir. Official Timetable 1603; further information ☎ 094/88 12 22.
Biasca Transport centre of bus services for Blenio Valley: Autolinee Bleniesi, CH-6710 Biasca, ☎ 092/72 31 72.
Miglieglia Small village important as site of chairlift to Monte Lema summit (Timetable 1660 ☎ 091/77 11 68).
Morcote Nearest rail station to this popular small resort is 5km (3 miles) away, Melide (which is also where the district tourist office is). Morcote is served by boat and by bus from Lugano (Timetable 633.64).
Ponte Tresa Swiss-Italian frontier town on arm of Lake Lugano. Linked to Lugano by excellent narrow-gauge rail service (Timetable 635).

6

GRAUBÜNDEN

For those who have travelled into the Ticino by the Gotthard route, alternative routes are available for the return north. It is very interesting to leave the Ticino by travelling further east or north-east and sample the different landscape and atmosphere of the large neighbouring canton, Graubünden. English-speakers commonly call canton Graubünden by its French name, Grisons. This may seem a curious thing to do, since in fact, French is not one of the mother tongues in that canton although it has more native languages (in its various regions) than other cantons: Swiss-German (60 per cent), Italian (13 per cent) and the several dialects of Romansch (22 per cent). The latter is a language distinct from Italian yet descended from the vernacular Latin once spoken here when it was part of a Roman province, *Rhaetia*. (Linguists give the name Rhaeto-Romanic to the group of languages that includes Romansch and if you travel around in Graubünden you may notice that the network of railways in the canton is known as the *Rhätische Bahn*, Rhaetian Railway or RhB). The canton's name in German is 'Graubünden', in Italian 'Grigioni' and in Romansch 'Grischun'.

Graubünden's mountainous nature and the isolation of its high valleys until comparatively modern times give a clue both to the survival of the Romansch language in this region and to its historical isolation for many centuries. It was not until 1803 that Graubünden came into the Swiss Confederation as the eighteenth canton, although the communities of the 'Grey League' ('Graues Bund' from which the canton's name derives) and like-minded leagues involved in independence struggles against the Austrian Hapsburgs had made common cause with the Central Swiss Confederates at the end of the fifteenth century.

In area Graubünden is the largest canton of all, but the most thinly populated, being predominantly mountainous. Paradoxically, although some of its individual villages and towns figure prominently among the names of well-known and highly fashionable Swiss resorts — especially for winter sports — such as St Moritz, Davos and Arosa, the great variety of landscape and atmosphere in the canton as a whole is not at all so well

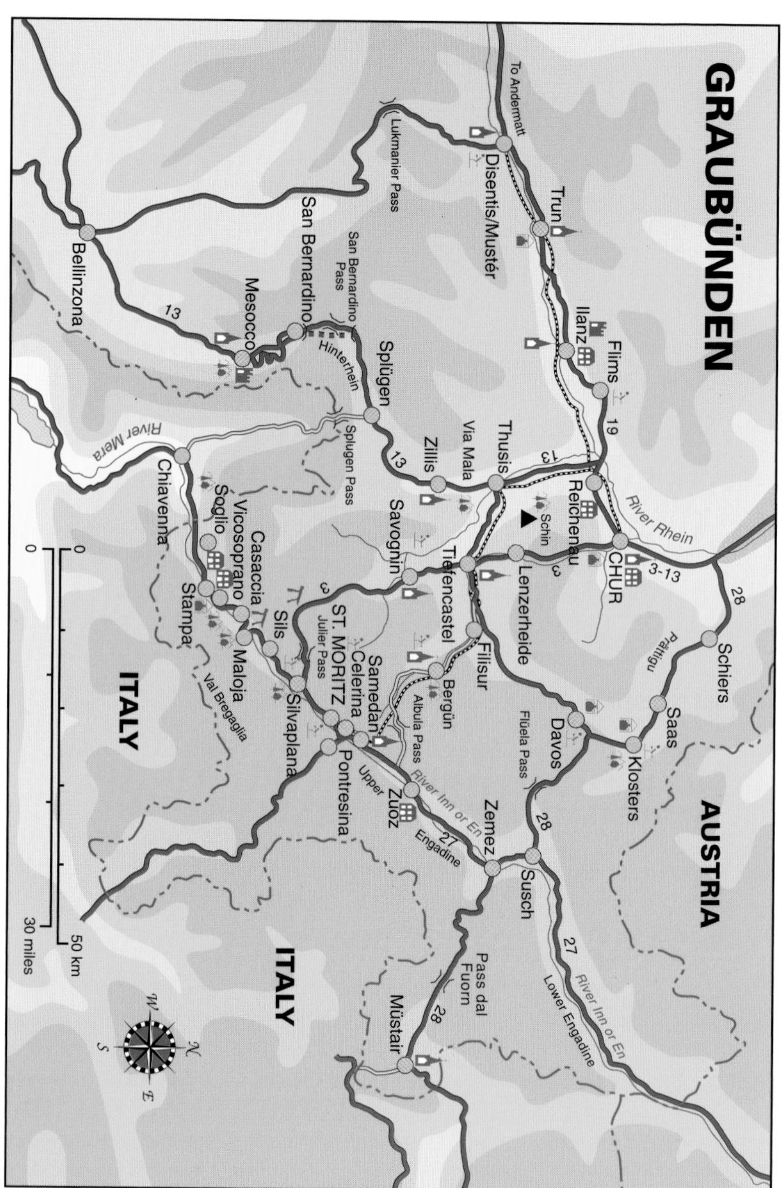

known to the average English or American traveller as are, say, the areas of Central Switzerland, the Berner Oberland or the Lake Geneva region.

Two-thirds of its frontiers bound with Italy and Austria. Its Alpine passes have been of great importance historically but its own economic resources have been poor until recent tourism (which accounts for 50 per cent of its income and 50 per cent of its employment) and the generation of hydro-electric power (of which this canton provides one-fifth of the

The cathedral, Chur

Arcas Square, Chur

country's supply but only consumes less than one twenty-fifth!) made their contribution.

6.1 From Andermatt to Chur and St Moritz

Andermatt, is the centre of the crossroads of rivers flowing north, south, east and west from the great Gotthard massif carved out of the mountain core of Switzerland. So it makes a suitable gateway into Graubünden for travellers whether they have just come south up the Gotthard route to Göschenen from Lake Luzern, north from the Ticino via the Val Leventina, or east from the Valais by way of the Furka Pass. Nor does it matter whether they have travelled by road or by rail. Indeed if they have travelled from Zermatt or Brig by the 'Glacier Express' their halt in Andermatt station will be quite brief before continuing.

From Andermatt rail and road alike tackle a 610m (2,000ft) ascent to the summit of the Oberalp Pass by taking a series of wide zigzag sweeps up the face of the harsh mountain wall. (The train uses spiral tunnels into the mountain face at the end of each zigzag to ease the climbing bends, even although it is assisted by cogwheel gearing for the 11km [7 miles] of the way to the Oberalp lake station where westbound and eastbound trains pass.) In the course of climbing there are good views backward to Andermatt below in its high pastoral valley rimmed with the clusters of rocky debris, evidence of past avalanches.

The watershed of the Pass (2,044m, 6,706ft), boundary between canton Uri and canton Graubünden, coincides with the kilometre-long seemingly sterile Oberalpsee. Beyond it is a long tunnel that serves as an avalanche shield for road and rail. (The pass road is usually blocked with snow from November to May; but cars can be transported by rail between Andermatt and Sedrun.) As the road descends to the east in serpentine bends there are fine views to the south towards the bare mountain zone where the sources of the River Rhein spring. **Sedrun** (23km, 14 miles from Andermatt) is the chief village of the Tavetsch district and is a small resort with winter sports facilities (1,441m, 4,728ft) above sea level). Nine kilometres (5½ miles) further on the road reaches **Disentis** (Mustér in Romansch). It is famed for its Benedictine monastery which quite dominates the place from its shelf on the hillside to the north. Founded in the eighth century, it is a prominent centre of Romansch culture. The present abbey-church of St Martin is early eighteenth century; its two tall towers are surmounted with onion domes. It has a bright baroque interior.

The town that grew up under its wing is now the capital of what is known as the Surselva region, consisting of the catchment area of the Vorderrhein (Anterior Rhine) along with its southern side valleys. It stands on a natural terrace above the junction of the two sources of that river, one having come down from the Lukmanier Pass in the south, the other from the Oberalp watershed. Disentis also caters for winter sports; there is quite a network of skilifts.

The next village, in 11km (7 miles), is a handsome one, **Trun**, made famous when the member communities of the Grey League (Graues Bund) took the founding oath under a maple tree at the entrance to the village, on 16 March 1424. In the entrance of the baroque St Anna Chapel opposite the railway station is a fairly modern wall painting of that historic occasion. Meetings of the Grey League took place in a handsome three-storied building known as the Disentiser Hof which today serves as a Surselva Museum.

From now on the stark austerity of the high Alps begins to give way to green woods, pastoral slopes and side valleys. In 18km (11 miles) **Ilanz** is reached, a picturesque little place, market town for the surrounding Surselva region and an early key member and former capital of the Grey League; it prides itself on being (rather ambiguously, 'the first town on the Rhine'. Two handsome towers survive of what were once its defensive fortifications. It has a fine late Gothic church to which a former medieval fortified keep has acted as bell-tower since 1438; and a number of handsome baroque residences including one, the Casa Gronda, which — like others in Central Switzerland — had as temporary occupant, the apparently ubiquitous Russian General Suvorov in the course of his 1799 retreat.

After Ilanz the road and rail part company for some 22km (14 miles), when the main road makes a sweep towards the north of the river to pass through the village of **Flims** (in 11km, 7 miles), from which several lifts ascend to the northern heights. It is a popular family resort, both winter and summer. Six-and-a-half kilometres (4 miles) beyond Flims is the village of **Trin**. Shortly after passing through it the motorist has excellent views on the right-hand to the south over the valley of the Hinterrhein (the valley known as the Domleschg in Romansch) and also of the Vorderrhein Gorge. The road continues downhill for 4km (2½ miles) to Tamins. Thereafter it descends to cross the river bridge and shortly enters Reichenau.

In the meantime the railway has taken a much more daring path — through the extraordinary **Flims Gorge** that lies between Ilanz and Reichenau. In a late Ice Age period a really gigantic landslip had filled and dammed the river valley here but the river managed to carve a twisting path through the still unconsolidated material of the landslip, so creating a unique gorge with contorted overhanging cliffs. It is along the slopes of this gorge, between river and cliffs, that the railway makes its way to the point where it meets a second railway line coming down at right angles to join it from the right (south). After this junction the line crosses a girder bridge where the Vorderrhein is also joined also from the right by another river. This is the meeting point of the two principal branches, the Vorderrhein (Anterior Rhine), and the Hinterrhein (Posterior Rhine), which together make up what, from this point downstream, is simply called the Rhine. The junction railway station opposite is Reichenau-Tamins. The rail which has come down from the Hinterrhein Valley is the Rhaetian Rail line from St Moritz to Chur.

The Old Town, Chur

Opposite: Klosters

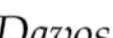

Davos

18
51

Reichenau has a seventeenth-century castle, probably linked with the little settlement's former function as a toll station at an important junction where the roads from the Domleschg and the Surselva meet.

Chur is 10km (6 miles) from Reichenau.

Public Transport Option

The route described above can be covered by train from Andermatt (or indeed from Brig or even Zermatt) (Timetable 920). For the section from Ilanz where the road via Flims deviates from the rail route, Postbus services reach Flims either from Ilanz or from Chur/ Reichenau (Timetable 920.30 and 900.75 respectively). Rail passengers on the 'Glacier Express' might wish to complete the journey by continuing onward from Chur to St Moritz; that route will be described in a subsequent section.

Chur

The capital of canton Graubünden may appear to be situated off-centre. In fact it is admirably placed at a key site for communications in a canton much divided up by high mountains and deep valleys. For the main communications lines from Graubünden Passes come together at Chur with those from North Switzerland, South Germany and Austria. The city's long history (and Chur is claimed as Switzerland's oldest city) is the history of the Rhaetian Mountain Passes. They were the foundation of its trading prosperity and at times the cause of its involvement in international embroilment.

The city is also sited near the linguistic frontier between Germanic and Rhaeto-Romanic speech, having been the capital of the Roman province of *Rhaetia Prima* stretching from what is modern Upper Bavaria to Lake Maggiore. The city lies where the Rhine's tributary river, the Plessur, had built up deposits of debris and silt near their junction. As one approaches Chur from the north one first sees its modern buildings. The Old Town has to be sought out at the foot of the Mittenberg Hill, stretching south to the River Plessur. It is grouped round the Martinsplatz, St Martin's Square, where so many enchanting alleys with fifteenth- to eighteenth-century patrician houses and guild halls mingle.

It is not difficult to find your way there from, say, the station. The local Tourist Office has marked out the route with red-painted footprints on the pavements. (Not an original idea, but one with a classical pedigree; a similar device was used in the cosmopolitan ancient Asia Minor city of *Ephesus*!)

Beside the square stands the Reformed parish church of St Martin, dating to the second half of the fifteenth century but built on the foundations of an earlier, Carolingian basilica. Rising picturesquely to the east above this medieval centre is a combination of fortress and ecclesiastical precinct, the complex of buildings known as the Bischöflicher Hof, Episcopal Court surrounding an inner Hofplatz where there was once a Roman fort. The Bishop's Palace (Bischöfliches Schloss) was reconstructed in Austrian baroque style in 1732-3. This imposing complex is reached from the Old Town below through the Torturm, Gate Tower.

Before starting on the principal visit, to the cathedral which stands to the east of the Episcopal Court, it may be worthwhile to leave the complex temporarily by the Schloss gateway, and cross the St Luzistrasse to visit the Kirche St Luzi (St Luke's Church), which stands in the grounds of what is now a theological college. The special interest of this much restored church is its round crypt of eighth-century Carolingian origin.

The cathedral itself, dedicated to the Assumption of St Mary, is basically a late Romanesque pillared basilica, twelfth and thirteenth century, with quite a severe exterior, although it has some Gothic features. The rich interior exemplifies a wide range of periods of decoration from the Carolingian to the baroque. The Cathedral Museum has priceless treasures including reliquaries of Carolingian and medieval periods. There is also a Rhaetian Museum, housed in the seventeenth-century Buol mansion immediately east of St Martin's Square with interesting prehistoric and historical exhibits relating to the canton.

But even for the tourist who has little time to pursue the details of these monuments, simply to stroll through the courtyards, the old town squares with their flowers and fountains, past handsome historic residences and perhaps also the fifteenth century Town Hall, is an experience that cannot fail to charm, and to impress the realisation that there is more to Chur than a junction to the skiing resorts.

Excursions from Chur

1 *The Brambrüesch*

A favourite local excursion is to a skiing and rambling area called Brambrüesch. It is easily reached by an aerial cableway which has its bottom station in the west of Chur on the Kasernenstrasse (Timetable 1880). Brambrüesch (1,600m, 5,250ft) provides impressive views over the Rhine Valley and interesting walks.

2 *Klosters and Davos*

A longer excursion but still within easy reach of Chur takes in the well-known resorts of Klosters and Davos. Heading north from Chur take the N13 motorway down the Rhine Valley in the St Gallen/Zürich direction. Across the Rhine on the left is the ridge of Chur's neighbourhood heights, the Calanda (2,806m, 9,206ft). In about 10km (6 miles) on the right (at the point where the road crosses the railway that has until then been running between road and river) you should glimpse the impressive castle of Zizers. Five kilometres (3 miles) further on take the exit for Landquart and turning sharply east follow road No 28 which enters the narrow mouth of what opens out into the River Landquart's valley, the lovely wooded and pastoral district of the Prättigau.

Public Transport Option

The Rhaetian Railway closely follows the road from Chur to Klosters and Davos (Timetable 910). It also completes the circuit by continuing to Filisur where the junction station provides a connection with the St Moritz-Chur line's spectacular journey via Tiefencastel and the Schin Gorge (to be described in a later section) to Chur (Timetable 940).

However, from Davos a well-frequented route runs east to the popular holiday region of the Inn Valley, the Engadine. Road No 28 runs the 43km (35 miles) to Susch in the Engadine by way of the Flüela Pass (2,383m, 7,819ft), through a rather barren landscape of large-scale rock debris relieved only by two little mountain tarns and, to the south just beyond the pass, a near view of the rock pyramid of the Schwarzhorn (3,147m, 10,325ft).

The Davos-Susch route is classed as a mountain post road and is served from the end of May until mid-October by a Postbus (Timetable 910.75). From Susch this bus route continues to Zernez (9km, 5½ miles) (where the great Swiss National Park lies) and at Zernez Post Office passengers can transfer to another bus (Timetable 960.20) which, a few minutes later, heads south-west to cross the Pass dal Fuorn or Ofenpass (2,149m, 7,051ft) to the frontier village of Müstair in its valley. The 46km (29 mile) journey takes about 1¼ hours. The unique feature of Müstair is that it is the site of one of the most ancient buildings in Switzerland. Charlemagne founded a monastery there which in the twelfth century became a Benedictine convent. The convent church of St Johann has Carolingian wall paintings of about AD800 which are a magnet for art lovers.

Obviously visitors with their own transport may be interested in taking the excursion to Zernez and Müstair. Road No 28 from Zernez to Müstair passes the offices of the National Park or Nature Reserve. Here, detailed information including maps can be obtained of the various marked paths (which may not be departed from) in this extensive park, rich in very varied topography, flora and fauna.

Until the late Middle Ages the district was inhabited by Romansch speakers but with immigration of Walsers (from the Valais) in the fourteenth to sixteenth century it became German-speaking. To its north lies the Rätikon massif which separates the Prättigau from the Austrian Vorarlberg province. In fact the Prättigau itself was, nominally at least, an Austrian district until 1649.

The first village in the Lower Prättigau is attractive **Grüsch**, with several fine patrician mansions in one of which, the seventeenth-century Rose Garden House, is a worthwhile district museum. A few kilometres on lies **Schiers**, the principal village of Lower Prättigau.

Road No 28 goes on climbing steeply past Saas, standing on its attractive

Angling by the lake at St Moritz

terrace over the river, and finally at 1,206m (3,957ft) above sea level reaches **Klosters**, 32km (20 miles) from Landquart. This world famous resort derives its name from a former Premonstratensian monastery, founded in 1215. There is a local museum in a fine sixteenth-century residence. It is long-established for its winter sports, some enthusiasts preferring it to Davos as it is smaller and more intimate. It has a fine setting, in the shelter of the Parsenn ski-fields to which its ski-lifts ascend, and has views of the Silvretta range (3,124m, 10,250ft) on the frontier with Austria.

Immediately on leaving the village the road climbs steeply south to the Wolfgang Pass (1,631m, 5,351ft), watershed between the Landquart and the Landwasser Valleys. Just beyond the wooded pass summit lies the Davoser See and behind it opens out the broad high valley. Davos Dorf (1,558m, 5,112ft) and Davos Platz, once separate villages, now merge to form **Davos**. The community of just over 10,000 inhabitants is an all-seasons resort, which first became world-known as a climatic centre, site of Europe's most important sanatorium for tuberculosis (inspiration for Thomas Mann's great novel *The Magic Mountain*) but is now one of the country's leading resorts catering for foreign tourists of all nations with more than 100 hotels, enough aerial cableways and lifts to convey about 35,000 people an hour and international conference facilities. However, it also has a *Heimatmuseum* dedicated to the Davos of earlier days in the old Prebendary House. Davos's 'local mountain' (most Swiss cities claim one) is the Weissfluhjoch (2,693m, 8,836ft) served by a funicular (Timetable 1865), and in winter is the starting point for the legendary Parsenn Ski Run.

From Davos there is no need to return to Chur by the same route. A round trip is possible by the road leading south-west down the Landwasser Valley to Tiefencastel (31km, 19 miles), and then via Lenzerheide to Chur in 28km (17 miles) by road No 3.

The Engadine

The little village of Susch lies in the Engadine, the principal tourist region of Graubünden canton. The Engadine, valley of the River En or Inn, extends for about 100km (62 miles) from the Maloja Pass to the Austrian border. Driving from Susch to Zernez and then continuing straight ahead on road No 27 one soon climbs into the Upper Engadine. This does not resemble the ravine-like form of most Alpine valleys, it more resembles a long, level trough-shaped plateau, in places over a kilometre wide, bounded by mountains and beautiful glaciers. The valley floor itself is 1,500 to 1,800m above sea level and has a very individual inner-Alpine situation that keeps it sunny, remarkably free from rain and, with its dry air, retentive of snow. As the valley is nearly level, lakes have formed to enhance the landscape. The language — outside of major towns — is Romansch.

Zernez to St Moritz

Road No 27 runs south-west, for some 16km (10 miles) to reach **Zuoz**, the one-time capital of the Upper Engadine, very attractive with its characteristic yet individual buildings. Very typical too is its spacious village square with fountain and flowers. Some of the houses have portions of medieval residential keeps incorporated in their building. Four kilometres (2 miles) further is La Punt, where the road from the Albula Pass enters the valley. **Samedan** is reached after 7km (4½ miles), the modern principal village of the Upper Engadine, with a population of 2,500. Many attractive Engadine houses catch the eye. There is the Planta House, bearing the name of a very influential Engadine family whose emblem, a bear, recurs in decorative forms in the valley. The Planta House contains a Romansch Culture Centre with a large library. A prominent viewpoint over the village is occupied by the late Gothic church of St Peter.

Celerina lies 5km (3 miles) on, falling rather into the 'dependence' area of St Moritz which is only 3km (2 miles) away and shares the same skiing area. In the old nucleus of the village, by the river, are some nice Engadine houses.

St Moritz, another twin town (St Moritz-Dorf and St Moritz-Bad) is probably the best-known of all the Swiss cosmopolitan and fashionable mountain centres. Little remains of the original village that has been smothered by hotels, winter sports facilities and summer tourism. The spa quarter, St Moritz-Bad, on the Inn Valley floor, reminds one that the curative waters from the springs have been used for centuries and were visited by the medical writer Paracelsus in the sixteenth century.

From St Moritz-Dorf, near the School Square, a funicular conveys you to Corviglia (2,496m, 8,189ft); from there an aerial cablecar lifts you to Piz Nair (3,030m, 9,941ft) where from the terrace there is a splendid view over the Upper Engadine and its lakes.

Chur to St Moritz by 'Glacier Express'

From Chur the train route follows the Rhine upstream to **Reichenau-Tamins** (see above). Here the 'Glacier Express' crosses the Hinterrhein and turns off south along its west bank through the fertile **Domleschg**, a once strategically important area, richly endowed with castles. With its favourable climate, and with valley slopes only moderately steep, maize and walnut trees do well here.

The valley gradually narrows as the train runs south until at Thusis the rock walls of the mountains apparently threaten any further advance. Then a giant-size gorge appears to the right, the notorious **Via Mala** with near perpendicular rock faces to a height of 305m (1,000ft), out of which flows the Hinterrhein. To the left from a second ravine flows its tributary river, the Albula. The railway enters this gorge by curving round to bridge the Hinterrhein and then bores through a series of tunnels, climbing all the while, to pass along the cliff face above the river swirling down below on the left. At **Solis**, halfway along the gorge, the train emerges into a somewhat wider part, but still high above the river. Then suddenly the line swings over from one side of the gorge to the other running at first along the edge of the precipitous rock wall but later along pastoral slopes

The village of Bergün *Opposite: Tiefencastel*

that look down upon the village of **Tiefencastel** with its typically Italian-style white church belfry.

An even more dramatic experience awaits just beyond Alvaneu station at the point where yet another stream, the River Landwasser, joins the Albula. The train travels into the Landwasser Valley high up on the slope that gradually develops into the rock face of another narrowing gorge. Suddenly the train swings out from the cliff face on to a curving viaduct high above the stream and heads straight into a tunnel mouth that gapes on the opposing rock face. Emerging from the tunnel shortly after at **Filisur** the line has been joined by the branch line from Davos. A series of spiral tunnels lift the line, inside the mountainside, sufficiently high to clear a great step in the valley floor and move into the typical high pastoral bowl, girt with woodlands and **Bergün**, a village of 400 inhabitants. Bergün is a popular little resort with good opportunities for excursions and summer and winter sporting activities. It has a typically Engadine village bell-tower (1200).

But as the journey proceeds the high pastoral bowl is also transformed into a further gorge-like landscape. And after Bergün comes the most

Hotel Julier

spectacular section of the line, when in a stretch of 12½km (8 miles) it climbs to reach the summit tunnel. How it achieves this with many turns, loops, two galleries, seven viaducts and four spiral tunnels can be traced out by road travellers looking down over the valley from the Albula Pass summit.

The descent from the summit tunnel is rather an anti-climax but gives beautiful views over the Upper Engadine on the way down to Bever where the line enters the valley, only 10km (6 miles) east of St Moritz.

Note: The route of this rail journey can also be taken substantially by road, and although the route will be longer, more demanding of the driver, and certainly not so fast as the more direct Julier Pass route from Chur to St Moritz, it will also be less busy. The road route via the Albula Pass finally enters the Engadine further east at La Punt.

6.2 From St Moritz through the Val Bregaglia

Nowhere is the contrast in landscape more pronounced than in the transition from the Upper Engadine to its apparent continuation west, the Bregaglia Valley (Bergell in Swiss-German). On one side the wide valley trough and the table-land with lakes, on the other a deeply cut, narrow ravine; on this side larch woods, on the other chestnut trees. The difference is not just geographical, it is also cultural, for, Waldensians apart, the people of Bregaglia are the only Italian-speaking people of Protestant faith. The Bregaglia lies almost entirely in Switzerland yet its inhabitants are largely of Italian stock speaking a Lombard dialect with some Romansch. Drained by the River Mera, which runs into Lake Como, its landscape is picturesque with chestnut trees at low level, meadows and coniferous forests on the heights, surrounded by lofty mountains with short glaciers.

The 20km (12 mile) stretch of road from St Moritz to the Maloja Pass is a scenic treat: a harmonious blend of lakes and mountains. Road No 27 leaves St Moritz along the foot of the valley slopes, soon skirting on the left the Champferer See and Silvaplaner See. It arrives after 10km (6 miles) at **Silvaplana**, the well-known resort sited on the peninsula separating the two lakes just at the point where the road coming down south-east from the Julier Pass joins road No 27. (On the left, facing Silvaplana across the lake causeway, is the village of Surlej with the valley station of the Corvatsch cablecar line which serves the north-east slope of Piz Corvatsch (Timetable 1965.) From Corvatsch upper station (3,303m, 10,837ft) there are magnificent panoramas of the neighbouring snowfields (which provide summer skiing) and the Bernina range further south-east, as well as the Upper Engadine Valley.

In 4km (2½ miles) the road reaches the twin quiet resorts of **Sils-Baselgia** and **Sils-Maria** (where last century the great philosopher Nietzsche was a frequent visitor) and for 7km (4 miles) skirts the Silser See before reaching the village of **Maloja** and shortly thereafter Maloja Pass.

The infant River Inn flows into the Silser See from the wooded north-west slopes of the valley, having descended from a mountain tarn on the east side of Piz Lunghin.

From the Engadine side the **Maloja Pass** is hardly perceptible, the gradient is so minimal. The other side is a very different story. The Mera torrent has gouged a formidably deep ravine. To look at it at leisure one can take a 15-minute walk from the little resort of Maloja to the Castello del Belvedere which sits on the very brink of a precipice over-hanging the ravine which is the southern aspect of the pass. From here is an awe-inspiring view down over the Bregaglia Valley and the road from it which climbs up in such tortuous twists and turns to ascend the formidable rock.

From Maloja village begins the track which is part of the remaining traces of the Septimer Pass road built in the fourteenth century. It is thought to have been one of the first Alpine pass roads to take vehicles. It is now only a minor mule track but in the medieval period was much used as, in combination with the Muretto Pass to the south, it linked Chur with the Valtellina region (now Italian) which was then subject to the dominion of Chur.

The descent of a pass such as the Maloja is somewhat more alarming than an ascent — when your eyes are glued to the steep road facing you! But it does give a better chance to appreciate what problems the road builders had to contend with. One can see how the road starts to climb up in the valley of the Orlegna torrent down below but, meeting the obstacle of a cliff-like step in the valley floor, it has to climb this in a sequence of thirteen steep hairpin bends cut into the face.

Having zigzagged down this precipitous step in the valley floor, a more normal rate of descent leads in 5km (3 miles) to **Casaccia**, passing en route (on the right) the picturesque ruins of a pilgrimage church which was destroyed in the troubled early eighteenth century. In those 5km (3 miles) the altitude of the road above sea level has fallen by 355m (1,165ft)! Casaccia is situated below the ruins of the castle of Turatsch and at the mouth of the Marozzo Valley from which the River Mera flows. From Casaccia too is a mule track road which makes a zigzag ascent through the woods into the Marozzo Valley and ultimately reaches the ancient Septimer Pass (2,310m, 7,579ft) to Bivio (village on the better-known modern Julier Pass road from the Engadine to the north). The Septimer Pass was used by the Romans and still shows traces of paved road in places.

Then comes a series of descending bends on to level, green pastureland through which runs a straight stretch of road. On the descent there is a clear view of the impressive high dam wall of the Lago da l'Albigna in its lofty site on the southern valley slope; it is a reservoir supplying a large hydro-electric power station.

Next is **Vicosoprano**, main village of the valley, holiday and excursions centre, with a fine sixteenth-century Town Hall and patrician houses of the same period. Then follows another straight stretch of road with impressive

Andeer, south of Chur

Opposite: Zillis, south of Cur

views of Piz Badile (3,308m, 10,854ft) and Sciora (3,238m, 10,624ft) to the south and Piz Duan (3,131m, 10,273ft) towering on the right.

Soon **Stampa** village comes into sight, a holiday resort that enjoys stupendous panoramic views of the jagged peaks to the south. The village warrants a stop to visit its Ciasa Granda, the Big House. In this four-storeyed former patrician mansion of 1581 is a very informative museum devoted to the Bregaglia way of life.

After Stampa the road drops down from the fairly level pastureland and passes through coniferous woodlands. Then, very shortly before reaching **Promontogno** village the road enters a narrow defile between the river and a towering rocky crag. This is known as the Porta ('gateway') and marks the boundary between the Upper Bregaglia Valley and the Lower. On the crag stands a picturesque group of buildings, the ruins of the medieval tower of Castelmur whose predecessor was a Roman post (excavations have revealed remains of bathhouses and living quarters). Slightly below the tower stands the mother church of the region, the Chiesa di Nossa Donna, Church of Our Lady, abandoned in the mid-sixteenth century and restored in the mid-nineteenth.

After passing through the hamlet of Promontogno in its sheltered site at the mouth of the Val Bondasca, the main valley road shortly crosses to the north (ie right) bank of the River Mera. Very soon after a side road goes off to the right which makes a worthwhile detour. It leads after 3½km (2 miles) of climbing bends to **Soglio**, nearly 300m (984ft) higher, a particularly picturesque village situated on a level terrace amid fir and larch woodlands with a spectacular panorama back over the main valley to the granite peaks in the Bondasca Valley away to the south. Rising above the compact outlines of the tightly grouped houses in Soglio are a number of distinguished mansions of the sixteenth and seventeenth century, built by members of the powerful Salis family. One of these mansions, the Palazzo Salis, is now a hotel.

Twenty-two kilometres (13½ miles) from the Maloja Pass the road reaches the village of **Castasegna** at the far end of which is the frontier and customs post. Running along the valley floor, now among chestnut groves and vineyards, the road shortly enters the first Italian village, Villa di Chiavenna.

Note: those who do not wish to return by the same road from Castasegna to St Moritz or continue on to Lugano via Lake Como have another option giving a round trip largely in Graubünden. Continue to Villa di Chiavenna (7½ km, 4½ miles) in Italy and there turn off right, to the north, up the Valle San Giacomo for 39km (24 miles) to join the Swiss N13 motorway at Splügen, having passed the Italian-Swiss frontier at the Splügen Pass (2,133m, 6,998ft). From Splügen one can travel by N13 motorway down the Hinterrhein Valley to Thusis and Chur — or, taking the opposite direction, up that valley to the San Bernardino tunnel through to Bellinzona — which is in fact a part of the route to be described in the following section

.Public Transport Option

Maloja to Castasegna is classed as a mountain post road. There is a Postbus service (Timetable 940.80) between St Moritz and Castasegna Post Office. The frequency varies according to season (information available from ☎ 082/3 30 72). From the end of May to mid-October there is also a daily express Postbus service from St Moritz via Maloja, Chiavenna and Italian Lake Como through to Lugano and Ascona. There is even a winter service as far as Lugano. (Timetable 940.75 and 633.80). Further Information is available from St Moritz, ☎ 082/3 30 72 or Lugano, 091/21 95 20). For a connection to Soglio there is a mountain Postbus service from Promontogno (which lies on the main road bus route St Moritz-Castasegna) (Timetable 940.82).

6.3 From St Moritz via Tiefencastel and Thusis to the Misox

From Silvaplana via the Julier Pass to Tiefencastel

Busy road No 3 is the first section of the usual route from St Moritz to the cantonal capital of Graubünden, Chur, and is usually kept open all year round. It climbs steeply from Silvaplana in zigzags giving grand views to the south over the Bernina range and over the Engadine lakes. It first reaches the Julier Mountain Refuge Hut and then the Julier Pass (Passo del Giulio) (2,284m, 7,494ft) in its splendid Alpine setting between Piz Lagrev to the south and Piz Julier to the north. The pass was used in Roman times and there are still traces of its paving and the stumps of two Roman columns stand by the roadside. The zigzag descent on the far side of the pass leads through a rather austere valley to **Bivio** (1,769m, 5,804ft) the village once a staging post at the fork where the Septimer Pass track goes off to Casaccia in the Val Bregaglia.

From Bivio the road descends the valley, passes the artificial lake of Marmorera and continues to descend in steps the Oberhalbstein Valley past Tinizong with its baroque church of St Blasius, to the main town of the valley, **Savognin** (at 1,210m, 3,970ft). Savognin shows many features of a typical modern winter sports centre, although the older parts of the town include no less than three seventeenth-century churches worth visiting. A seasonal exhibition marks the town's association with the favourite Swiss nineteenth-century painter of Lombardy and Graubünden, Giovanni Segantini. After passing some small villages there is a rapid descent to **Tiefencastel** (851m, 2,792ft) in its key position at the junction of the Albula and Giulia streams and the corresponding pass roads. Its landmark is its handsome white baroque church of 1652 which crowns the craggy spur above the river junction.

Note: This is the point at which those travellers who have followed this excursion as part of a return homeward will probably wish to continue

The post-bus halts in San Bernardino village after passing through the tunnel

their journey direct to Chur via Lenzerheide on road No 3 and on to Zürich or some other destination further north.

Public Transport Option

The route from St Moritz to Chur via the Julier Pass and Lenzerheide is covered by a good Postbus service (Timetable 900.85). The railway follows a different route (Timetable 940) via the Albula tunnel and the Schin Gorge that is more spectacular, and has been described (in reverse direction) in a previous section. For the continuation of the excursion — as described below — via Thusis, Splügen and San Bernardino to Bellinzona, there is a Postbus service (Timetable 900.80) from Chur to Bellinzona which follows this route but it does not pass through Tiefencastel. Would-be passengers should reserve seats on it and join it either from Chur or from Thusis.

Tiefencastel to Bellinzona

Motorists interested in continuing this excursion from St Moritz by private car to the Ticino will turn east from Tiefencastel. Crossing to the north side of the Albula, turn left into the Alvaschein road. On a knoll near the entrance to the gorge of the Albula is a unique church, marked out by its bell-tower. The little church of St Peter in **Mistail** is the only unspoiled surviving example of a Carolingian single-aisle church with three late eighth-century apses; the tower dates from about 1400.

From this point the road has to negotiate the spectacularly wild but undoubtedly picturesque **Schinschlucht** (**Schin Gorge**) of the River Albula. This it does by a series of tunnels into the cliff-like south-face of the gorge; there is a particularly spectacular — if brief — view to be had half-way up the gorge where the road has to bridge a lateral tributary stream, the Mutten.

Clear of the gorge, the road gives a glimpse, to the north, of the castle of Baldstein below, bypasses Sils-im-Domleschg, and east of the small market village of Thusis joins the N13 motorway coming south from Chur along the Hinterrhein Valley.

Heading south through the tunnel and up the east bank of the Hinterrhein through an area of land reclaimed from the river-flats, the motorway now enters the Via Mala, another notorious gorge of limestone cliffs, 500m (1,640ft) high. From this it emerges into the open Schons valley lying between Piz Beverin (2,998m, 9,836ft) to the west and Piz Curver (2,972m, 9,751ft) to the east. Halfway along the Schons Valley lies the village of **Zillis** which justifies making an exit from the motorway. It has a remarkable Protestant church of St Martin which possesses the rarest wholly-painted twelfth-century ceiling, in the form of 153 painted panels attached to the roof beams. Nearby in the village is an ethnographic museum in a sixteenth-century peasant house, exhibiting tools, textiles, furniture, agricultural equipment etc.

Five kilometres (3 miles) from Zillis is **Andeer**, the main village of the district, nowadays a climatic resort. Here the motorway can be rejoined. Soon one arrives at Roffla ravine with its Rhine cataract, better seen from the old road. The N13, shortly after passing through a tunnel, has an exit road at Avers that climbs into the particularly enchanting high valley of the tributary torrent Averserrhein. This little-frequented road climbs into the high massif firstly in a southerly direction through a Romansch-speaking valley, the Val Ferrera. Then, after skirting a salient of Italian territory (there is a joint Italian-Swiss hydroelectric dam to the right) it swings south-east through the German-speaking Averstal. It ends its 27km (17 mile) course at the glacier-girt village of Juf, deemed to be the highest agricultural hamlet in Europe that is occupied all year round, at 2,133m (6,998ft).

The main road swings south-west to enter the Rheinwald Valley, skirts a small reservoir and reaches the village of **Splügen**. Here the left-hand fork is for the Splügen Pass road leading south to Chiavenna in Italy (referred to at the end of the previous section dealing with the Val Bregaglia route). The N13 motorway however here continues west, giving a distant view of the Rheinwaldhorn on the Graubünden-Ticino border. Eleven kilometres (7 miles) from Splügen the N13 enters the **San Bernardino tunnel** (6 ½ km, 4 miles long; opened 1967) which pierces the massif below the historic pass of the same name. The pass honours the name of the fourteenth-/fifteenth-century preacher; in former times it was called the Passo Uccello or Vogelberg Pass, ie, the Bird Pass, after the name of a nearby mountain, Piz Uccello). Since the tunnel was completed the Chur-Bernardino motorway has been considered the fastest route from South Germany to North Italy.)

Both motorway and old road have access to the village of **San Bernardino**, lying as it does beyond the tunnel. From this point onward the sweeping curves and viaducts of the motorway offer better views than the old road, including a fine view to the left of the hill-top Castello di Misox (or Mesocco) which gives its name to this valley, Val Mesolcina. At about this point, too, the change of climate and vegetation from an Alpine to a southern character becomes apparent with the appearance of vines and mulberries. **Mesocco**, the principal village of the Val Mesolcina, is well worth a visit, although in general appearance has suffered from the motorway constructions. The now-ruined Castello, referred to above, on its commanding crag above the River Moesa, was a medieval fortified place of refuge for the local population, extended in the twelfth century by the Counts Sax, the local magnates, and is an impressive reminder of this valley's history. The castle's outer works also take in, at the bottom of the crag, the twelfth-century church of Santa Maria al Castello which, with its well-preserved fifteenth-century interior paintings, ranks among the most precious art treasures of Graubünden. The Val Mesolcina, in which the local language is Italian and the religion Catholic, nonetheless still belongs to Graubünden.

In the valley there are some attractive waterfalls. There is a good view soon, on the right, of a particularly fine one, the Buffalora Cascade. With every passing kilometre the outlines of the villages, their Romanesque bell-towers and their other stonework are more and more evocative of the Ticino, the cantonal boundary of which is crossed shortly before the site of the Battle of Arbedo (see Chapter 5). At the next crossroads the left-hand turn leads into the suburbs of Bellinzona; the right-hand bends back north to the Gotthard; while the road straight ahead leads shortly to the N2 motorway for Lugano.

Additional Information

Places to Visit

Chur
Dommuseum Kathedral (Cathedral Museum of church treasures)
Hof 19, CH-7000 Chur
☎ 081/22 23 12
Open: Monday to Friday 10am-12noon by arrangement with Sacristan, Hof 2 ☎ 081/22 92 50.

Rätisches Museum
(History Museum of the Canton)
Hofstrasse 1/Museumplatz
CH-7000 Chur
☎ 081/22 82 77
Open: Tuesday to Sunday 10am-12noon, 2-5pm. Closed Monday.

Bündner Kunstmuseum
(Cantonal Fine Arts Museum)
Postplatz, CH-7000 Chur
☎ 081/22 17 63
Open: Tuesday to Sunday 10am-12noon, 2-5pm (Thursday continues 10am-8.30pm). Closed Monday.

Bündner Natur-Museum
(Cantonal Museum of Natural History)
Masanserstrasse 31
☎ 081/22 15 58
Open: Tuesday to Sunday 10am-12noon, 2-5pm. Closed Monday.

Kutschensammlung Hotel Stern (Coach Museum)
Reichsgasse 11
☎ 081/22 35 55
Open: daily 9am-12noon, 1.30-5pm or by arrangement.

Davos
Bergbaumuseum
(History of Mining Museum)
Schmelzboden
CH-7270 Davos-Monstein
☎ 083/3 57 12
Open: only mid-June to mid-October, Wednesday 2-4pm and Saturday 4-6pm.

Disentis
Culture-historical exhibition at Benedictine abbey (recently reconstructed)
☎ 086/7 51 45

Grüsch
Heimatmuseum Prättigau
Haus Rosengarten, Grüsch
☎ 081/52 12 30
Open: Saturday and Sunday 2-4pm, Wednesday 8-10pm; groups by arrangement.

Klosters
Nutli Hüschi (old Walliser house)
Monbielerstrasse
CH-7250 Klosters
Conservator's 083/4 21 53
Open: July to mid-October Wednesday and Friday 4-6pm (July-August also Saturday 4-6pm) mid-January to mid-April only Friday 4-6pm.

Müstair
Klostermuseum (Benedictine Convent of St John; museum)
Benediktinerinnen-Kloster St Johann, CH-7531 Müstair
☎ 082/8 52 65
Open: Monday to Saturday 9-11am, 2-5pm; Sunday 10.30-11am, 3-5pm.

St Moritz
Engadine Museum
Via dal Bagn, CH-7500
St Moritz
☎ 082/3 43 33
Open: June-October Monday to Friday 9.30am-12noon, 2-5pm; Sunday 10am-12noon; Saturday closed: December to April, Monday to Friday 10am-12noon, 2-5pm; Sunday 10am-12noon; closed Saturday.

Samedan
Chesa Planta
CH-7503 Samedan
Romansch cultural centre and library. Library open: July-August, Monday to Friday 10am-12noon, 2-4pm; Guided visits to collections Monday/Wednesday/Thursday at 4.30pm.

Savognin
Oberhalbstein Regional Folk Museum
CH-7451 Savognin
Conservator's ☎ 081/74 18 61
Open: July-August and Christmas-Easter Sunday and Tuesday 7.30-9pm, Thursday 2-4pm.

Stampa
Ciasa Granda
(Val Bregaglia Museum)
Stampa
Conservator's ☎ 082/4 12 92
Open: June to mid-October, 2-5pm daily.

Trun
Cuort Ligia Grischa (Sursilvan Museum of the Grey League)
CH-7166 Trun
Conservator's ☎ 086/8 11 26
Open: April to November daily 10am-12noon, 2-5pm. Closed Sunday morning.

Zernez
Nationalparkhaus (Information/Exhibition Centre, National Park)
CH-7530 Zernez
Conservator's ☎ 082/8 13 78
Open: June to mid-October daily 9am-12noon, 2-6.30pm; Sunday closed except from approx 5 July to 9 August.

Zillis
Schams Valley Museum
(beside famous church)
Zillis
Custodian's ☎ 081/61 14 19
Open: July/August daily 10am-12noon, 2-5pm; September only on Sunday. (In immediate vicinity is St Martin's church, with oldest timber ceiling wholly covered with panel paintings in Western Europe.)

Sport and Recreation

Outdoor activities and sports are extremely popular in Graubünden; facilities are abundant, even in quite small communities. Local tourist offices invariably can supply information, usually in leaflet form, on tennis, swimming, golf, outdoor and indoor sport centres, and the popular 'Fitness Parcours' tracks for jogging as well as the recommended cycle tracks that now exist widely.
River Rafting especially in broken water is a popular sport and facilities are good on Graubünden rivers such as the Rhine branches and the Inn. See local tourist offices for details.
Guided Hiking Excursions are regularly organised in June/July-September by local tourist offices in Arosa, Bergün, Celerina, Chur, Davos, Disentis, Klosters, Portresina, St Moritz, Samedan, Savognin, Silvaplana, Zernez, Zuoz (addresses listed below).

Tourist Information Offices

Cantonal
Verkehrsverein für Graubünden
Alexanderstrasse 24
CH-7001 Chur
☎ 081/302 61 00

Engadine Region
Oberengadiner Verkehrsverein
CH-7504 Pontresina
☎ 082/6 65 73

Local

Arosa
Kurverein
CH-7050 Arosa
☎ 081/31 16 21

Bergün
Verkehrsbüro
CH-7482 Bergün
☎ 081/73 11 52

Celerina
Verkehrsbüro
CH-7505 Celerina
☎ 082/3 39 66

Chur
Verkehrsverein
Ottostrasse 6
CH-7000 Chur
☎ 081/22 18 18

Davos
Verkehrsverein
CH-7270 Davos
☎ 081/45 21 21

Disentis/Mustér
Verkehrsbüro
CH-7180 Disentis
☎ 081/947 58 22

Klosters
Verkehrsbüro
CH-7250 Klosters
☎ 081/69 18 77

Müstair
Verkehrsverein Val Müstair
CH-7537 Val Müstair
☎ 082/8 55 66

Pontresina
Kur u. Verkehrsverein
CH-7504 Pontresina
☎ 082/6 64 88

St Moritz
Kur- und Verkehrsverein
CH-7500 St Moritz
☎ 082/3 31 47

Samedan
Verkehrsbüro
CH-7503 Samedan
☎ 082/6 54 32

Silvaplana
Verkehrsverein
CH-7513 Silvaplana
☎ 082/4 81 51

Zernez
Verkehrsbüro
CH-7530 Zernez
☎ 082/8 13 00

Zuoz
Verkehrsbüro
CH-7524 Zuoz
☎ 082/7 15 10

7

Geneva, Lausanne and the Lake Geneva Region

7.1 Geneva

The Swiss call their largest lake Lac Léman; English-speakers call it Lake Geneva — often to the affront of citizens of the largest canton on the lake's shores, the canton of Vaud whose principal city of Lausanne is sited fairly centrally on the north shore.

Geneva itself lies at the extreme south-west horn of this crescent-shaped lake. It occupies a site typical of several Swiss historic settlements which developed into cities of power and influence, namely, at the first bridgable section of the outflow of an important river from a great lake — Zürich and Luzern are other notable examples. Modern Geneva lies on both banks of the River Rhône and fronts onto the lake basin. The small canton of Geneva is surrounded by French territory except for a narrow lakeside corridor which links it with the Vaud, its large neighbour to the west.

So situated, Geneva is a principal gateway into Switzerland for visitors from the west and indeed from the whole world. The city's main railway station, the Gare de Cornavin, has many international express connections. Geneva's international airport is served by forty-eight regular and ninety-nine charter companies linking it with fifty-four countries. Recently its airport railway station has been providing a direct train link with the city and the rest of Switzerland every ten minutes, with many through services to major cities such as Zürich, St Gallen, Basel, Luzern, Lugano.

Archaeologists date occupation of the Geneva area back to about 3000BC. The hill on which the 'Old Town' of Geneva was later to grow was first stockaded as the fortified hill town of a Celtic tribe, the Allobroges. When they were subjected by the Romans in the second century BC, their hill town became a Roman stronghold and in the mid-first century BC was actually defended by the great Gaius Julius Caesar against attack by the Helvetii tribe (who were ironically later destined to give their name to the Roman province corresponding to modern Switzerland — *Helvetia* — the name which nowadays appears on Swiss postage stamps).

By the end of the fourth century Geneva had become a Christian episcopal seat. This status stood it in good stead by providing a measure of independence under its bishops during many turbulent centuries. With the Reformation, Geneva took the political status of a republic. Under the guiding — and, indeed, often dictatorial — spirit of John Calvin, who had settled there, Geneva earned the title 'Rome of the Protestants'. The city also became a sanctuary for Protestants fleeing persecution in other lands, notably France and Italy. And, as not infrequently happens, the host city's economy and influence gained strength from the knowledge, skills and crafts brought to it by talented refugees. What was to be the Duke of Savoy's final attempt to storm the city's walls in a night attack in 1602 failed — and is to this day commemorated annually in the city's December weekend Fête of the Escalade.

In the eighteenth century Geneva, home of Rousseau among other prominent thinkers, was a considerable intellectual centre. When the French Revolution came here it was welcomed and indeed echoed. The city became capital of a French *département*. But, like other Swiss regions, it found that French *liberté* apparently involved a highly centralised and authoritarian form of government; at the end of the Napoleonic Wars Geneva applied to become a member of the Swiss Confederation, becoming the twenty-second canton in 1815.

Each Swiss city has an atmosphere very much its own. It could be said that Geneva just missed being a French city rather than a Swiss one. Much more obviously it has the atmosphere of an international city. Its own history as a notable political sanctuary combined with the international recognition of the neutrality of the Swiss Confederation have led to the city's role as the home of a long list of international agencies and organisations. Today a visitor may be forgiven if he finds that this cosmopolitanism prevails over either the French or the Swiss inheritance. Both in city proper and in the canton, statistics show that fully one-third of the population consists of foreigners. Because of the expansion of function as well as of population there has been much modern building in and around the city.

Yet it also serves an unofficial but real Swiss role too. Geneva's own canton is small, indeed tiny, but the city *de facto*, if unofficially has become the economic as well as the intellectual and cultural centre of Suisse Romande, the French-speaking west of Switzerland. Its cultural as well as its shopping facilities reflect this.

First-time visitors, perhaps a little overwhelmed by some of the grey modernity of parts of the city, should, as soon as possible, find their way to the historic heart, the Vieille Cité on the hill.

A Walk through the Heart of the Old Town

To reach the Old Town from the **Gare de Cornavin** (main railway station) on foot the most direct and instructive route is to follow the Rue du Mont Blanc straight ahead. It leads past Post Office buildings and the English

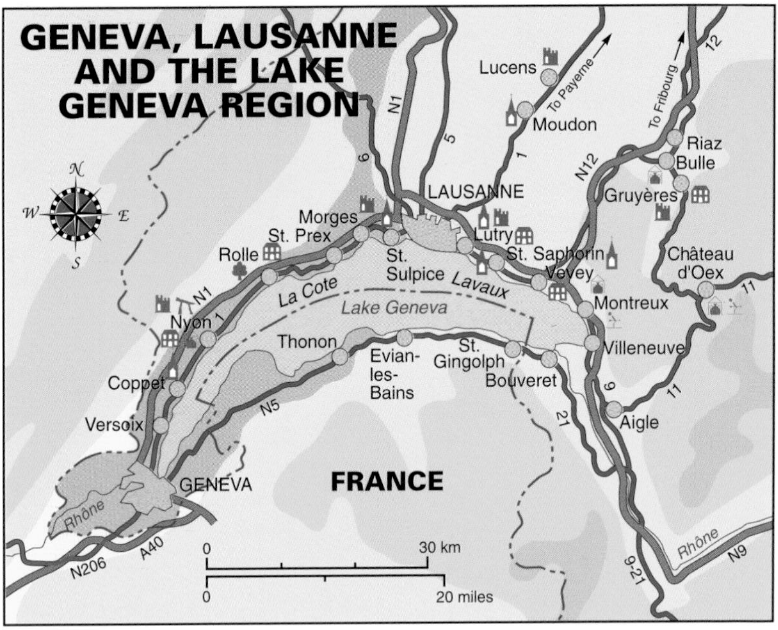

GENEVA, LAUSANNE AND THE LAKE GENEVA REGION

church to the city's principal traffic artery, the Pont du Mont Blanc, outermost of the eight bridges which span the River Rhône as it leaves the lake. The bridge provides visitors with a good orientation point for the city, offering views left and right of the lakeside and riverside quays. From its right-hand pavement one can view the **Ile Rousseau**, the tree-decked islet with the statue of the seated philosopher (to which access can be gained by a footbridge from the neighbouring bridge downstream, the Pont des Bergues). From the left side of the Pont du Mont Blanc one has a fine clear view of the city's notable landmark, the **Jet d'Eau** water fountain which, shooting to a height of 145m (476ft), can in favourable circumstances be seen even from passenger aircraft.

At the southern end of the bridge, on the left is the lakeside promenade with the English Garden behind. Turning right, however, on to the Quai Général Guisan, pass the south ends of the Pont de la Machine bridge and thereafter of the twin Ponts de l'Ile which span an island on which stands the thirteenth-century **Tour de l'Ile**, a surviving tower from the medieval city fortifications. The Tourist Office is adjacent, also on the twin bridge.

On the south bank opposite the island and twin bridges is the Place Bel-Air, a square which you cross to ascend the Rue de la Cité and, beyond the colourful Place du Grand Mézel with its flower-decorated fountain, its continuation as the well-conserved Grand' Rue of the Old Town. In this and the neighbouring streets and alleys are charming antique shops, bookshops, handsome eighteenth-century mansions and changes of level that provide great variety of interest within a small area. No 40 Grand' Rue

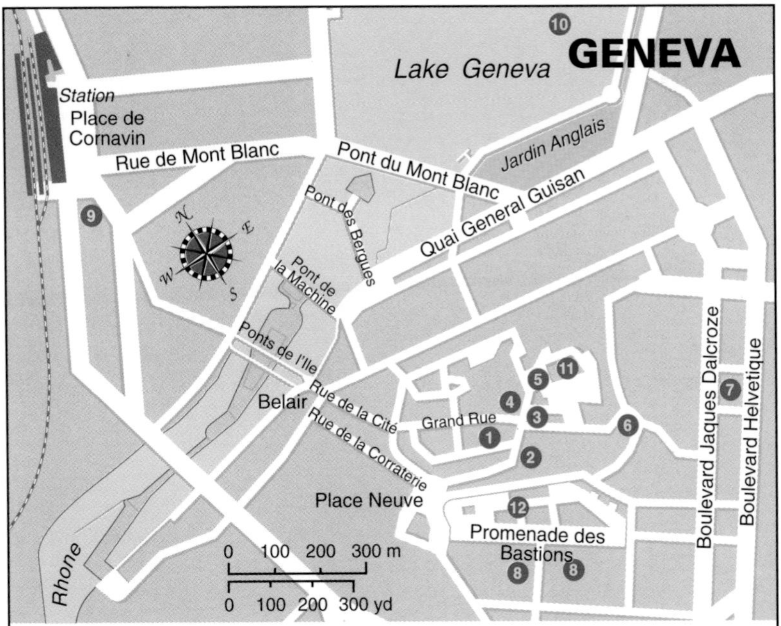

GENEVA

1 St Germain Church
2 Hôtel de Ville
3 Old Arsenal
4 Maison Tavel
5 Courtyard St Pierre
6 Place du Bourg-de-Four
7 Museum of Art And History
8 University & Library
9 Nôtre-Dame Church
10 Jet d'Eau Fountain
11 Cathédrale St Pierre
12 Monument de la Réformation

is Rousseau's birthplace. Halfway up the street is an alley through to the **Eglise St Germain**, in origin a fourth-century basilica, rebuilt and extended in the fourteenth century and restored last century.  Resuming on the Grand' Rue, at the next main crossing a turn to the right leads to the **Hôtel de Ville**, the Town Hall dating from the sixteenth and seventeenth  century, now seat of cantonal government. Its fifteenth-century tower, the Tour Baudet, now holds the cantonal archives. The courtyard has a cobbled ramp leading to upper floors where one might expect a staircase. Was this for horsemen? Or for sedan-bearers? The ground floor of the Hall includes the Alabama Room where the initial Geneva Convention of the Red Cross was signed in 1864.

Immediately facing the Hôtel de Ville at the top of the Grand' Rue is the arcaded **Ancien arsenal**, sixteenth-century corn hall, eighteenth-century  arsenal, now official archive. Past the Arsenal, the alley at right-angles to the Grand' Rue is the Rue du Puits-St-Pierre. No 6 is the oldest house in  Geneva, the fourteenth-century **Maison Tavel** with its carved Gothic façade and its corner turret. Just beyond, a right turn leads into the Cour St Pierre, the courtyard which is dominated by the lofty cathedral. In recent times extensive archaeological excavations have been carried out here to uncover ruins and remains of the cathedral's several predecessing sanctuaries, the earliest of which goes back to the late fourth century. Excavated areas are now accessible to visitors.

The **Cathédrale St Pierre** stands on a site that was once occupied by a Roman temple and thereafter by earlier Christian churches, as the adjacent excavations have confirmed. It was built between the mid-twelfth and mid-thirteenth centuries but has undergone alterations and restorations — among which the most surprising is the neo-classical columned portico which in the eighteenth century replaced the west front. The interior accords with the plain style of Calvinist tradition but with austerity it combines impressive dignity and grandeur. Capitals of pillars throughout the nave, choir and aisles have conserved the beautiful artistic quality of their Romanesque and early Gothic workmanship. Look out, too, in the north aisle for the triangular chair which is supposed to be the one used by Calvin.

On the south side of the cathedral is a former church of Nôtre-Dame which was used by the Reformers for preaching and teaching and is known as the Auditoire de Calvin; it is now used by Protestant congregations of other nationalities such as Dutch and Scottish.

On leaving the cathedral it is worthwhile to climb to the south to the Rue de l'Hôtel de Ville and from it to pass round to the quaint **Place du Bourg-de-Four** which may be considered the heart of the Old Town having been the market place in the medieval period (and before that probably the Roman forum). It is particularly picturesque with its fountain and its art and antique shops. From the Place du Bourg turn south to reach the Rue St Leger, passing under the bridge and on reaching (right) the gateway to the Promenade des Bastions enter this Promenade which follows the old fortification line. On the left stand the buildings of the university and library. On the right, however, extends a 100m (328ft) wall, impressive in its austerity, built against one-time ramparts of the fortifications. This was erected in 1917 as a **Monument de la Réformation.** At its centre, larger than life, stand statues of the Reformers most closely associated with this city, the Genevan Reformers Farel, Calvin and Bèze and the Scottish Reformer Knox; the six other statues, left and right of the central figures, include William the Silent of the Netherlands, Oliver Cromwell of England, and Roger Williams of New England, champion of freedom of conscience in the New World. Background reliefs and text illustrate the history of the Reformation.

On leaving the monument, head west from the Promenade to reach the Place Neuve, a square served well by public transport. From Place Neuve it is but a short walk down the Rue de la Corraterie to the Place Bel-Air from which the ascent to the Old Town began.

But before departing from the Old Town you may be interested to visit Geneva's great **Musée d'Art et d'Histoire**. This famed collection is particularly strong in the spheres of archaeology and of painting. It is housed in (and overflowing from) a site to the south-east of the Old Town's hill. It can be easily reached by descending south-east either from the Place du Bourg-de-Four or from the Reformation Monument, to the Boulevard Jacques Dalcroze. The museum occupies a site lying between that boulevard and the parallel Boulevard Helvétique. In the same district, about half a kilometre further east, the **Muséum d'Histoire Naturelle** is to be found and, beside it, a fascinating Musée de l'Horlogerie, a **Watch and Clock Museum**.

Geneva has many other aspects to attract the visitor, not least a stroll or drive along the west bank of the lake (Rive Droite), starting where the Rue du Mont Blanc and the Pont du Mont Blanc meet and are intersected by the Quai du Mont Blanc. A walk in a northerly direction on a clear evening will explain these names by revealing a distant view of the Mont Blanc range (4,807m, 15,772ft) on the south-eastern horizon, the far French-Italian frontier.

Beyond the lake steamer landing stages, the modern casino and the breakwater which shelters the bathing area, the Quai du Mont Blanc continues into the Quai Wilson in which stands the **Palais Wilson**, the home of the headquarters of the League of Nations for 16 years. The Quai Wilson eventually leads into the series of three great lakeside parks which are the pride of Geneva, the parks of **Mon Repos**, **Perle du Lac** and **Villa Barton** with handsome mansions scattered through them and their surroundings. Beyond the last of these there is the Conservatoire et Jardin Botanique, which in 1993 celebrated their 175th anniversary. (The botanical gardens are open to the public every day, while greenhouses are closed on Fridays.) Inland from these stand the extensive buildings of the **Palais des Nations**, built as the post-1936 home of the League of Nations and since World War II serving also as the United Nations' second centre to its main seat in New York.

However, for most visitors, this part of Geneva, which also houses the highly regarded **Musée Ariana** with its impressive collections of porcelain and other ceramics, European and Oriental, and other institutions, can be more conveniently reached by public transport routes from the vicinity of the Gare de Cornavin (bus route line 8 which starts at Cornavin, or line 5 which begins at the Place Neuve near the Old Town and runs by way of Cornavin and Place des Nations to the Palais des Expositions). The Place des Nations, lying immediately south-west of the Palais des Nations, is a helpful destination, being the key traffic intersection of this northern part of Geneva.

To the north-west from the Place des Nations the Avenue de la Paix sweeps round having on its right the Ariana Museum and the extensive extra-territorial parkland area of the Palais des Nations. West of the Avenue at no great distance from the western or rear entrance to the Palais des Nations a prominent site is occupied by the headquarters of the International Committee of the Red Cross and the impressive, instructive and very moving Musee International de la Croix-Rouge, International

Geneva lies on both banks of the River Rhône

Opposite: On Lake Geneva, near the head of the lake

Museum of the Red Cross.

Anyone interested in nuclear energy would be fascinated by a visit to CERN, the European Centre for Nuclear Research where a permanent exhibition is open every day except Sunday. It lies west along the Route de Meyrin and is reached by bus line 15. Guided visits only available on Saturday must be booked at least a week in advance (☎ 767 4052).

Local Excursions

1 *Mont Salève*

Like most Swiss cities, Geneva has its 'neighbourhood' mountain which is the destination of a favourite excursion, the Mont Salève ridge to the south-south-east. It is only a short distance (6km, 4 miles) from city centre to the village of Veyrier on the French frontier. (Visitors who use public transport should note that bus route line 8 runs there from Cornavin via Rive.) At Veyrier there is a French cablecar (passports should be carried) which ascends to an upper station at 1,143m (3,750ft) providing a good panorama of the lake, the city, the Rhône, the Jura heights and the Alps.

2 *Lake Excursions*

These are provided by the Compagnie Générale de Navigation ships and range from 1½ hour local cruises to a 10-11 hour tour of the whole lake — or a crossing to the French lakeside spa resorts of Evian and Thonon with time ashore there (passports).

7.2 Geneva to Lausanne along the North Shore of Lake Geneva

Lake Geneva, the largest of the Alpine lakes, lies in the shape of a huge crescent between the French Savoy Alps to the south and the Jura and Vaud Alps to the north. So its shores and waters are shared in the proportion of 3:2 between Switzerland and France. It is fed by the turbid waters of the Rhône surging down from the Valais. It enters the lake at Bouveret, between the small towns of Villeneuve and St Gingolph, and flows out again at Geneva, some 72km (45 miles) distant. The French shore, backed by the Savoy Alps, is sparsely inhabited except for the spa resorts of Evian-les-Bains and Thonon-les-Bains. The north shore, however, facing the sun and enjoying a mild climate has long been famed for its vineyard slopes and historic wine villages producing white wines to rival those of the Valais. The principal grape grown is the variety known in France as Chasselas, in Germany as Gutedel, in the Valais as Fendant and here on Lake Geneva its name is Dorin.

From Geneva the modern N1 motorway, running at some distance inland from the lake is the most rapid route to Lausanne, but the shore road passes through places of interest to the tourist. Once clear of Geneva's built-up area the road soon reaches (9km, 5½ miles) the pleasant little residential town of **Versoix** — with its charming promenade on the lake, a favoured short excursion from the city — and shortly afterwards crosses the canton boundary of the Vaud. The first substantial little town in the Vaud is **Coppet**, best known perhaps even today because its eighteenth-century *château* was the home of Madame de Stael (daughter of Louis XVI's Minister of Finance) whose salon was the hub of a famed literary and philosophical circle at the turn of the century.

Nine kilometres (5½ miles) on is an interesting and attractive town that deserves a visit. **Nyon**, nowadays a place of some 13,000 inhabitants, having doubled its population in the post-World War II era, was a tribal fortified hill site of the Helvetii in Julius Caesar's day. Romanised, it received from its conquerors the municipal status they awarded to towns settled by veterans. It has an interesting Roman Museum with finds from the area, on the excavated site of a first century basilica. Not far away, further east, on a broad terrace above the lake, is the medieval castle of twelfth-century foundation that was substantially restructured in the sixteenth century as a square building with picturesque towers, for occupation by the bailiffs of the Bernese when by force of arms they took over the town along with the surrounding Vaud. It now houses a museum which includes an important collection of the fine porcelain which was produced in Nyon around the turn of the eighteenth and nineteenth centuries. There are splendid outlooks from the castle terrace over the lake. The Rive lake front area below the castle, lying between road No 1 and the lake, is a delightful parkland of flowers and trees for relaxation, adjacent to a colourful little harbour, with views to France, across the narrow end section of Lake Geneva which is called the Petit Lac. Nyon also has good swimming facilities at a well laid-out beach complex.

From now on until Morges (27km, 17 miles away) the road runs through the classic wine-growing region known simply as La Côte, meaning a shoreline or a hill slope — very apt for this picturesque region of delightful villages and hamlets set among vineyards and orchards. Delightful to drive through, it presents the visitor with the quandary of whether to remain on coastal road No 1 after Nyon or to take the opportunity of moving up the hillside to the corniche road which passes through or past distinguished wine villages such as Luins or Féchy. La Côte is equally enchanting to see from the deck of one of the lake steamers which call at Nyon and the next substantial small town of **Rolle** (12km, 7½ miles on).

Rolle too has its thirteenth-century castle built by the Duke of Savoy on the edge of the lake; today it has an important role in the wine trade and has some handsome traditional vintner's houses among the sixteenth-century buildings of the straggling main street. Ten kilometres (6 miles) further on is **St Prex**, a picturesque old market town with cobbled streets which has preserved its ancient defensive gate tower; it also has very attractive lake front gardens. Five kilometres (3 miles) beyond St Prex the shore road enters **Morges**, a town of around 13,000 inhabitants, an important centre of the wine trade. In the era before railways it was a key port for transport by water; the harbour once used by the Bernese fleet is now used by colourful pleasure craft. It has a Vaud Military Museum in the rather gaunt square castle, founded in the thirteenth century by the Princes of Savoy as a counterpoise to Lausanne's bishops, and after 1536 used as the headquarters of the Bernese bailiffs. Those with a special interest in medieval castles might also be tempted to drive inland for 2½ km (1½ miles) to visit the white brick Château de Vufflens, built for a Savoyard vassal around the turn of the fourteenth and fifteenth centuries. It has a lofty square keep and imposing towers, the whole walled with machicolated ramparts.

The lakeside road carries on after Morges, passing in 4km (2½ miles) **St Sulpice** where there is a church founded in the eleventh century as part of a Cluniac priory (dissolved in the fifteenth century). Substantial parts of the original eleventh-century building, including its three apses, survive in the present, restored building.

From Morges harbour and from St Sulpice shore there are clear views across the lake at about its maximum width of 14km (9 miles) to the imposing mountains of Savoy, and also, looking sharply east, to Lausanne.

The road soon reaches the junction where the choice has to be made of entering Lausanne's centre, which is on the hillside, or of continuing along the lakeshore road into Ouchy, the lakeside port and resort with which it is now effectively merged. In either case Lausanne is reached within 7km from St Sulpice.

Lausanne, capital of the large French-speaking canton of Vaud, is another city of notable antiquity. It too was an important Roman station,

CAISSE D'EPARGNE ET DE CREDIT
fourrures KRISS

Lausanne Cathedral

Opposite: The cantonal capital of Lausanne

commanding routes north into Gaul over the rolling plateau of what modern Swiss call their Mittelland, and also the Great St Bernard Pass route south into Italy. With the collapse of the Roman Empire, in the ensuing troubled period of tribal incursions the settlement was moved from the lakeside to the defensible craggy hill on which the cathedral now stands. The cathedral was the site of earlier church buildings from the end of the sixth century when Bishop Marius moved his see there from pillaged *Aventicum* (modern Avenches). This has remained the centre of the city and is an extraordinary, if picturesque, site for a modern city, two hills with gorges between, nowadays spanned by bridges and viaducts, making Lausanne very much a city of many levels since modern expansion has taken place on a series of terraces that dot the hillside. At lakeside level is the little port and the resort of **Ouchy**, which has inevitably become linked so closely with the cantonal capital further up the hillside that the hyphenated form of the name, Lausanne-Ouchy, has come commonly into use.

Visitors to Lausanne arriving either by railway at the Main CFF Station or by road (whether at the Place de la Gare or at Ouchy's lakeside level) do well to make their first reconnaissance of the city by using the Métro which has a station facing the Main CFF Rail Station across the Place de la Gare.

A Walk through the Heart of Lausanne

As was indicated above the cathedral is the historic heart of the city. To reach it on foot from the Métro's upper station, Gare du Flon, is a good start to a tour of Lausanne. Only a short distance east of the Place Gare du Flon is the **Place St François** which has been described as the hub of the city's traffic. Certainly the main traffic axis in the citadel quarter lies between the Place St François and the Place Bel-Air to its north-west which is marked out by a modern twenty-storey skyscraper block called the Tour Métropole. The two points are separated by a valley, bridged by the busy Grand Pont which provides an impressive outlook, to the north, of the hill crest on which the cathedral stands.

(Those determined to reach the Place St François by foot from the main Railway Station without using the Métro can do so by using the fairly steep Rue du Petit-Chêne). The square takes its name from the church of St François. In origin the church of a Franciscan monastery, it was built in the thirteenth century, rebuilt after a fire in the fourteenth, converted to Protestant use in the sixteenth and underwent nineteenth-century alterations. From the Place St François' north corner the Rue de Bourg leads off east through a pedestrian precinct section into the wider Rue Caroline. From this turn left on to the Pont Bessières which bridges the valley over to the Place de la Cathédrale. The south-facing terrace of the cathedral gives a splendid viewpoint over the city and the lake. The **Cathedral of Nôtre-Dame** is recognised as Switzerland's most magnificent and finest Gothic building. The south entrance, first met by this approach, known sometimes as 'The Apostles' Doorway', sometimes as the 'Painted Portal', is thirteenth century and has fine sculpture work in the original colouring, including figures of apostles and prophets. The main façade has two towers of which one is complete, the other incomplete and the main (west) portal dates from early sixteenth century. The carvings are modern copies while the originals are kept under cover; sixteenth-century murals illustrate the life of the Virgin.

The interior of the building exhibits beautiful proportions and harmony of style, with the tower at the transept crossing marking the point at which the Gothic style took over from the Romanesque of the earlier east end, where there is a rose window of thirteenth-century stained glass. The end of the south aisle gives access to the south tower by a stairway of 232 steps. The view over lake and Alps from the top of the tower justifies the climb!

From the east end of the cathedral the Rue Cité Derrière runs to the left, ie, northwards. It is a picturesque medieval street leading to the **Château St Maire** (named after sixth-century Bishop Marius or Maire), a massive fifteenth-century sandstone and brick building, with four corner towers. It was originally the residence of the Bishops of Lausanne, but after 1536 when the Vaud lands were conquered by the Bernese it became the seat of the Bernese bailiffs for more than two-and-a-half centuries. Today it is the seat of the cantonal government.

Return to the Place de la Cathédrale. A covered flight of steps can be found called the Escalier du Marché which lead down to the Place de la Palud (on the second level of terrace that was developed after the Bourg or citadel quarter). This was the medieval market area and remains a bustling scene of such activity. The **Hôtel de Ville** (Town Hall), with its seventeenth-century façade in Renaissance style, was built here on the site of a fifteenth-century predecessor. Proceeding further north on this level from the Place de la Palud one arrives at the spacious Place de la Riponne, site of the nineteenth-century **Palais de Rumine** that was built to house the cantonal museums, library and university. From the Place de la Riponne take the Rue Haldimand which runs south-west to the Place Bel-Air, crowned by the modern tower block 'Tour Métropole'. From here the Grand Pont leads back across the valley to the Place St François and the nearby Gare du Flon, completing the walk circuit.

It is worth pointing out that a number of other places of interest can be easily reached by extending the circuit. For example, from the Place de la Riponne it is little more than a kilometre to the **Palais de Beaulieu**, the modern convention and exhibition centre with its attached sports complex and the spacious pavilions where the 'Comptoir Suisse' National Fair is held each September.

Since 1915 Lausanne has been the seat of the International Olympics Committee (CIO). In 1993 the CIO installed an Olympic Games Museum at Ouchy in a new building in stately parkland, 'Petit Ouchy', near the lake. This lively, modern museum, a showplace of the Olympic ideal, has aroused immense interest.

St Gingolph

The lake promenade, Montreux

Public Transport Option

The Palais de Beaulieu can be reached from the Main CFF Station Square by trolley-bus route 3, or by trolley-bus route 2 from Ouchy via Place St François.

Local Excursions

1 *Le Signal*

The favourite elevated viewpoint is sited north of the cathedral by just over a kilometre: Le Signal (647m 2,123ft above sea level, compared to Place St François, 475m 1,558ft, and Ouchy lake front's 377m 1,237ft).

Public Transport Option

Bus route 16 runs to Le Signal from Place St François. Indeed it continues to the Lac du Sauvabelin just beyond, a small lake in a wooded park which is a favourite local excursion or picnic spot.

2 *Roman Site*

About 2km (1½ miles) to the west of Ouchy, south of the La Maladière roundabout where the N1 motorway from Geneva ends, is an interesting archaeological site in the suburb of Vidy where Roman *Lousonna* was situated. The site reveals the forum, a temple and first-century basilica and from it an underpass beneath the motorway leads to a museum displaying finds from the site.

3 *Lake Excursions from Ouchy*

But the principal local excursions are taken from Ouchy. For Lausanne's lakeside resort, as well as having over a kilometre of tree-shaded promenade 'quays' with flowers and tropical plants, along the lake front, has a yacht harbour, boating and other sports facilities. But above all its lake steamer jetties have a more extensive programme of calls and departures than any other port on the lake, including Geneva. Destinations include **Evian-les-Bains** and **Thonon-les-Bains** across the lake in French Savoy as well as the Swiss ports in both directions along the north shore of the lake. A great favourite is the excursion along the north shore calling at all ports, including Vevey and Montreux, to the head of the lake. See below for the land route.

Lausanne to Montreux and the Head of the Lake

Proceeding west from Ouchy road No 9 passes close by **Lutry**, once a possession of Lausanne's bishops and fortified in the third century. Its attractive sixteenth-century church of St Martin embodies remnants of an earlier Romanesque priory-church. The fifteenth-sixteenth-century castle has an imposing sixteenth-century defensive entrance gate. From Lutry to Vevey the road passes through what is commonly considered one of the country's most delightful landscapes, the steep Lavaux slopes covered with vineyards running down to the lake.

It is possible to pass through the midst of these vineyards by leaving road No 9 just beyond Lutry, turning left uphill onto the 'Lavaux Corniche' road that traverses the brow of the hill through Grandvaux and the wine village of **Epesses**, a name familiar to wine-lovers. Near the little climatic resort of **Chexbres** on the hill there is a spectacular viewpoint with views over the upper reach of the lake to the Rhône-mouth at Bouveret, with the snow-tipped peaks of the Dents du Midi as a backcloth. From Chexbres a turn-off right from the corniche road descends to the lakeside rejoining road No 9 just beyond St Saphorin.

The snag to making that corniche diversion through Chexbres is that one then misses a specially enticing section of the lakeside road which firstly passes the renowned Dézaley vineyards between Lutry and Rivaz, and secondly the equally renowned wine-growing village of **St Saphorin** with its charming old-world houses, including the arcaded sixteenth-century priest's house. The origin of the village's obscure name is clarified when you visit the sixteenth-century church of St Symphorien. Its porch is flanked by two Roman relics, a first-century Claudian milestone, and a pagan Romano-Gallic altar.

Nineteen kilometres (12 miles) from Lausanne, **Vevey** is reached, which together with neighbouring Montreux, has, since the early nineteenth century, been a favourite resort of English-speaking visitors. This former prominent Roman and medieval lake port is most attractive in its lake front setting, backed by the slopes of the Lavaux vineyards which are crowned in turn by Mont Pèlerin (806m 2,644ft) and the Pléiades (1,348m

4,423ft); in the foreground at the quayside is the surprisingly extensive Grand' Place, the market square where the spectacular Fête des Vignerons is held every 25 years — and every Saturday there is a lively weekly market.

Vevey has many interesting and attractive buildings, including the *château* in the Rue d'Italie 43, built on the site of a former castle which underwent eighteenth-century alterations when it housed the Bernese bailiffs. It is now the home of two museums: a folk museum of 'Old Vevey' and one of the Vintners' Confraternity. The Gothic church of St Martin — built in phases in the thirteenth, fifteenth and sixteenth centuries — stands apart a little on its historic terrace site overlooking town and railway.

Vevey also houses the headquarters of the Swiss milk and chocolate industry, known world-wide as Nestlé, including their research division. The 'Alimentarium' in the Rue du Léman is a Nestlé foundation, a Museum of Nutrition and Nutritional Sciences of considerable contemporary interest.

A favourite local excursion is to the viewpoint of Mont Pèlerin, either by road or using the Mont Pèlerin rack railway (Timetable 1050). Another is to the former independent village now joined with Vevey to the east, **La Tour de Peilz**, with an unusual sixteenth- to eighteenth-century church that has part of the former town wall and town gate-tower built into its structure. The lakeside castle from which the village derives its name, originally built in the thirteenth century by the Count of Savoy and later destroyed by the Bernese, was rebuilt in the eighteenth century.

The road continues from Vevey to **Montreux** (7km 4½ miles). Montreux's splendid situation, sheltered from north and east winds, and its consequent mild 'Mediterranean' climate have long made it a favourite resort on the lake and it has extended its lake frontage to about 6km (4 miles) by swallowing up former separate villages such as Clarens. Its popularity is ascribable not only to its climate but also to the variety of scenery in which it is set, from the sub-tropical lakeside gardens to the high pasturelands, forests and peaks of its immediate hinterland, accessible by good transport provision. It has a full range of recreational facilities: golf, riding, all manner of water sports, even skiing on the Rochers-de-Naye ski grounds. The Montreux Oberland Bernois (MOB) rack railway runs an hourly service to Rochers-de-Naye via Caux.

Montreux also has a lively name for the events it hosts, notably, each spring the 'Golden Rose' Television Contest, and July's International Jazz Festival. Montreux and Vevey also jointly sponsor a classical music festival from the end of August through September.

Local Excursions from Montreux and Vevey

First and foremost is the **Château de Chillon** which lies 3km (2 miles) to the east. This excursion can be carried out by car, by ship from Montreux or Vevey to the Chillon jetty, by rail to Veytaux-Chillon station (200m from the jetty) or by bus route 1 from Montreux or Vevey (with final

Château de Chillon near Montreux

destination Villeneuve CFF Station). The castle, familiar to many from its photographs and pictures, occupies a rocky isle just offshore and is reached by a bridge. Although there were earlier structures on such a key site, the castle's present form dates to the twelfth and thirteenth century when it had become the preferred residence of the Counts of Savoy. The shoreward east wall of the castle is heavily fortified by semi-circular towers while the residential section is on the lakeward side. Rock-cut cellars served as dungeons such as that featured in the well-known Byron poem *The Prisoner of Chillon* (said to be written in two days at Vevey), based on the imprisonment at Savoyard hands of the Genevan Prior Bonivard, freed when the castle was taken by the invading Bernese in 1536.

Other half-day excursions easily undertaken are to the **Rochers-de-Naye** by cogwheel train (Timetable 121); **Mont Pèlerin** by train and then by funicular (Timetable 100 and 1050); **Les Pléiades** by train (Timetable 112).

As in the case of other principal resorts on the lake, a range of excursions is available by lake steamers (Timetable 2150). A favourite short afternoon trip from Vevey and Montreux is the excursion to the head of the lake, calling at **Chillon**, **Villeneuve**, **Bouveret** (where the Rhône enters the lake) and **St Gingolph**. The last-mentioned is the town divided by the Swiss-French frontier and the excursion call is to its Swiss jetty.

A favourite excursion that can be carried out by motorists, and which gives a good idea of Montreux's hinterland is the short (9km, 6 miles) but somewhat tortuous climb to **Les Avants** on its terrace site overlooked by the Rochers-de-Naye. A simpler approach, however, is to use the train

Above and below: The medieval walled town of Gruyères

service of the Montreux-Oberland-Bernois railway (Timetable No 120) that makes a stop at Les Avants while crossing the hill country between Lake Geneva and the Berner Oberland (see below).

7.3 Between Lake Geneva and Bernerland

The relationship between the Bernerland and Lake Geneva is a fascinating one. Visitors to the lakeside region of Vaud are often surprised at the evidence, in the substantial form of castles and governors' residences, of the subjugation of this region to Bernese rule for the two-and-a-half centuries between 1536 and the French Revolution. This seems so much out of keeping with modern perception of the neutral, non-aggressive character of the Swiss Confederation.

It is helpful to recall that just as the original Central Swiss cantons acquired martial skills in meeting the threats of domination from the Austrian Habsburgs, so too in the west the Bernese gained military prowess in the series of victories in defence of their independence against the predatory and powerful armies of Burgundy. So, when in 1536 the Protestant city and republic of Geneva, under threat from the powerful and ambitious House of Savoy which held so many strategic points in the Vaud lands, called for help from Bern, the Bernese complied — mopping up Savoy strongholds as they went, including Chillon.

In the preceding era Bern had at times been in temporary alliance with Savoy, at times the contrary. The interesting thing to note is that Savoy was always on the horizon for the Bernese. The reason for this is easy for any visitor to West Switzerland to understand if he makes a journey from Montreux, Vevey or Lausanne north-east towards Bern. For once he has made the ascent through the vine-clad slopes of Lake Geneva's shores he finds himself travelling through a great wide corridor of the rolling plateau country, settled and mostly well-cultivated, that the Swiss call Mittelland, a corridor offering no natural obstacles or defensible barriers to migrant tribes or invading armies.

Even today the ease and speed of travel from Lake Geneva to Bern through the Mittelland corridor rarely fails to surprise the visitor who has recently carried out tours involving Oberland passes or their like. And most visitors to Lake Geneva are likely to include among their longer excursions perhaps one that will take them up the neighbouring canton of the Valais and another that will lead to destinations in the Mittelland such as Fribourg or Murten briefly described in Chapter 3.

For the motorist there are interesting possibilities.

To Bulle and Gruyères

Gruyères is probably the favourite excursion beyond Lake Geneva. From Lausanne, Vevey or Montreux use the N9 motorway to reach the junction into the N12 motorway north of Montreux which climbs north from the lake with Les Pléiades on the right and then passing Châtel St Denis on the left. The road passes Bulle, visible away to the right; take the exit (26km, 16 miles) for Riaz, only then turning south for 3km (2 miles) to **Bulle**, an important market and processing town in the attractive Gruyère cattle-grazing and cheese-producing district. Bulle has a folk museum for this region and in many ways is a prelude to the extraordinary little fortified walled town of Gruyères that perches on its hilltop 6km (4 miles) south-east. **Gruyères** is out of bounds to motor traffic. An immense parking area is available at the foot of the ascent ramp to the town.

The adjacent castle was the seat of the Counts of Gruyères, feudal vassals of Savoy, from the eleventh to mid-sixteenth century; the Gruyères estates were subsequently sold to meet debts, and divided between Bern and Fribourg, to which latter canton the castle nowadays belongs. The walled town, with its huge open 'square' (which is nearer oval in shape) is possibly Europe's most picturesque example of a small town that has retained its medieval look. It has numerous eye-catching features including some fine houses from the fifteenth to seventeenth century, wrought-iron signs, and above all really elegant proportions. The existing fortifications are mostly fifteenth century. The castle immediately behind the town, on the hill summit, has one of the round thirteenth-century keeps that are typical of Savoyard structures; for nearly three centuries it was the seat of the Fribourg governors.

Gruyères has such a magnetic attraction that during the main tourist season it is very frequently over-crowded. It is well worth the additional effort of trying to organise a visit to it in an off-season period or in less than clement weather!

Public Transport Option

One of Gruyères' charms is its pastoral setting; its public transport services primarily serve the purposes of the rural community. On Wednesdays, however, in the summer season (June, August, September) a special excursion train service operates from Montreux to Gruyères and Bulle; but note the preceding remark about high season crowds. Gruyères station is normally served by a country line, narrow-gauge, which runs from Montbovon (Timetable 256) taking 20 minutes to do the journey. As Montbovon is also a main station on the Montreux-Oberland Bernois railway (see below) (Timetable 120) — 45 minutes' travel from Montreux — that connection offers a chance to make the journey at off-peak times.

Lausanne via Payerne to Avenches and Murten

It is a fairly steep climb from Lausanne on road No 1 until it levels off and makes a descent into the Broye Valley along which it continues. At 25km (15½ miles) it passes through **Moudon**, once a Savoyard possession. A little, medieval town with some interesting sixteenth- and seventeenth-

The MOB train climbs from Montreux to Oberland

century houses, it also has a church that incorporates a part of the town fortifications in its fifteenth-century bell-tower. Further on by 5km (3 miles) is **Lucens** with its imposing castle (thirteenth century) of the Lausanne Bishops. The older part has a round keep that dominates the valley. Extensions were added during the Bernese governors' era of occupation. In 17km (10½ miles) is **Payerne**, an ancient town associated with a Cluniac abbey going back to the tenth century. This town, too, became a Savoyard possession in the thirteenth century. But the townspeople were allies of Bern during the wars with Burgundy and espoused the Protestant cause in 1536. The former abbey church remains an outstanding example of its type, one of the most renowned Romanesque churches in the whole country, the present building having its origins in the eleventh century. There are also fine sixteenth-century fountains.

From Payerne, 11km (7 miles) on is **Avenches** — which was the Roman *Aventicum* from which the good Bishop Marius or Maire fled (in the aftermath of the Western Empire's collapse) to Lausanne. *Aventicum* in the first and second centuries AD was the large and prosperous capital of the Roman province of *Helvetia* (before which it had been the hill town tribal capital of the Helvetii). It never quite recovered from its destruction by Germanic tribesmen in the third century. In the medieval period the extensive Roman town remains were used as a source of building material. Even so, the existing remains are remarkable, including one of the best-preserved Roman amphitheatres (accommodating 12,000 spectators). There are also remains of baths, a theatre and many parts of the Roman walls, gates and towers have been preserved. Next to the amphitheatre is an eleventh-century fortified tower, no doubt once part of the medieval town defences; well-maintained, it now serves as a Roman Museum, containing many of the Roman antiquities found here.

Apart from the Roman remains Avenches preserves interesting buildings from the medieval period. In the market place stands the *château*, formerly the bishop's residence, which was enlarged in Renaissance style in the sixteenth century by the governor who ruled the town after it had become subject to Bern in 1536.

From Avenches it is only 8km (5 miles) to **Murten** which lies just beyond the linguistic frontier, falling within the German-speaking area of Mittelland. Murten is an exceptionally fine example of a small fortified town with well-preserved and accessible rampart walks. It too was a Savoyard possession — and as such uncomfortably close to Bern (see chapter on the Berner Mittelland).

Public Transport Option

The three principal destinations of the excursion can be reached by rail from Lausanne (Timetable 251). Trains are at approximately hourly intervals, taking just over an hour to Payerne; Payerne to Avenches, some 13 minutes, and to Murten just over 20 minutes. By continuing on the same line from Murten to Kerzers, too, one can count on a ready connection there on the adjacent platform to travel onward to Bern (Timetable 220).

Winter on the road from Zweisimmen to the Vaud

Between Lake Geneva and the Oberland By Rail

To the east of the swathe of Mittelland country, is Oberland country which links the Berner Oberland, by way of some notable resorts of the Vaudoise Alps, with Montreux at the head of Lake Geneva. Travellers who continued on to Bern by train from Avenches or Murten will find it no great detour but a rewarding one to take the trip of 31 minutes by train from Bern to **Spiez** in its splendid position above the Thuner See (Timetable 310); and from there to travel by the BLS rail up the serpentine course of the sparkling River Simme to **Zweisimmen** (Timetable 320) (see final section of Chapter 3).

At the Zweisimmen junction station (already 314m, 1,030ft higher above sea level than Spiez station) awaits the blue train of the Montreux-Oberland Bernois railway. The standard of its notably comfortable coaches gives no clue to the fact that it operates on narrow-gauge rail track; in fact the tightness of the curves it has to take on its climb through the mountain landscape rules out standard track. The climb starts at once as it leaves Zweisimmen; and the first tight curve is a half-spiral tunnel to enable it to double back on its tracks higher up on the steep hillside to breast the crest of the high pasture watershed between the the valley of the Simme and that of the River Sarine. Incidentally, this change of direction high up the mountainside presents an unexpected view down upon Zweisimmen at its valley junction.

The watershed — and the highest point of the line — is reached at 1,279m (4,196ft), at the little Alpine resort of **Saanenmöser**. At this height there is a glimpse of snow-clad tops away to the south near Diablerets, in the area where the mountain frontiers of cantons Bern, Vaud and Valais come together. The line now descends and makes another long, tight loop south to take in the station of **Gstaad**, world-famous summer and winter resort, in its saucer-like site where four wide valleys slope gently together. Here, near the boundary between canton Bern and canton Vaud, the winter sports facilities can hardly be rivalled.

Having regained the Sarine Valley the track now swings west, through the resort of **Saanen**. Then comes a long run in a westerly direction, after crossing the Bern-Vaud boundary (and with it the linguistic one) through a brief but very narrow gorge. The next village bears the unambiguously French name of **Rougemont**, a charming little place with a fine church — twelfth-century Romanesque — that was once part of a Cluniac priory before the Reformation reached the Vaud. Rougemont too is the valley station of a two-stage aerial gondola cablecar to La Videmanette (2,140m, 7,021ft) with an extremely fine panorama of Bernese and Vaudoise heights.

Nine kilometres (6 miles) further west is another main station, **Château d'Oex**, capital of the Enhaut mountain district of the Vaud and a very characteristic family holiday resort with typical chalets and hotels dotting its wide, sunny valley situation. It offers a wide range of facilities for winter and summer sports, and has of late been specialising in the sport of hot-air ballooning, including an annual international competition in the sport. It has an exceptionally rich collection of exhibits in its extensive folk museum reflecting the history of this district which once was part of the Gruyère.

Road and rail continue in parallel down the valley of the River Sarine, shortly turning sharply north to cross into canton Fribourg to **Montbovon** where another narrow-gauge line runs north (following the valley) in the Gruyère district while the MOB line shortly performs another of its loops and heads south-west again climbing now into the narrow valley of the River Hongrin and finally entering a tunnel of some 2½ km (1½ miles).

Its emergence from the tunnel leads to perhaps the most theatrical moment of the MOB journey. The tunnel has taken the line under the Col du Jaman and incidentally across the cantonal boundary into Vaud; and the line now runs downhill to Les Avants with, ahead and 595m, 1,952ft below, Montreux spread out against the brilliant background of glistening Lake Geneva and the distant gleaming Dents du Midi — a near blinding contrast to the dark green forests and hill slopes of the other side of the tunnel. Descent to lake level involves the most serpentine twisting and looping of the whole journey, but each turn presents now left-, now right-hand broadside views of the lake, the vineyards and the city and suburbs until, after two final half-spiral tunnels the train is in Montreux station.

Note for Motorists

Although over some stretches of the route, road and rail run together, there is no road journey that replicates the MOB rail route. A general impression of the region can be gained, however, by taking the road Spiez-Boltigen-Zweisimmen-Saanen (as outlined in the final section of Chapter 3) then continuing Saanen-Rougemont-Château d'Oex. However, from Château d'Oex turn south, crossing the Sarine and following road No 11 south by way of the Col des Mosses Pass and so to Aigle, and from Aigle entering the N9 motorway to return west to Montreux or whichever is your appropriate Lake Geneva resort.

Additional Information

Places to Visit

Avenches
Musée Romain
(Museum of Roman Antiquities)
CH-1580 Avenches
☎ 037/75 17 30
Open: March to October daily 9am-12noon, 1-5pm; November to February daily, except Tuesday, 9am-12noon, 1-5pm.

Bulle
Musée Gruyérien (local museum of Gruyère region's farming traditions)
Place du Cabalet
CH-1630 Bulle
☎ 029/2 72 60
Open: Tuesday to Saturday 10am-12noon, 2-5pm; Sunday 2-5pm.

Château de Chillon
CH-1820 Veytaux-Montreux
☎ 021/963 39 11

Open: summer, 9am-12noon, 1.30-4pm; winter, 10am-12noon, 1.30-4pm.

Château de Coppet
CH-1296 Coppet
☎ 022/76 10 28
Open: March to end October Tuesday to Sunday 10am-12noon, 2-6pm.

Château-d'Oex
Musée du Vieux Pays-d'Enhaut
Chalet de l'Etambeau
CH-1837 Château-d'Oex-Les Bossons
☎ 029/4 65 20
Open: Tuesday/Thursday/Friday2-4.30pm; Saturday/Sunday 11am-12 noon, 2-4.30pm.

Geneva
Musée d'Art et d'Histoire
rue Charles-Galland
CH-1200 Genève
☎ 022/311 43 40
Open: daily except Monday morning, 10am-12noon, 2-5pm (2-6pm in summer).

Musée d'Histoire des Sciences
128 rue de Lausanne
CH-1202 Genève
☎ 022/731 69 85
Open: daily (except Monday 1-5pm), or by arrangement; closed November to end March.

Musée Philatélique des Nations Unies
Palais des Nations
8-14, avenue de la Paix
CH-1211 Genève 10
☎ 022/907 48 82
Open: Monday to Friday 9-11am, 2-4.30pm. Closed 23 December-2 January.

Musée d'Instruments Anciens de Musique
23 rue François Le-Fort
CH-1206 Genève
☎ 022/346 95 65
Open: Tuesday 3-6pm, Thursday 10am-12noon, 3-6pm, Friday 8-10pm or by arrangement.

Musée de l'Horlogerie et de l'Emaillerie
15 route de Malagnou
CH-1208 Genève
☎ 022/736 74 12
Open: daily except Tuesday 10am-5pm or by arrangement. Five centuries of clockmaking.

Musée Internationale de la Croix-Rouge
Avenue de la Paix 17
☎ 022/734 52 48
Open: Wednesday to Monday 10am-5pm (closed Tuesday).

Musée de l'Ariana (ceramics)
Avenue de la Prix 10
☎ 734 29 50
Open: daily, except Monday 10am-5pm. Entry free.

Lausanne
Musée Cantonal d'Archéologie et d'Histoire
Palais de Rumine, place de la Riponne
CH-1005 Lausanne
☎ 021/222 83 32
Open: daily 10am-12noon, 2-5pm.

Jardin Botanique
14 av. de Cour
CH-1007 Lausanne
☎ 021/26 24 09
Open: March to end October, 8am-12noon, 1.30-5.30pm.

Musée Romain de Vidy
Ch. du Bois-de-Vaux
CH-1007 Lausanne
☎ 021/25 10 84
Open: Wednesday to Saturday 2-5pm (until 4pm winter); Sunday 10am-12noon, 2-5pm (until 4pm winter). 'Archaeological Promenade' open permanently.

Musée de la Cathédrale, and Musée Historique de l'Ancien Evêché
2 place de la Cathédrale
CH-1005 Lausanne
☎ 021/312 13 68
Open: summer, Tuesday to Sunday 10am-12noon, 2-6pm (until 8pm Thursday); July to August 10am-6pm (until 8pm Thursday); winter, Tuesday to Sunday 2-5pm (until 6pm Thursday).

Musée Olympique
1 Quai d'Ouchy
CH-1006 Lausanne
Information: ☎ 021/621 65 11

Lucens
Musée Sherlock Holmes
Château
CH-1522 Lucens
☎ 021/95 80 32

Open: March and November, Saturday and Sunday, 10am-5pm; April-October Wednesday to Sunday 10am-6pm.

Morges
Musée Militaire Vaudois
Château
CH-1110 Morges
☎ 021/801 26 15
Open: Monday to Friday 10am-12noon, 1.30-5pm; Saturday/Sunday/public holidays 1.30-5pm. Closed mid-December to end January (weapons, uniforms, toy soldiers).

Musée Alexis Forel
Grand' Rue
CH-1110 Morges
Open: Tuesday to Sunday 2-5pm (dolls, eighteenth-/nineteenth-century toys.)

Nyon
Musée Historique et des Porcelaines
Place du Château 5
CH-1260 Nyon
☎ 022/361 58 88
Open: April to end October daily 9am-12noon, 2-6pm; November to end March Tuesday to Sunday 2-5pm or by arrangement.

Basilique et Musée Romains
Rue Maupertuis
CH-1260 Nyon
☎ 022/361 75 91
Open: April to October daily 10am-12noon, 2-6pm; November to March Tuesday to Sunday 2-5pm.

Payene
Abbey Church (11th century)
Open: daily 10.30am-12noon and 2-6pm.

Vevey
Alimentarium (Scientific Museum of Food of Mankind)
Musée de l'Alimentation
Quai Perdonnet
CH-1800 Vevey
☎ 021/924 41 11
Open: Tuesday to Sunday 10am-12noon, 2-5pm.

Musée Suisse d'Appareils Photographiques
5 Grande Place
CH-1800 Vevey
☎ 021/51 94 60
Open: Tuesday to Sunday 2-5pm; July/August Saturday 10am-12noon, 2-5pm. Old cameras etc.

Musée Historique du Vieux Vevey and Musée de la Confrérie des Vignerons
Le Château
43 rue d'Italie
CH-1800 Vevey
☎ 021/51 07 22
Open: Tuesday to Sunday 10am-12noon, 2-5pm; Sun 11am-12noon, 2-5pm.

Sport and Recreation

Hot air ballllooning organised by clubs in Geneva, Lausanne and Château d'Oex:

Groupe Aerostatique de Genève rue Pestalozzi 27B, CH-1202 Genève
☎ 022 738 52 00

Club Aerostatique du Léman
Case postale 291, CH-1001
Lausanne
☎ 021/38 32 46

Centre Alpin International de Ballons à Air Chaud
Office du Tourisme, CH-1837
Château d'Oe
☎ 029/4 77 88

Guided Hiking Excursions organised in June/July to September by local Tourist offices in Château d'Oex, Lausanne, Montreux and Vevey (addresses below).

Tourist Information Offices

Cantonal Offices
Office de Tourisme du Canton de Vaud
60 Avenue d'Ouchy
CH-1002 Lausanne-Ouchy
☎ 021/617 72 02

Office du Tourisme de Genève
Tour de l'Ile
CH-1211 Genève 11
☎ 022/310 50 31

LOCAL OFFICES

Avenches
Office du Tourisme d'Avenches

Place de l'Eglise 3
CH-1580 Avenches
☎ 037/75 11 59

Château-d'Oex
Office du Tourisme de Château d'Oex
CH-1837 Château d'Oex
☎ 029/4 77 88

Lausanne
Office du Tourisme
2 ave de Rhodanie
CH-1000 Lausanne 6
☎ 021/617 14 27

Morges
Office du Tourisme de Morges
Grand' Rue 80
CH-1110 Morges
☎ 021/801 32 33

Montreux
Office du Tourisme de Montreux
Case Postale 97
CH-1820 Montreux
☎ 021/963 12 12

Nyon
Office du Tourisme de Nyon
avenue Viollier 7
CH-1260 Nyon
☎ 022/361 62 61

Payerne
Office du Tourisme de Payerne
Hotel de Ville
CH-1400 Payerne
☎ 037/61 61 61

Vevey
Office du Tourisme de Vevey
Place de la Gare 5
CH-1800 Vevey
☎ 021/921 48 25

Public Transport

Shipping services on Lake Geneva are run by:
Compagnie Générale de, Navigation sur le Lac Léman
(usually CGN)
17 av. de Rhodanie, Case Postale 252
CH-1000 Lausanne 6
☎ 021/617 06 66

Geneva branch
Jardin Anglais
CH-1204 Genève
☎ 022/311 25 21

TRAVEL GUIDE LIST

Airline ....
....
....
....
....

Telephone No. ....

Tickets arrived ☐

Travel insurance ordered ☐

Car hire details ....
....
....

Visas arrived ☐

Passport ☐

Currency ☐

Travellers cheques ☐

Eurocheques ☐

Accommodation address ....
....
....
....

Telephone No. ....

Booking confirmed ☐

Maps required ....
....
....

SWITZERLAND FACT FILE

Accommodation

The Swiss Hotel Association publishes annually a comprehensive Swiss Hotel Guide listing detailed information (including rates) some 2500 Swiss hotels, annotated in English as well as French, German and Italian. This is available on request from main offices of the Swiss National Tourist Organisation. (SNTO offices are listed in this Fact File.) It should be noted, however, that SNTO does not make hotel reservations. This should be done direct with the hotel or through a travel agent or hotel representative. See page 236 for lists of recommended hotels and restaurants.

For camping and caravanning enthusiasts camping guides can be purchased from SNTO. There are some 450 recognised camp sites. A comprehensive brochure 'Camping in Switzerland' can be had from Verband Schweizerischer Campings, Im Sydefaedeli 40, CH-8037 Zürich.

Information about furnished apartments, chalets and houses for holidaymakers is available from local tourist offices (and also estate agents) in Switzerland. A list of contacts can be obtained from SNTO.

Youth Hostel accommodation is available to tourists up to the age of 25. (Hostellers above that age are admitted if there is room). Those tourists wishing to use them must hold a membership card of their national organisation. (A list of these can be obtained from YHA Service Ltd., 14 Southampton Street, London, WC2E 7HY.) A list of Youth Hostels can be obtained from SNTO; and a Youth Hostel Guide from the Schweizerischer Bund fuer Jugendherbergen (SBJ), Postfach, CH-3001 Bern.

Banks and Currency

Banks open at 8.30am, close at 4.30pm, Monday to Friday. (It is useful to remember, however, that travellers' cheques can be cashed and money exchanged also at any railway station of reasonable size; the appropriate desk usually shows a sign in picture language — of notes and coins. These desks are open for much longer hours than the banks).

The unit of Swiss currency is the Swiss franc (Sfr); 100 centimes = 1 Sfr. (Note: in German-speaking areas centimes are commonly known as 'Rappen'). Coins are in currency for 5, 10 and 20 centimes, for ½ Sfr, 1 Sfr, 2 Sfr and 5 Sfr; notes for 10, 20, 50, 100, 500 and 1000 Sfr.

Average monthly rainfall

Zurich
Average Rainfall (centimetres)
15
14
13
12
11
10
9
8
7
6
5
4
3
2
1
0
J F M A M J J A S O N D
Month

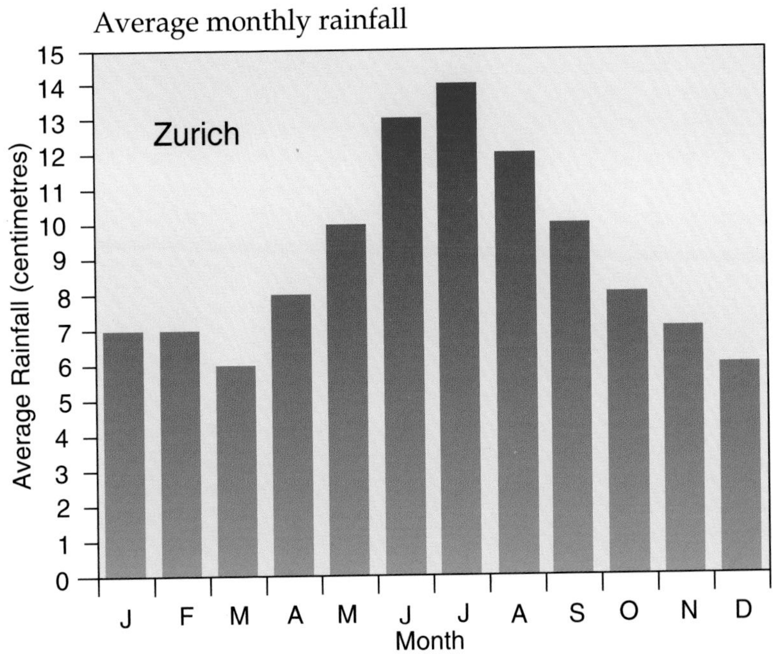

Maximum and minimum daily temperatures

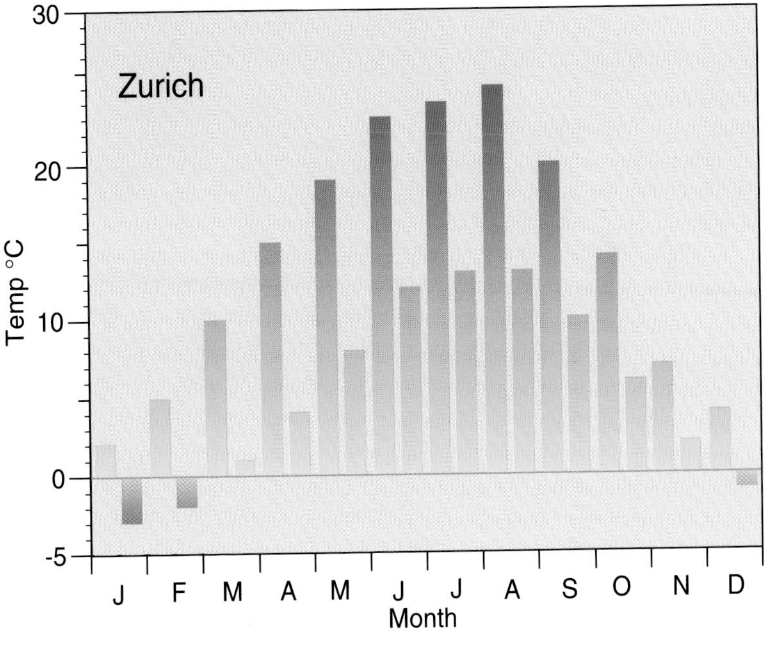

Zurich
Temp °C
30
20
10
0
-5
J F M A M J J A S O N D
Month

Eurocheques (backed by the cheque card) are used like ordinary domestic cheques and widely accepted in Swiss establishments, including for withdrawal of cash in banks. (They must of course be made out in Swiss francs — and the maximum limit per cheque is 300 Swiss francs (written 'CHF300' in this context). The use of major credit cards also can supplement cash and traveller's cheques. For instance, Swiss Federal Rail stations will accept American Express, Diners Club, Eurocard/Mastercard and Visa. The SNTO also accepts Eurocard/Mastercard and Visa credit cards for ticket purchases over the counter.

Business Hours

In Switzerland the usual hours for business are 8am to 12noon and 2-5pm Monday to Friday. Shops are usually open 8am to 12noon and 1.30 to 6.30pm (on Saturday to 4pm). They are often closed on Monday mornings. Post offices in large towns are open 7.30am to 12noon and 1.45 to 6.30pm, Saturday closing at 11am except for a few major city offices which may close later.

Chemists (Pharmaceutical)

Open during normal shopping hours. But note that in German-speaking areas the sign indicating a pharmacy is Apotheke, in French areas Pharmacie, Italian Farmacia. A Drogerie (drugstore) does not dispense medicinal prescriptions, but sells vitamin tablets, insect repellents etc.

Climate and Clothing

In climate Switzerland is a microcosm of Europe — no other European country combines within so small an area such marked contrasts of climate: the Mittelland surrounded by mountains has a mild temperate climate; south of the Alps under Mediterranean influence is warmer; the Valais is noted for dryness.

During spring, summer and autumn the golden rule is to take similar clothing as for a holiday in Britain — including a warm jacket and good walking shoes, as some of the best excursions take you to mountains still snow-clad in summer. It goes without saying that in winter stout shoes and anorak-type outer garments are advisable.

Customs

All personal belongings needed for a holiday visit are duty-free. Tobacco and alcoholic beverages are only exempt from duty to persons of at least 17 years of age.

Disabled/Handicapped

A list of hotels that cater specially for disabled tourists can be supplied by the Swiss Association for the Disabled (Schweizerische Invalidenbund) Froburgerstrasse 4, CH-4600 Olten; ☎ 062/21 10 37. Special town guides for the larger cities (Basel, Bern, Lausanne, Luzern, St Gallen, Zürich) can be had through any SNTO office — or from the organisation Pro Infirmis, Postfach 129, CH-8023 Zürich.

Electricity

Swiss electric current is supplied at 220 volts AC. The socket outlets take two pin plugs. British travellers should take an adaptor if they wish to use appliances of their own equipped with British made plugs.

Emergencies

Regardless of which Swiss town or city you are visiting, if confronted with an emergency there are universal telephone dialling codes that enable the appropriate service to be contacted quickly.

Important Telephone Numbers for Emergencies
117 Police (only for emergencies)
118 Fire brigade
120 In winter, snow reports and avalanche warnings
140 Motoring assistance
152 Weather report
163 Information on road or traffic conditions, passes etc.

A 24-hour English-speaking information line exists, Anglophone, prepared to answer any queries in English. Dial 157-5014 from anywhere in Switzerland.

Entertainment and Festivals

For theatre, ballet, music and other entertainment, which are generally provided in the Swiss cities, it is best to obtain up-to-date information from the weekly or monthly 'What's on and When' tourist bulletins, especially for the larger resorts. Some exceptional items are listed below, however.

Altdorf
William Tell historical plays in dedicated theatre, July to September, information from Tellspielbüro, 6460 Altdorf, ☎ 044/2 22 80

Luzern
September International Festival of Music; precise details from Tourist Office available in early May annually.

Weggis
'Chilbi' Fair on 3rd Sunday of October.

Interlaken
For August Music Festival consult local publicity.

Ascona
International Music Festival, autumn. Check date each year.

Bellinzona
'Espo' Trade Fair in month of May.

Locarno
Fiesta dei Fiori (Flower Festival), May. International Film Festival.

Lugano
Open-air Jazz Festivals: June-July. Wine-growers procession, 1st Sunday October (Wine Festival Weekend).

Food and Drink

As pioneers of catering for tourists for more than 150 years the Swiss have become known not only as highly experienced in hotel-keeping and hotel management, but also as exporters of these skills to other countries. Even so, although Switzerland can boast many examples of world-famous hotels in the international class, it is the well run family-owned hotel that is still very characteristic of Switzerland today. The kind of hotel accommodation likely to be sought by the majority of readers of this book is likely to be a small-town inn or hotel-café-restaurant (as they often proclaim themselves comprehensively), family run, that caters for the local inhabitants having an evening meal out, a Sunday lunch or a weekly evening meeting of some local club; and where the foreign visitor can have the inestimable privilege of seeing a little of the life of the people.

Swiss hotel cooking is fairly international because they have exported much of it to others. The dishes they do most often and do best are likely to be made from what they are best at rearing — veal and pork. With their agricultural economy based on dairy production, they also tend to favour dishes with a cheese content such as the familiar veal *cordon bleau;* or one with a full foundation of cheese such as the *fondue* for which each Swiss chef or humble cook has his or her personal secret recipe for the proportions of each type of cheese and the variety of wine. Their really unique delicacy, however, which falls into the same category as smoked salmon in Scotland and Parma ham in Italy is the air-dried meat, served cut wafer thin with the translucency of autumn leaves, that comes from the high Alpine valleys of the canton Graubünden and is accordingly known as *Bündnerfleisch.* Their patriotic bias towards dairy produce also shows on the dessert table, where cream plays a prominent role, as does the meringue (which some enthusiasts would derive etymologically from the east Berner Oberland village of Meiringen!)

Until recently, breakfast in Swiss hotels was the so-called 'continental breakfast' of coffee/tea, bread rolls or something similar with butter and jam. In recent years hotels in most areas have changed over to the 'buffet breakfast' which also includes a choice of fruit or fruit juices, cereals, *aufschnitt,* ie sliced cooked ham, meat and/or sausage and cheese.

There is a fair amount of orchard land — compatible with grazing of course — in the Mittelland. Their masterpieces of distilled spirituous liquors are produced from stone-fruits by classic pot-still distillation: *Kirsch* from black cherries, and *Pflümli* from plums — both best from the orchard country of cantons Zug and Schwyz. Need it be stressed that these are not sweet liqueurs but bone dry distillates made in the same type of still as classic brandy. They are reputedly an acquired taste; an easy acquisition if sampled with an after-dinner coffee of comparable quality. Of Swiss wines, mention is made in the chapters dealing with the cantons of Valais and Vaud, the major wine-producing regions. Their average quality is excellent; their only defect is that their total production falls far short of the demand; it can only meet something like one-third of the requirement of the home market.

Health Insurance

There is no state medical health service in Switzerland and medical treatment must be paid for. So it is advisable to take out insurance cover against personal accident and sickness — and indeed for loss and damage to personal effects etc as well. Special winter sports policies also exist. Consult travel agent or the SNTO.

Health Resorts and Spas

Information can be had from Verband Schweizer Badekurorte (VSB), Postfach 1456, CH-5400 Baden, and from many SNTOs.

Languages

The distribution of languages spoken in Switzerland is dealt with in the Introductory chapter of this guide. But here it should be emphasised that in addition to the three official languages (German, French, Italian) English is for all practical purposes regarded almost as a fourth as far as all documentation for travel and tourism is concerned — and is widely understood and spoken in officialdom, in commerce and the catering industry.

Maps

A really good map is very helpful even for the general-interest tourist; for the motorist it is well nigh indispensible. Quite a choice is available of one-sheet maps of Switzerland issued by a variety of publishers. When it comes to the problem of variations in the spelling of place names in a country where there are four national languages (two of which have dialect variants as an additional complication) the prudent course is to use maps reproduced with the imprint of authorisation of the Federal Topographical Office (the equivalent of the British Ordnance Survey). Bern, the capital of Switzerland is the home of one of Europe's most distinguished specialist cartographical publishers, Kümmerly and Frey, who in fact print such maps. So top recommendation for a map would be the one printed by Kümmerley & Frey as the TCS (Touring Club Suisse)'s *Carte Routiere Officielle* — in German, *Offizielle Strassenkarte*. One final thought: particularly for the motorist it is important to have a map with the place names showing the same spelling as you can expect to find on the local road-signs and signposts. The map recommended is of the scale 1:300 000, ie 1cm representing 3km.

A Caution: Place names with variants
Even with the use of a good map there is still some risk of puzzlement over place names when you are passing from one language area to another. Proceeding north in the Ticino you are not likely to have problems in recognizing northern cities under their Italian names of Basilia, Zurigo or Lucerna. Problems are more likely to occur along the French/German linguistic divide in the Mittelland or the Valais. Freiburg for Fribourg is scarcely a problem, but Neuenburg has a rather different ring from Neuchatel, and Sitten from Sion in the Valais (or Wallis), or — from the opposite angle — Morat as the French version of Murten, so near Bern.

Measurements

The metric system is used in Switzerland. The following conversions apply:

1 kilogram (kg) - 2.2lb
1 litre = 1¾ pints
4.5 litres = 1 gallon
8 kilometres (km) = 5 miles

Motoring

The two principal motoring associations in Switzerland are a) the TCS Touring Club Suisse (or Touring Club der Schweiz) which is affiliated to the British Automobile Association, and b) the ACS Automobil Club der Schweiz which is affiliated to the Royal Automobile Club. Both have offices in major centres but their head offices are:-

TCS, Rue Pierre-Fatio 9, CH-1200 Geneva and
ACS, Wasserwerkgasse 39, CH-3000 Bern

Regulations for Motorists
In poor visibility (including heavy rain) driving with side-lights only is not permitted under any circumstance; the use of headlights, dipped headlights or twin fog-lights is obligatory. Dipped headlights are also compulsory in road tunnels. The use of seat belts is obligatory. Children under 12 years must travel in the rear seats. And police have the power to inflict on-the-spot fines (quite substantial) for infractions of such rules and regulations, including speed restrictions. In built-up areas the Swiss speed limit is 50km (31.5 miles) per hour; on the open road it is 80km (50 miles) per hour and on motorways the limit is 120km (75 miles) per hour. When driving in the mountains, if you meet another vehicle on a narrow road, it is for the

vehicle travelling down hill to give way to the other and if need be to reverse to make passing possible. If you meet a postal vehicle — recognisable by its yellow colour, post horn emblem and with horn sounding the characteristic post-horn triple note — you are required to obey the instructions of the postal driver.

In the event of a breakdown you should lay out a hazard-warning red triangle at least 150m (164yd) behind the halted vehicle if on a motorway and at least 50m (55yd) behind if on another road. You should also switch on the vehicle's own hazard-warning lights. Motorists needing assistance can dial the dedicated telephone number 140 from any telephone booth.

Another telephone number motorists should note is 163, which is dialled for reports on road and traffic conditions.

The tourist offices of most large cities can supply pamphlets for the guidance of visiting motorists on matters such as parking facilities, one-way traffic systems and pedestrian precincts. Incidentally, British motorists should note that the word 'car' in Switzerland is used to mean a touring or excursion motor-coach even in German-language areas. Be on guard not to make a costly mistake by parking a private automobile where a notice reads 'Reserviert fur Cars'! Parking space for private transport is often indicated by the abbreviation 'Pkw' — short for *Personenkraftwagen*, private car.

Motorway Tax (Vignette)

An annual tax of Sfr 30 is levied on all cars and motorcycles using Swiss motorways. (An additional tax of Sfr 30 is applied to caravans and trailers). This tax can be paid by visiting motorists at point of entry to Switzerland but most find it time-saving to make the payment to a Swiss National Tourist Office in advance, receiving as a visible sign of receipt of the tax a so-called 'vignette' sticker to display on the vehicle windshield. (Sterling price available from SNTO on request). These permits are valid for multiple re-entry to Switzerland and are valid for one year plus two months from the fixed date of 1 December.

Passports and Visas

Holders of valid British passports do not require visas for travel in Switzerland. They are valid for visits (excluding employment) of up to three months. Similarly with holders of valid Australian, USA, Canadian, South African and New Zealand passports.

Post and Postages

Correspondence can be forwarded to Swiss Post Offices for collection. Such envelopes must be clearly addressed to the addressee 'Poste restante', giving the name of the town preceded by its Swiss (CH-) postcode; the sender's address should be marked on the back of envelope. Unclaimed mail is returned to sender if not collected within 30 days.

Public Holidays

New Year's Day
Easter
Ascension Day
Whitsun
Christmas
1 August is the National Holiday

Local tourist offices can give information on cantonal and local holidays — and festivals.

Sport and Recreation

Local tourist offices invariably can supply information, usually in leaflet form, on tennis, swimming, golf, outdoor and indoor sports centres, and the popular 'Fitness Parcours' tracks for jogging as well as cycle tracks.

Swiss National Tourist Offices (SNTO)

Reference has already been made to these as a source of information. For tourist information in general the Swiss National Tourist Offices (SNTO), whether at national, cantonal or local level, are models of efficiency and helpfulness; they can be recommended wholeheartedly. So the addresses of regional offices and of many local offices will be found listed in the appropriate 'Additional Information' section which follows each chapter of this guide. Principal offices are listed below:

Head Office
Bellariastrasse 38
CH-8027 Zürich
☎ 01/288 11 11

Principal offices in English-speaking countries are:

UK
Swiss Centre
Swiss Court
London W1V 8EE
☎ 071/734 1921

USA
Swiss Center
608 Fifth Avenue
New York, NY 10020
☎ 212/757 59 44

260 Stockton Street
San Francisco
CA 94108
☎ 415/362 22 60

150 North Michigan Avenue
Suite 2930
Chicago, IL 60601
☎ 312/630 58 40

Canada
154 University Avenue
Suite 610 Toronto
Ontario
Canada M5H 3Y9
☎ 416/971 97 34

Australia
203-233 New South Head Road
PO Box 193, Edgecliff
Sydney, NSW 2027
☎ 02/326 17 99

Telephones

When phoning from Switzerland remember after dialling the international code to omit the first zero of the number you are ringing.

Main international direct dialling codes:
Australia 00 61
Britain 00 44
Irish Republic 00 353
New Zealand 00 64
USA and Canada 00 1

Public phone-booths are all automatic, coin operated with digital display. But larger post offices have separate departments of telephone cabins where the amount is indicated on the electronic display and can be paid for afterwards at the counter. This is particularly helpful for long-distance calls when it is difficult to be sure of having the right number of coins for a public phone-booth. Another way out of difficulty with coins is to purchase PTT phone cards (available from post offices and rail stations) for use in appropriately equipped public phone booths. Phone calls made from hotel rooms involve a surcharge which is often considerable.

Tipping

Tips are automatically included on all hotel and restaurant bills, as well as on most taxi fares. It is neither necessary nor expected to leave an extra tip.

Travelling to Switzerland

Most English-speaking visitors from overseas will travel by air to Switzerland which has air links with the whole world through the international airports of Zürich and Geneva; and if thereafter they wish to do any motoring will hire from one of the well-known firms. Overseas visitors intending to make maximal use of Swiss Federal Railways should note that there are through trains to many major destinations from Zürich Flughafen (ie, airport) Rail Station.

Travellers from the United Kingdom and Eire will also find scheduled services to Zürich and Geneva provided from London Heathrow by their national air companies and Swissair in cooperation. Swissair offices also exist in the following cities and will deal helpfully with enquiries: Boston, Chicago, Cleveland, Dallas, Detroit, Houston, Los Angeles, Miami, Milwaukee, Minneapolis, Montreal, New Jersey, New York, Philadelphia, San Francisco, Sydney, Toronto and Washington.

Passengers to Switzerland travelling by air from a number of provincial airports in Britain can benefit greatly from recent new possibilities. Thanks to the 'consolidation' of ticketing and connecting flights between the British carriers Air UK operating from these provincial airports and the specially timetabled connecting services operated from Schiphol, Amsterdam, by KLM (Royal Dutch Airlines), one can travel to Basel, Geneva and Zürich on a 'consolidated' ticket without having to give any thought at Amsterdam to the luggage one had checked-in at the British airport. The provincial airports in question, served by Air UK include Norwich, Newcastle, Belfast, Leeds/Bradford, Aberdeen, Edinburgh, Glasgow.

In recent years more and more people going to Switzerland on tour or holiday from the UK (or from USA via the UK or the Low Countries) have been attracted by the opportunity now available of starting the holiday with a cruise of some days' duration up the River Rhine on a 'hotel-ship' style of river cruise vessel from Holland to Basel. As this book's opening chapters deal with places on the Swiss course of the Rhine, this leisurely alternative approach to Switzerland from the North — which sets Switzerland in its geographic and historic perspectives in Europe — might appeal to readers of this guide. Such cruises are carried out by two German companies:

1. KD Deutsche Rheinschiffahrt AG, Frankenwerft 15, D-5000 Koeln 1, Germany; ☎ 0221 2088-318. English address for information: KD German Rhine Line, 28 South Street, Epsom, Surrey KT18 7PF; ☎ 03727/4 20 33. In USA, KD German Rhine Line, 150 Hamilton Avenue, White Plains NY 10601; ☎ 914-948-3600.

2. Peter Deilmann Reederei, with its headquarters address at Am Hafensteig 17-19, D-23730 Neustadt in Holstein, Germany. Its English agency and address for information is Cunard, 30/35 Pall Mall, London SW1Y 6LS; ☎ 071/930 4321. In USA it is Cunard, 555 Fifth Avenue, New York NY 100017; ☎ 212-880-7466.

Motorists intending to take their own private transport from the United Kingdom to tour in Switzerland have a wide choice of services available to them by Channel car ferries or by rail tunnel.

Motorists who travel from the United Kingdom by car ferry to French Channel ports are most likely to take one of the choices of routes to Switzerland through France. It is worth noting that routes from Belgian and Dutch ports traversing Limburg or Flanders respectively and then up the valley of the Rhine to Basel can offer an interesting variety of landscape without significantly increasing the time taken for the journey.

Information and assistance in making bookings, arranging travel documents and itineraries for motorists are available from the well-known motoring organisations.

Special Luggage Facilities by Rail for Air Passengers

Passengers arriving at Zürich, Geneva or Basel airports who then intend to travel on to Swiss destinations by rail (or by principal lake-boat services or postbus) can register their baggage for forwarding through to their destination by an accelerated service. There is a standard charge for luggage up to 30kg. Further, travellers returning home by flights from Basel, Zürich or Geneva can check their luggage through to their final flight destination in their own country direct from the railway station of many Swiss towns and resorts. (Indication of availability of this 'Fly Luggage' facility appears under the town name in the index of the Swiss Official Timetable. An explanatory leaflet *Fly Luggage* is obtainable at stations and SNTOs).

Travelling in Switzerland: by Public Transport

Despite formidable terrain problems no other country has such a comprehensive and efficient network of rail, autobus, lake boats and aerial cableways services — and all integrated with one another. In particular the services of the yellow Postbuses provide an extremely comprehensive network especially in mountainous country. To take an extreme example, there is a regular Postbus service, winter and summer, to Juf (in canton Graubünden), deemed to be the highest agricultural hamlet in Europe at 2,133m (6,199ft) above sea level. The Swiss Postbus network extends to about 8,000km (nearly 5,000 miles) in length, which is 1½ times the length of all Switzerland's public railways put together.

As a result, more visitors to Switzerland are willing to depend on public transport than visitors to the neighbouring countries. And the incentive to do so is particularly strong for overseas visitors in possession of Eurorail or similar tickets. But even among those visitors who do make much use of Swiss railways, Postbus services etc, a surprisingly large number do not realise how useful is the *Offizielles Kursbuch, Indicateur officiel* (the *Official Timetable for Switzerland*) published jointly by the Swiss Transport Undertakings. It contains full details of services and fares of all railways, Alpine Postbuses, lake boats, cableways and chairlifts, and main international connections. An annual publication, it is issued at the end of May each year and can be purchased from the Swiss National Tourist Office abroad or at any railway station in Switzerland.

It is published in three volumes, one containing trains, cable railways and boat services, the second dealing entirely with bus services and the third with international connections. Every route timetable has a number for identification, eg, 600 for the Gotthard rail route. These numbers are encoded on the synoptic maps which illustrate the routes in the volumes. Explanatory notes and hints on how to make best use of the timetabled information are given in each of the national languages and also in English. The detailed information about connected services that is included in the individual timetables goes far beyond the expectation of visitors from most other countries.

In the chapters of *The Visitor's Guide to Switzerland* describing routes, the sections giving public transport options will specify these timetable references using the official numbers for ready reference by readers. It is sound advice to take three basic preliminary steps when you contemplate an excursion by public transport in Switzerland.

1. Look up the destination you have in mind in the index of Volume 1 of the *Official Timetable*. It will give you the relevant table numbers for as many transport means as apply to the particular destination, not only trains, but buses, ships, cableways so that you can then study the tables and assess all the options and opportunities as well as the timings and frequencies from the outset.

2. Next, take a look at the route or routes on a good map.

3. If you find it would be possible — and might also add interest — to work out a route that would take you partly by rail, partly by bus or ship (or outward by one means and return by a different means or route), enquire at the Tourist Office or the Railway Station Information desk if any special type of ticket can be issued.

Here is a brief outline of the main framework of the Swiss railway system.

1. The principal north-south line runs from Basel to Chiasso on the Italian frontier, through Luzern, the Gotthard tunnel, Bellinzona and Lugano. At Arth-Goldau, east of Luzern, its traffic is increased by a second direct line coming in from Zürich by way of Zug.

2. A second cardinal route runs through Zürich, crossing the country in a roughly west-east passage from Geneva in the south-west to St Gallen in the north-east, via Lausanne, Bern and Zürich. These north-south and west-east main lines cross one another at Olten, key rail junction about 40km (25 miles) south of Basel.

3. A third cross-route of great importance is that from Basel to Chur, using the track of the Bern-Zürich main line between Brugg and Zürich. Trains from Basel to Austria use this line.

Not only foreign visitors but the Swiss themselves take excursions — including excursions where you travel part of the way by train or bus or both, then do a cross-country ramble or a hill walk that finishes in a different place from where it started, so that you can return by a different rail or bus service. Very frequently special excursion 'round tickets' are available to meet this very need for tourists. Enquire at the rail station, boat station, etc and keep your eyes open for free pamphlets with 'special excursion offers' of this kind. These pamphlets are usually printed in whichever is the principal national language of the area but many also appear in English in the regions frequented by English-speaking visitors.

So far as the Postbus services are concerned, for each of ten regions they issue an annual edition of a *Postbus Excursion Guide*, well illustrated, with regional road maps and with sketch maps of walks, rambles and hill climbs made accessible by bus; they also give prices of excursions, including 'round ticket' excursions. Examples of the regions covered by these guides are: Engadin; Surselva/Via Mala; Calanda/Julier/Flüela; Appenzell/Toggenburg; Central Switzerland/Gotthard; Berner Oberland; Vaud Alps; Valais central and lower; Upper Valais; Ticino.

Travel Passes

Visitors to Switzerland using public transport should also give consideration to the purchase of a Swiss Pass or a Regional Pass.

The Swiss Pass entitles the holder to unlimited travel by Swiss Railways, boats and most alpine posbuses for the period of its validity. It also allows travel on the transport services of 30 Swiss cities. In addition, reductions of 25 per cent are offered on many privately owned funiculars and mountain railways on production of the Card. It is issued for periods of 4 days, 8 days, 15 days or 1 month, and is available for either Second Class or First Class travel. It offers very good value indeed for the visitor interested in seeing the diversity of the country. Other advantageous tickets include:

The Regional Pass which is popular with visitors who wish to make excursions in a particular region. These are available during the summer season for the following regions: Montreux/Vevey; Bernese Oberland; Lake Luzern; Graubünden; Locarno/Ascona; Lugano; Churfirsten/Saentis; Chablais (Vaud Alpine region). Details available from SNTO.

Rail Europe Senior (RES). Holders of a British Rail Senior Railcard can obtain from British Rail a RES card for a modest price. It entitles the holder to purchase reduced-fare tickets to Switzerland.

Hotels and Restaurants

(If a hotel is known to have a restricted annual season, the months of opening are indicated after the number of beds).

*** Expensive
** Moderate
* Inexpensive

Chapter 1 • The Northern Cities

Hotels

Appenzell
Romantik Hotel Säntis **
CH-9050
☎ 071/87 87 22
60 beds. Open all year. Good restaurant; local wines, fish dishes.

Hotel Appenzell **
Landsgemeindeplatz, CH-9050
☎ 071/87 42 11
31 beds. Pleasant modern hotel on town's historic square. Moderate rates. Has restaurant and cafe.

Baden
Hotel Ochsen **
Badstrasse, CH-5400
☎ 056/22 52 51
50 beds. Part of a complex of hotels in the spa precinct. Rates include full board.

Basel
Hotel Drei Könige am Rhein ***
Blumenrain 8, CH-4001
☎ 061/261 52 52
144 beds. One of the world's really grand hotels, yet charming with it. Expensive, of course. Distinguished restaurant.

Hotel Basel ***
Münzgasse 12, CH-4001
☎ 061/261 24 23
108 beds. Conveniently sited in heart of city.

Hotel Victoria am Bahnhof ***
Centralbahnhofplatz 3-4, CH-4002
☎ 061/271 55 66
150 beds. Good position opposite Station. Conducted in the great tradition — both hotel and restaurant.

Hotel Admiral **
Rosentalstrasse 5, CH-4021
☎ 061/691 77 77
Good middle class. 200 beds.

Kunsthotel Teufelhof ***
Leonhardsgraben 47, CH-4061
☎ 061/261 10 10
Small but artistic. 16 beds. Stylish bohemian lodging attached to gourmet restaurant.

Basel/Liestal
Hotel Bad Schauenburg **
Liestal-Schauenburg, CH-4410
☎ 061/901 12 02
Good middle class. 42 beds.

Brugg
Hotel Rotes Haus **
CH-5200 Brugg
☎ 056/41 14 79
40 beds. Open all year. Comparatively inexpensive.

Neuhausen (by Schaffhausen)
Hotel Bellevue above Rhine Falls **
Bahnhofstrasse, CH-8212 Neuhausen
☎ 053/22 21 21

50 beds. Open all year. Terrace overlooking the Rhine falls. Well-favoured restaurant. Moderate prices.

Rapperswil
Hotel Schwanen ***
12 Seequai, CH-8640
☎ 055/21 91 81
31 beds. Open all year. Centrally sited; historic and comfortably modernised.

Hotel Freihof **
Hauptplatz
CH-8640 Rapperswil
☎ 055/27 12 79
Comfortable. 33 beds. Open all year. Picturesque building with modernised interior. Good value accommodation.

Rheinfelden
Hotel Schiff am Rhein **
CH-4310 Rheinfelden
☎ 061/87 60 87
80 beds. Open all year. Quiet surroundings.

Schaffhausen
Hotel Kronenhof **
Kirchhofplatz 7, CH-8200
☎ 053/25 66 31
54 beds. Open all year.

Schwägalp (Urnäsch)
Hotel Schwägalp **
CH-9107 Schwägalp
☎ 071/58 16 03
54 beds. Open all year. Moderately priced.

St Gallen
Hotel Walhalla ***
Bahnhofplatz, CH-9001
☎ 071/22 29 22
80 beds. Open all year. Conveniently situated, modernised hotel with good restaurants (two). In the expensive category.

Hotel Dom (Garni) **
22 Webergasse, CH-9001 St Gallen
☎ 071/23 20 44
No restaurant. Breakfast only. Comfort at moderate cost.

Stein am Rhein
Hotel Adler **
Rathaus Plat
☎ 054/42 61 61
59 beds. Open all year. At heart of Old Town, comfortably modernised interior and picturesque exterior.

Trogen
Hotel Krone *
CH-9043 Trogen
☎ 071/94 13 04
Simple, homely. 20 beds. Open March-January.

Zürich
Hotel Schweizerhof ***
7 Bahnhofplatz, CH-8001
☎ 01/211 86 40
150 beds. Open all year. Modernised grand hotel opposite main station. Caters largely for singles.

Hotel Ascot ***
9 Tessinerplatz, CH-8002
☎ 01/201 18 00
First class plus. 120 beds. Open all year. Stylishly renovated in recent time. Also good restaurant.

Hotel Ambassador ***
6 Falkenstrasse, CH-8008
☎ 01/261 76 00
70 beds. Open all year. Reasonable for its category. Near lake.

Hotel Glockenhof **
31 Sihlstrasse, CH-8021
☎ 01/211 56 60
166 beds. All year. Rates moderate for category; central situation convenient for tourists.

Hotel Seidenhof **
9 Sihlstrasse, CH-8021
☎ 01/211 65 44
142 beds. Open all year. Well situated for tourists; well-run by the Zürich 'Frauenverein' (Women's League) as an alcohol-free establishment.

Hotel Bristol (Garni) **
34 Stampfenbachstrasse, CH-8035
☎ 01/261 84 00
100 beds. Open all year. Moderate rates for its category. Breakfast only.

Hotel Krone-Limmatquai * (There is more than one Krone!)
88 Limmatquai, CH-8001
☎ 01/261 42 20
Comfortable. 40 beds. Open all year. Good value on this central riverside site.

Zürich-Erlenbach
Hotel Erlibacherhof **
83 Seestrasse, CH-8703
☎ 01/910 55 22
Country inn. 34 beds. Open all year. Residential village along Lake Zürich. Inn recommended for comfort and typical regional cuisine.

Restaurants

(Additional to those indicated under Hotel entries above)

Appenzell
Restaurant Säntis **
At Hotel Säntis, CH-9050
☎ 071/87 87 22
Open: 11.30am-2pm; 6.30-10pm. Variety of menus including regional dishes; popular fixed price and *a la carte* meals.

Basel
Bahnhof Buffet Basel SBB **
Centralbahnstrasse 14, CH-4051
☎ 061/271 53 33
Three restaurants including Cellar-Tavern l'Escargot (bistro). Hot dishes until 11.30pm. Alsatian cuisine.

Restaurant Börse */**
Marktgasse 4, CH-4051
☎ 061/261 87 33
Hot dishes till 11pm, closed Sundays in summer. Central site, opposite tourist office.

Restaurant Chez Donati ***
St Johanns-Vorstadt 48
CH-4056 Basel
☎ 061/322 09 19
Closed Monday and Tuesday. Fashionable Rhine terrace. Italian cuisine but not to excess.

Kunsthalle Restaurant **
Steinenberg 77, CH-4001
☎ 272 42 33
Warm dishes till 10.45pm. Open every day. Meeting place of art and theatre types. In summer large garden below chestnut trees. No credit cards.

Restaurant Löwenzorn **
Gemsberg 2, CH-4051
☎ 061/261 42 13
Hot dishes till 11.30pm. Closed Sundays. Garden-restaurant with charcoal-grill.

Olten
Bahnhofbuffet Restaurant **
Am Bahnhof, CH-4600 Olten
☎ 062/26 54 54
Open until 11.30pm. Three dining rooms. Swiss and international cuisine.

Rapperswil
Hotel Eden Restaurant **/***
CH-8640 Rapperswil
☎ 055/27 12 21
Open: 12noon-2.30pm, 5-10.30pm. Closed Monday. High quality food in the Old Town area. Gastronomic and fish dishes.

Schaffhausen
Restaurant Gerberstube **/***
8 Bachstrasse, CH-8200
☎ 053/25 21 55
Open: 12noon-2pm, 6.30-10pm. Closed Monday. Specialises in Italian dishes.

Stein am Rhein
Restaurant Sonne ***
127 Rathausplatz, CH-8260
☎ 054/41 21 28
Open: 12noon-2pm, 6-9.30pm. Closed Thursday. Fine food and fine wines in heart of town.

St Gallen
Restaurant Bahnhof Buffet SBB */**
2 Bahnhofplatz, CH-9001
☎ 071/22 56 61
Open until 11pm. Regional and international modern cuisine.

Restaurant Kongresshalle Schützengraben **
38 St Jakobstrasse, CH-9001
☎ 071/24 71 71
Open until 11.30pm. Large establishment. Fondue speciality.

Zürich
Restaurant Agnes Amberg ***
5 Hottingerstrasse, CH-8000
☎ 01/251 26 26
Open until 11.30pm excluding Saturday and Monday. Closed Sunday. Presided over by one of Switzerland's best chefs.

Restaurant Fischstube Zürichhorn **
160 Bellerivestrasse
☎ 01/422 25 20
Open 12noon-2pm; 6-11pm. On lakeside. First-class quality. As name indicates, fish specialities, including lobster.

Restaurant Bahnhofbuffet (various prices)
Hauptbahnhof
☎ 01/211 15 10
Open until 11.30pm. Comprises group of restaurants beneath same roof and suits a variety of purses — and of tastes.

Restaurant Le Dezaley **
7-9 Romergasse
☎ 01/251 61 29
Open 9am-2.30pm, 6-12 midnight. Closed Sunday. French-Swiss atmosphere; 'fondue', Vaud dishes and great variety Vaud wines.

Restaurant Bierhalle Kropf *
16 In Gassen
☎ 01/221 18 05
Open 11.30am-1.45pm; 6.45-9.45pm. Closed Sunday. Not far from Paradeplatz and Bahnhofstrasse. Attracts wide range of patrons including students, with reliable cooking.

Restaurant Hilti Vegi *
28 Sihlstrasse
☎ 01/221 38 70
Open 6.30-11am; 11am-9pm. All imaginable vegetarian dishes of season.

Chapter 2 • Luzern and Central Switzerland

Hotels

Altdorf
Hotel Goldener Schlüssel **
9 Schützenstrasse, CH-6460
☎ 044/2 10 02
50 beds. With restaurant, inexpensive. In heart of town.

Amsteg
Hotel Stern u. Post **
Gotthardstrasse, CH-6474
☎ 044/6 44 40
40 beds. Former post-house. Good atmosphere. Good cuisine.

Andermatt
Hotel Krone **
CH-6490 Andermatt
☎ 044/67206
85 beds. Good cuisine.

Brunnen
Hotel Seehotel Waldstätterseehof ***
160 beds. Grand style, own lakeside grounds; many facilities.

Hotel Bellevue au Lac **
2 Axenstrasse, CH-6440
☎ 043/31 13 18
90 beds. Lakeside site, well renovated, has Kursaal (Casino) nightlife.

Hotel Ochsen *
Ochsen-platz, CH-6440
☎ 043/31 11 59
17 beds. Old-world inn, hospitable, well run. Restaurant with good Swiss traditional fare.

Engelberg
Hotel Restaurant Hess **
CH-6390 Engelberg
☎ 041/941366
85 beds. Closed first half May, mid-October to mid-December. Good restaurant.

Entlebuch
Hotel Drei Könige **
CH-6162 Entlebuch
☎ 041/72 12 27
Country inn. 24 beds. Recommended for comfort and typical regional cuisine.

Flüelen
Hotel Flüelerhof-Grill Rustico **
38 Axenstrasse, CH-6454
☎ 044/2 11 49
50 beds. Splendid outlook. Modern, comfortable.

Gersau
Hotel Mueller ***
CH-6442 Gersau
☎ 041/84 19 19
60 beds. Recently modernised. Splendid outlook.

Langnau im Emmental
Hotel Hirschen **
CH-3550 Langnau
☎ 035/2 15 17
Country inn. 36 beds. Recommended for comfort and typical regional cuisine.

Luzern
Hotel Schweizerhof ***
3 Schweizerhofplatz
CH-6002 Luzern
☎ 041/50 22 11
214 beds. Elegant, old-style traditional.

Hotel Monopol and Metropole ***
1 Pilatusstrasse
CH-6002 Luzern
☎ 041/23 08 66
183 beds. Hotel restaurant.

Hotel Flora ***
5 Seidenhofstrasse
CH-6002 Luzern
☎ 041/24 44 44
40 beds. Modern style, central. Good restaurant.

Hotel des Alpes **
5 Rathausquai
CH-6002 Luzern
☎ 041/51 58 25
90 beds. Quiet situation; cafe-restaurant on riverside terrace.

Hotel Tourist-Hotel *
12 St Karliquai
CH-6002 Luzern
☎ 041/51 24 74
100 beds. Not far from station.

Schwyz
Hotel Wysses Rössli ***
3 Hauptplatz
CH-6430 Schwyz
☎ 043/21 19 22
45 beds. Attractively restored; traditional central situation.

Seelisberg
Hotel Bellevue **
CH-6377 Seelisberg
☎ 043/31 16 46
75 beds. Spectacular site, quiet, own grounds.

Trubschachen im Emmental
Hotel Hirschen **
CH-3555 Trubschachen
☎ 035/6 51 15
Country inn. 10 beds. Recommended for comfort and typical regional cuisine.

Vitznau
Hotel Seehotel Vitznauerhof ***
Hauptstrasse
CH-6354 Vitznau
☎ 041/83 13 15
90 beds. Lakeside, on own property.

Weggis
Hotel Rössli **
2 Aegeri-strasse
CH-6353 Weggis
☎ 041/93 11 06
30 beds. Peaceful site centrally on lakeside road.

Worb
Hotel Gasthof zum Löwen **
3 Enggisteinstrasse
CH-3076 Worb
☎ 031/83 23 03
60 beds. Handsome traditional inn building. Has good rustic yet stylish restaurant.

Restaurants

(Additional to those indicated under Hotel entries above)

Gersau
Cafe Mueller and Gero Restaurant ***
At Hotel Mueller
☎ 041/84 19 19
Open 11am-2pm, 5.30-9.30pm. Very fine cuisine.

Luzern
Arbalete (Hotel Monopole) ***
1 Pilatusstrasse
CH-6002 Luzern
☎ 041/23 08 66
Open 6am-12.30am. Elegant; French cuisine.

Kunst-u. Kongress-Haus Restaurants **
Am Bahnhof
CH-6002 Luzern
☎ 041/23 18 16
Open 12noon-2.30pm and 6.30-11pm. At large convention centre beside main station; facilities for handicapped. Three restaurants in complex.

Chapter 3 • Bern, Oberland and Mittelland

Hotels

Adelboden
Hotel Beau-Site ***
CH-3715 Adelboden
☎ 033/73 22 22
65 beds.

Bern
Hotel Schweizerhof ***
11 Bahnhofplatz
CH-3001 Bern
☎ 031/22 45 01
157 beds. Facing main station. Grand comfort, service, in elegance. For restaurant see under Schultheissenstube.

Hotel Hospiz zur Heimat *
50 Gerechtigkeitsgasse
CH-3011 Bern
☎ 031/22 04 36
70 beds. Perfect location for sightseeing in Old Town and good value.

Brienz-am-See
Hotel Bären **
50 beds. Closed mid-December to mid-March. Good lake-side site. Good restaurant.

Burgdorf
Hotel Touring Bernerhof *
Am Bahnhof
☎ 034/22 16 52
55 beds. Modern. At station yet reasonably quiet. Restaurants.

Château d'Oex
Hotel la Rocaille **
1837 Château d'Oex
☎ 029/46215
26 beds. Good value for its quality and pleasant atmosphere.

Fribourg
Hotel Elite **
Rue du Criblet 7
CH-1700 Fribourg
☎ 037/22 38 36
72 beds. Has restaurant.

Giswil
Hotel Krone **
CH-8074 Giswil
☎ 041/68 24 24
130 beds. Good value.

Grindelwald
Hotel Fiescherblick **
CH-3818 Grindelwald
☎ 036/54 33 54
50 beds. Also good local cooking.

Gstaad
Hotel Posthotel Rossli **
CH-3780 Gstaad
☎ 030/4 34 12
36 beds. Open June-October, December-April. Central position. Popular restaurant.

Gunten am Thunersee
Hotel Hirschen-am-See ***
CH-3654 Gunten
☎ 033/51 22 44
110 beds. March-October. Own grounds on lakeside adjacent lake-steamer jetty. Good cuisine.

Interlaken
Gasthof Hirschen **
CH-3800 Interlaken
☎ 036/22 15 45
36 beds. Situation convenient for touring drivers.

Pension Alfa *
CH-3800 Interlaken
☎ 036/22 69 22
26 beds. Convenient for West station.

Kandersteg
Waldhotel Dolderhorn **/***
CH-3718 Kandersteg
☎ 033/75 18 18
50 beds. Peaceful surroundings. Has restaurant. Moderate to expensive.

Meiringen
Parkhotel du Sauvage ***
CH-3860 Meiringen

☎ 036/71 41 41
140 beds. Traditional high standards.

Merligen am Thunersee
See-Hotel Beatus ***
CH-3658 Merligen
☎ 033/51 21 21
125 beds. Own lido beach, caters for watersports etc.

Mürren
Hotel Blumental **
CH-3825 Mürren
☎ 036/55 18 26
30 beds. Family-run; good facilities.

Murten
Hotel Krone **
Rathausgasse
CH-3280 Murten
☎ 037/71 52 52
65 beds. Closed mid-November to mid-December. Central in town. Several eating places. Reasonable.

Hotel Schiff **/***
CH-3280 Murten
☎ 037/71 27 01
30 beds. Quiet setting on lake. Comfortable. Good restaurant. Expensive.

Sigriswil
Hotel Adler **
CH-3655 Sigriswil
☎ 033/51 24 81
45 beds. Setting on sun-terrace with fine outlook over lake to Oberland peaks.

Spiez
Hotel Seegarten Marina (garni) **
CH-3700 Spiez
☎ 033/54 67 61
70 beds. Good position on strand. Family restaurant attached.

Thun
Hotel Seepark ***
47 Seestrasse
CH-3600 Thun
☎ 033/26 12 12
108 beds. Situated direct on lake at Schadau parkland. Restaurant.

Hotel Freienhof ***
3 Freienhofgasse
CH-3600 Thun
☎ 033/21 55 11
98 beds. Quiet location on Aare river bank, yet central town.

Wengen
Hotel Alpenrose **
CH-3823 Wengen
☎ 036/55 32 16
80 beds. Long-established family-run. Good restaurant.

Wilderswil
Hotel Baren **
CH-3812 Wilderswil
☎ 036/22 35 21
Reasonable rates. 80 beds. Traditional village-centre hotel. Handy for Jungfrau rail.

Restaurants

(Additional to those indicated under Hotel entries above).

Bern
Schultheissenstube ***
At Hotel Schweizerhof
11 Bahnhofplatz
☎ 031/22 45 01
Very expensive. Open 12noon-2pm and 6.30-12midnight. Closed Sunday. One of Switzerland's leading restaurants.

Goldener Schluessel **/*
72 Rathausgasse
☎031/22 02 16
Open: 11.30am-2pm; 6-10.30pm. Closed pm Friday and Saturday. Good value in typical traditional Swiss fare.

Gfeller am Barenplatz *
21 Barenplatz
☎ 031/22 69 44
Open: 10.30am-8pm. A favourite for generous lunches and afternoon teas.

Interlaken
Schuh **
Hoheweg 56
CH-3800 Interlaken
☎ 036/22 94 41
Closed Sunday. Conveniently sited in town, next door to its pastry-shop.

Mürren
Piz Gloria **
Schilthorn, above CH-3825 Mürren

☎ 036/55 21 41
Closes daily 6pm. Famous revolving restaurant at top-station of cableway.

Thun
Bahnhofbuffet **
3 Seestrasse
CH-3600 Thun
☎ 033/23 22 23
Open until 11.30pm. At station, facing lakeship quays. Fish specialities.

Chapter 4 • The Valais

Hotels

(If a hotel is known to have a restricted annual season, an indication is given after the number of beds).

Champery
Hotel Rose des Alpes **
CH-1874 Champery
☎ 025/79 12 18
Chalet pension. 45 beds.
Traditional homely style. Moderate.

Champex
Hotel Belvedere **
CH-1938 Champex
☎ 026/83 11 14
Country inn. 16 beds. Situation lives up to hotel's name.

Crans-Montana
Hotel Du Golf et Des Sports ***
CH-3963 Crans
160 beds. Open all year. Very expensive but the ultimate in style and amenities.

Martigny
Hotel de la Poste **
rue de la Poste 8
CH-1920 Martigny
☎ 026/2 14 44
65 beds. Homely restaurant also.

Saas-Fee
Hotel Saaserhof ***
CH-3906 Saas-Fee
☎ 028/57 15 51
100 beds. Open June-September, December-April. Apartments available for families/groups.

Sierre
Hotel Atlantic **
CH-3960 Sierre
☎ 027/55 25 35
64 beds.

Sion/Sitten
Hotel Du Castel *
rue du Scex 38
CH-1950 Sion
☎ 027/22 91 71
60 beds. Modern building, soundproof windows. No restaurant.

Hotel Du Rhone **
rue du Scex 10
CH-1950 Sion
☎ 027/22 82 91
80 beds. Modern style, local favourite.
Popular cafe-restaurant.

Verbier
Hotel Rosalp ***
Route de Tintaz
CH-1936 Verbier
☎ 026/31 63 23
40 beds. Open July-September, November-April.
Top-class accommodation and amenities. Restaurant with exceptional cuisine (see under 'Restaurants').

Zermatt
Grand Hotel Zermatterhof ***
CH-3920 Zermatt
☎ 028/66 11 00
155 beds. Closed November. Very expensive. Restaurants for hotel-guests only.

Hotel Touring **
CH-3920 Zermatt
☎ 028/67 11 77
38 beds. Closed November.
Inexpensive, homely; sited above town.
Matterhorn views.

Restaurants

(Additional to those indicated under Hotel entries above).

Verbier
Restaurant Pierroz (in Hotel Rosalp) ***
Route de Medran
CH-1936 Verbier

☎ 026/31 63 23
Open 7-11pm (dinners only).
This gourmet restaurant (advance booking essential) has a second restaurant at street level, La Pinte, fine food more moderately priced, at hours 12noon-2pm, 7-10pm.

Zermatt
Restaurant da Mario (in Hotel Schweizerhof) **
Bahnhofstrasse
CH-3920 Zermatt
☎ 028/66 11 55
Open 6.30-10.30pm.
'Trattoria' with touch distinction.

Chapter 5 • The Ticino

Hotels

Agno
Hotel La Perla ***
Via Pestariso
CH-6982 Agno
☎ 091/59 39 21
238 beds. All year. Moderate priced accommodation.

Ascona
Hotel Tamaro **
CH-6612 Ascona
☎ 093/35 02 82
56 beds. Waterfront situation. Fine lake views.

Hotel Piazza *
CH-6612 Ascona
☎ 093/35 11 81
44 beds. Good position on front. Small bedrooms, well-planned.

Bellinzona
Hotel Unione **
CH-6500 Bellinzona
☎ 092/25 55 75
67 beds. In own grounds, centrally. Good restaurant.

Biasca
Hotel Al Giardinetto **
CH-6710 Biasca
☎ 092/72 17 71
54 beds. Inexpensive, hospitable hotel. Very good and correspondingly priced restaurant.

Faido
Hotel Faido *
CH-6760 Faido
☎ 094/38 15 55
Comfortable. 30 beds. All year. Central.

Gandria (by Lugano)
Hotel Moosmann **
CH-6978 Lugano-Gandria
☎ 091/51 72 61
55 beds. March-November. Spectacular outlook on lake. Moderately priced.

Locarno
Hotel Reber au Lac ***
CH-6600 Locarno
☎ 093/33 02 02
140 beds. Open all year
Spacious amenity. Two restaurants. Noted regional food.

Hotel Belvedere **
CH-6601 Locarno
☎ 093/31 003 63
136 beds. Open February-December. All rooms face south. Two restaurants, the less formal offering moderately-priced Italian cuisine.

Lugano
Hotel Bellevue au Lac ***
10 Riva Caccia
CH-6900 Lugano
☎ 091/54 33 33
120 beds. April-October. Central site on lakeside promenade road. Swimming pool and sun-terrace. Good cuisine.

Lugano-Paradiso
Hotel Meister **
11 Via San Salvatore
CH-6902 Lugano
☎ 091/54 14 12
130 beds. Open March-November. Superior family hotel. Swimming pool in grounds. Well-equipped rooms.

Mendrisio
Hotel Milano **
CH-6850 Mendrisio
☎ 091/46 57 41
55 beds. Open-air pool. Moderately priced accommodation.

Morcote
Hotel Olivella au Lac ***

CH-6922 Lugano-Morcote
☎ 091/69 10 01
140 beds. Open March-December. Luxurious hotel, lakeside situation, watersports etc. Restaurant reputed one of the best in Switzerland.

Olivone (Val Blenio)
Hotel Olivone e Posta **
CH-6718 Olivone
☎ 092/70 13 66
46 beds. All year.

Piora
Hotel Lago Ritom *
☎ 094/38 16 16
24 beds. Simple.

Ponte Tresa
Hotel Del Pesce **
Via Cantonale
CH-6988 Lugano-Ponte Tresa
☎ 091/71 11 46
44 beds. All year. Lakeside situation. Prices moderate.

Vira Gambarogno
Hotel Touring Bellavista **
CH-6574 Vira Gambarogno
☎ 093/61 11 16
110 beds. March-November. Extensive parking area. Splendid views of L. Maggiore.

Restaurants

(Additional to those indicated under Hotel entries above).

Faido
Albergo Pedrinis **
Piazza Fontana
CH-6760
☎ 094/38 12 41
Open 11.30am-2.30pm, 6.30-10pm. Fine cuisine includes regional dishes.

Gandria/Lugano
Locanda Gandriese **
CH-6978 Lugano-Gandria
☎ 091/51 41 81
Open 12noon-2pm, 6-10pm. Has lakeside terrace. Popular for regional specialities.

Locarno
Saleggi **
38 Via Angelo Nessi
CH-6600 Locarno
☎ 093/31 41 71
Open until 12midnight. Local Ticinese cuisine.

Lugano
Locanda del Boschetto **
8 Via Boschetto
CH-6900 Lugano
☎ 091/54 24 93
Open: 12noon-2pm, 7-10pm. Closed Monday. Good value for simple dishes of excellent quality.

Restaurant Monte Ceneri *
44 Via Nassa
CH-6900 Lugano
☎ 091/23 33 40
Open 11.30am-2pm, 6.30-10pm. Family-run, popular for inexpensive fixed-price meals.

Chapter 6 • Graubünden

Hotels

Arosa
Hotel Waldhotel National ***
CH-7050 Arosa
☎ 081/31 15 51
180 beds. All amenities in this forest park retreat. Very expensive. Only demi-pension terms.

Hotel Alpensonne **
CH-7050 Arosa
☎ 081/31 15 47
62 beds. Closeed May. Central, near ski-lifts. Restaurant. Half-pension rates.

Celerina
Hotel Cresta Kulm ***
CH-7505 Celerina
☎ 082/3 33 73
76 beds. June-September, December-April. Quiet sunlit situation where Cresta run finishes.

Chur
Hotel Freieck **
Reichsgasse 50
CH-7000 Chur
☎ 081/22 17 92
80 beds. Near station. Has range of restaurants.

Hotel Stern **
Reichsgasse 11
CH-7000 Chur
☎ 081/22 35 55
90 beds. Three dining rooms, well regarded locally. Free carpark.

Davos-Platz
Hotel Davoserhof ***
Post-Platz
CH-7270 Davos-Platz
☎ 083/3 68 17
46 beds. Closed May. Attractive atmosphere, 2 very good restaurants (advance booking needed).

Flims-Waldhaus
Hotel Adula **
CH-7018 Flims-Waldhaus
☎ 081/39 01 61
180 beds. Closed November. Comfortable, good amenities and catering.

Guarda
Hotel Meisser **
CH-7549 Guarda
☎ 084/9 21 32
40 beds. Season June to November. Vernacular farmhouse transformed into hotel of great charm. Good food. Moderate tariff.

Klosters
Hotel Raetia **
CH-7252 Klosters-Dorf
☎ 081/69 47 47
42 beds. Quiet situation.

Hotel Chesa Grischuna ***
CH-7250 Klosters
☎ 081/69 22 22
42 beds. Very expensive, considering. But central with popular restaurant.

Maloja
Hotel Maloja Kulm **
CH-7516 Maloja
☎ 082/4 31 05
43 beds. Open May-October; December-April. Spectacularly sited historic hotel at pass-summit. Half-board included in reasonable room rates.

Samedan
Hotel Bernina ***
CH7503 Samedan
☎ 082/6 54 21
105 beds. Season mid-June to October and mid-December to April. Rates moderate for standards of service and amenity.

San Bernardino Villaggio
Hotel Brocco e Posta ***
CH-6565 San Bernardino Villagio
☎ 092/94 11 05
60 beds. Open June-October; December-April. Half-board inclusive in room rates.

Sils-Baselgia
Hotel Chesa Randolina **
CH-7515 Sils-Baselgia
☎ 082/4 52 24
65 beds. Season June-end October, Xmas-April. Typical Engadine farmhouse style. Restaurant.

Sils-Maria
Hotel Waldhaus ***
CH-7514 Sils-Maria
☎ 082/4 53 31
260 beds. Season June-October and December-April. Splendid views from this forest Palace above the lakes. Every amenity.

Hotel Maria **
CH-7514 Sils Maria
☎ 082/4 53 17
65 beds. Half-board included in room price. Hotel has sailing school and ice-rink.

Silvaplana
Hotel Albana **
CH-7513 Silvaplana
☎ 082/4 92 92
60 beds. Closed May, November. Moderate prices for this class.

Splügen
Posthotel Bodenhaus **
CH-7435 Splugen
☎ 081/62 11 21
51 beds. Open May-October; December-April. Sun terrace, restaurant. Moderate prices.

St Moritz
Hotel Waldhaus am See **
CH-7500 St Moritz

☎ 082/3 76 76
60 beds. Closed November. Set apart from bustle with outlook over lake and mountains. Restaurant with reasonable tariff.

Neues Posthotel **
CH-7500 St Moritz
☎ 082/2 21 21
110 beds. Open all year. Comfortable, good accommodation and cooking.

Thusis
Hotel Splügen **
CH-7430 Thusis
☎ 081/81 41 51
60 beds. All year. Moderate charges.

Tiefencastel
Hotel Albula **
CH-7450 Tiefencastel
☎ 081/71 11 21
85 beds. Open December-October. Moderately priced.

Zernez
Hotel Bettini *
CH-7530 Zernez
☎ 082/8 11 35
57 beds. On fringe of National Park, a typical straight forward local hotel (with restaurant) patronised by walkers.

Zuoz
Posthotel Engiadina **
CH-7524 Zuoz
☎ 081/39 01 61
70 beds. Season June-October, December-April. Moderate rates for first-class amenity.

Restaurants

(Additional to those indicated under Hotel entries above).

Celerina
Restaurant Stuvetta (at Hotel Misani) **
CH-7505 Celerina
☎ 082/3 33 14
Open 12noon-2pm, 6.30-9pm. Good food, good price, good service.

Chur
Restaurant Duc de Rohan ***
Masanerstrasse 44
CH-7000 Chur
☎ 081/22 10 22
Open 9.30am to 11.30pm. Restaurant of city's top hotel; meals and service both recommended.

Restaurant Stern (at hotel of same name) **
Reichsgasse 11
CH-7000 Chur
☎ 081/22 35 55
Open 11.30am-2pm, 6.30-9.30pm. Regional specialities in attractive surroundings.

Samedan
Restaurant Le Pavillon (in Hotel Bernina) **
CH-7503 Samedan
☎ 082/6 54 21
Open 9am-midnight. Closed mid-April to mid-June and 1 October to mid-December.

Sils-Maria
Restaurant Waldhaus (Restaurant of de-luxe Hotel Waldhaus) **
CH-7514 Sils-Maria
☎ 082/4 53 31
Open 12noon-2.15pm and 7-9.30pm. Highly regarded menus. Fixed-price meals not expensive considering standards of establishment.

Silvaplana
Restaurant Rustica *
Chesa Munterots
CH-7513 Silvaplana
☎ 082/4 81 66
Open until 11pm. Closed Monday. Local cuisine. Private parking.

St Moritz
Restaurant Steffani (at Hotel Steffani) **/***
CH-7500 St Moritz
☎ 082/2 21 01
Open 11.30am-11.30pm. Best value is the fixed price meal.

Restaurant La Marmite **/***
Corviglia Bergstation
CH-7500 St Moritz
☎ 082/3 63 55
Open 12noon-4pm and 6-10pm. Early June to mid-October, 20 November to 20 April. Top reputation of high altitude restaurants.

Chapter 7 • Geneva, Lausanne and the Lake Geneva Region

Hotels

Château-d'Oex
Hotel Bon Accueil **
CH-1837 Château-d'Oex
☎ 029/4 63 20
40 beds. Closed mid-October to Xmas. Good example country inn. Well-run.

Geneva
Hotel Metropole ***
Quai General-Guisan 34
CH-1204 Geneva
☎ 022/311 13 44
180 beds. Riverside, well placed for old town and also splendid style. Good restaurants and fashionable lounge.

Hotel Touring-Balance **
Place Longmalle 13
CH-1204 Geneva
☎ 022/310 40 45
100 beds. Well-run, convenient Left Bank situation. Attractive period dining room.

Hotel Bernina *
Place de Cornavin 22
CH-1211 Geneva
☎ 022/731 49 50
110 beds. Near rail station. Caters breakfast only.

Gruyères
Hotel Hostellerie des Chevaliers ***
CH-1663 Gruyères
☎ 029/6 19 33
34 beds. Closed mid-January to mid-February. Stands apart from tourist-throng. 3 dining rooms (see under Restaurants).

Gstaad
Posthotel Rossli **
CH-3780 Gstaad
☎ 030/4 34 12
36 beds. Open June-October, December-April. Central position. Popular restaurant.

Lausanne
Hotel Agora ***
Ave Rond-Point 9
CH-1006 Lausanne
☎ 021/617 12 11
180 beds. Top-class modernised hotel short distance from station. Famed restaurant (see entry under Restaurants).

Hotel Elite **
Ave Ste Luce 1
CH-1003 Lausanne
☎ 021/20 23 61
55 beds. Near station yet quiet site. Caters only breakfast.

Hotel La Residence ***
Place du Port 15
CH-1006 Lausanne-Ouchy
☎ 021/617 77 11
94 beds. Discreetly sited, genteel-stylish, expensive.

Jeunotel (Youth Hotel) *
36 chem Bois-de-Vaux
CH-1000 Lausanne
☎ 021/626 02 22
Large modern accommodation complex (325 beds) designed for young tourists visiting region/students in term time.

Les Diablerets
Hotel Les Lilas **
CH-1865 Les Diablerets
☎ 025/53 11 34
Small, 16 beds. In village. Comfortable. Good cuisine.

Montreux
Hotel Le Montreux Palace ***
Grand Rue 100
CH-1820 Montreux
☎ 921/963 53 73
De luxe and immense. 500 beds.

Eurotel Riviera ***
Grand Rue 18
CH-1820 Montreux
☎ 021/963 49 51
270 beds. Lake front, all amenities and comfort.

Hotel L'Ermitage
CH-1820 Clarens-Montreux
☎ 021/964 44 11
15 beds. Comfortable, family-run.

Nyon
*Hotel Beau-Rivage ****
rue de Rive 49
CH-1260 Nyon
☎ 022/61 32 31
100 beds. Lake-side, old town site. Traditional comfort.

Rolle
*Hotel De la Tete-Noire ***
Grand-Rue 94
CH-1180 Rolle
☎ 021/825 22 51
30 beds. Main street situation. Has good old-style restaurant.

Vevey
*Hotel Du Lac ****
rue d'Italie
CH-1800 Vevey
☎ 021/921 10 41
90 beds.
Period piece. Lakeside amenities include restaurant.

*Hotel de Famille ***
rue des Communaux
CH-1800 Vevey
☎ 021/921 39 31
100 beds. Central, near station, comfortable. Lives up to name.

*Hotel des Negociants **
rue du Conseil 27
CH-1800 Vevey
☎ 021/922 70 11
45 beds. Near lake, near market, comfortable. Inexpensive for this coast. Restaurant.

Restaurants

(Additional to those indicated under Hotel entries above).

Geneva
*Restaurant Les Armures **
Rue de Puits-St-Pierre
CH1204 Geneva
☎ 022/310 91 72
Wide range of Swiss specialities, in vicinity of cathedral in old town.

*Restaurant Brasserie Lipp ***
rue de la Confederation 8
CH-Geneva
☎ 022/311 10 11
Open 7.30-midnight (1am Friday and Saturday). Closed Sunday. Parisian ambience within modern shopping mall.

Gruyères
*Restaurant Hostellerie des Chevaliers **/****
CH-1663 Gruyères
☎ 029/6 19 33
Open 12noon-2pm, 7-9pm. Closed Wednesday. 3 dining rooms of Hotel of same name, set apart from throng of the town.

Lausanne
*Restaurant L'Agora ****
ave du Rond-Point
CH-1006 Lausanne
☎ 021/617 12 11
Open 12noon-2pm, 7-11pm. Closed Sunday. High reputation for food. Closed mid-July to mid-August.

Morges
*Restaurant Fleur du Lac ****
Route de Lausanne 70
CH-1110 Morges
☎ 021/802 43 11
Open 12noon-11pm. High repute in region.

Vevey
*Restaurant Cafe-Restaurant du Raisin ****
Place du Marche
CH1800 Vevey
☎ 021/921 10 28
Closed Sunday evenings and Monday. Choice restaurant. Choice wines. Cafe with superior food, moderate cost.

Index

Page numbers in **bold** type indicate maps

MPC Visitor's Guides To
SWITZERLAND
& Surrounding Countries

Belgium & Luxembourg
Northern Germany
Czech & Slovak Republics
Rhine & Mosel
Bavaria
Champagne & Alsace-Lorraine
Black Forest
Southern Germany
Tyrol & Vorarlberg
Austria
France
Switzerland
Alps & Jura
Italian Lakes
Northern Italy
Provence & Côte d'Azur
Southern Italy
Corsica

Visitor's Guides To:

Austria:
Tyrol & Vorarlberg

Belgium & Luxembourg

Corsica

Czech & Slovak Republics

France:
Alps & Jura
Champagne & Alsace-Lorraine
Provence & Côte d'Azur
Plus Many More.

Germany:
Northern Germany
Southern Germany
Bavaria
Black Forest
Rhine & Mose

Italy:
Northern Italy
Southern Italy
Italian Lakes

MPC

Visitor's Guides

Itinerary based guides for independent travellers

America:
America South West
California
Florida
Orlando & Central Florida
USA

Austria:
Austria
Austria: Tyrol & Vorarlberg

Britain:
Cornwall & Isles of Scilly
Cotswolds
Devon
East Anglia
Hampshire & Isle of Wight
Kent
Lake District
Scotland: Lowlands
Somerset, Dorset & Wiltshire
North Wales & Snowdonia
North York Moors, York & Coast
Northern Ireland
Northumbria
Peak District
Treasure Houses of England
Yorkshire Dales & North Pennines

Canada
Czechoslovakia
Denmark
Egypt

France:
Champagne & Alsace-Lorraine
France
Alps & Jura
Brittany
Burgundy
Dordogne
Loire
Massif Central
Normandy
Normandy Landing Beaches
Provence & Côte d'Azur

Germany:
Bavaria
Black Forest
Northern Germany
Rhine & Mosel
Southern Germany

Greece:
Greece (mainland)
Athens & Peloponnese

Holland
Hungary
Iceland & Greenland

India:
Delhi, Agra & Jaipur
Goa

Ireland

Islands:
Corsica
Crete
Cyprus
Gran Canaria
Guernsey, Alderney & Sark
Jersey
Madeira
Mallorca, Menorca, Ibiza & Formentera
Malta & Gozo
Mauritius, Rodrigues & Reunion
Rhodes
Sardinia
Seychelles
Tenerife

Italy:
Florence & Tuscany
Italian Lakes
Northern Italy
Southern Italy

Norway
Peru
Portugal

Spain:
Costa Brava & Costa Blanca
Northern & Central Spain
Southern Spain & Costa del Sol

Sweden
Switzerland
Turkey